Copyright © 2017 by Joachim Claes. All rights reserved.

No part of this book may be reproduced in any form or by any electronic, photographic, or mechanical means, or in the form of a phonographic recording; nor may it be stored in an information storage or retrieval system, transmitted, or otherwise be copied for public or private use, other than for "fair use" as brief quotations embodied in articles and reviews, without prior written permission from the author. To obtain permission or to contact the author email: joachim@fieldparadigm.com

The author of this book does not dispense medical advice or prescribe the use of any technique as a form of treatment for physical, emotional, or medical problems without the advice of a physician, either directly or indirectly. The intent of the author is only to offer information of a general nature. The author assumes no responsibility for actions taken based on the information in this book.

Claes, Joachim
　　The Field Paradigm: 20 Experiments That Can Change The World

Edited by: Lilla Nemeth, Howard Chandler

Cover Design: Razvan Petre

First edition, June 2017

Trade paper

Printed in the United States of America

Dedicated to all the messengers of the Field Paradigm throughout history...

...who were brave enough to try to tell us we are far bigger, far more beautiful, and far more powerful than we could imagine in our wildest dreams.

From Plato to Einstein...There are far more than you'd think.

Praise for *The Field Paradigm*

"one of the best, most well written, and compelling tours of Maharishi's knowledge I have ever read" **Raja Pat Barrett**

"I am totally amazed. It is exactly what is needed to bring TM to the public. Such clear use of simple logic that is accessible to people, such entertainment which will actually get them through it, and such deep understanding of the Knowledge, put in the language of the time.
I am reading it through program. It is a page turner." **Raja John Konhaus**

"I think this is the most important TM book ever written - from the point of view of making the incomprehensible promise of world peace obvious to anyone with any brains at all." **Richard Broome** (TM teacher, South Africa)

"fullest intro presentation to Maharishi's knowledge that I have seen...It is truly amazing you can do such a complete introduction to the Maharishi Effect that will be able to fully engage non-meditators in this knowledge. Congratulations." **Steve Herzfeld** (Uttar Kashi Purusha)

"I would like to congratulate you on your great work and achievement. Maharishi would have been very pleased with your presentation of the knowledge and events. Your story telling style is captivating; I couldn't let go. There is a magical flow to your thoughts and words; it felt exceptionally familiar instilling in me a pleasant feeling of connectedness.

I believe you have skilfully succeeded with a touch of humour and lightness to provide quite strong, persuasive answers and arguments to a great deal of frequently asked questions. **Sophia Bitar** (sidha from Lebanon)

Everybody (and I mean Everybody) should read this book...Well written, accessible, funny, intelligent. I'm convinced this is going to make a big Impact. **Eva De Roovere** (famous pop-star in Belgium)

" I have to admit I was never really open to the whole theory [of the Maharishi Effect]. For me TM was a technique that finally allowed me to meditate, but for the rest I didn't want anything too pie-in-the-sky.

Your book changed my mind, in the sense that I now realize it's not pie-in-the-sky at all.

Thomas [a friend who also just read the book] and I decided to start learning the advanced techniques and TM sidhi program as soon as possible, and I told my wife she should also absolutely learn TM."
Wannes Kappelle (another famous Belgian pop-star)

"One of the most inspiring books I've ever read...now that I know what the Global Country of World Peace stands for I'll do anything I can to help"
Joost Berghman (Owner/CEO of financial services company with 180 retail stores)

Table of Contents

Prologue: It's a kind of magic   1

Part 1: The Field Paradigm at a glance   9

- Meeting the president
- The Field Paradigm: how it works, how it was forgotten, and how it was rediscovered
- Rediscovering our true Selves
- The Field Effect

Part 2: The Field Paradigm as a new scientific reality   31

- The Field Paradigm, rediscovered in physics
- Everyday examples of unity in nature
- The science of miracles: how paranormal experiences make sense
- The law of action and reaction from a Field Paradigm perspective

Part 3: Using the Field Paradigm   97

- The power of silence
- The too-good-to-be-true problem
- Changing lives
- Twenty experiments that will change the world
- Five ways to make it happen – at virtually no cost
- Why we have good reason to hope

Part 4: Will you keep this a secret?   273

Prologue: It's a Kind of Magic

Have you ever experienced magic?

This may be a strange sentence to open what is essentially a story about a scientific revolution, but bear with me.

You'll see how this simple question will eventually lead us to a wide range of practical solutions, from learning to heal ourselves, or developing our full brain potential, to stopping terrorism and corruption on a global scale... even solve global warming.

It's all interconnected.

So...have you ever had magic in your life?

Not the David Copperfield stuff – I mean the real thing.

Here are some examples of what I'd define as "magic":

- Dreaming that something has happened to a loved one, only to find out it really happened.
- Thinking about a friend you haven't spoken with in years and he/she calls you shortly after.
- Having a strong intuitive feeling you have to do something, even if you can't explain why, and it later turns out to be the perfect decision.

And the ultimate one:

- Desiring something from the bottom of your heart and then watching events unfold around you as if being "organized" for the desire to be fulfilled.

I define such experiences as "magic" because they would indicate some kind of connection between our inner thoughts and outside events...

...Unless it was a coincidence.

We learned in school that there is no connection between our inner mind and the outer world. We are clearly isolated objects walking around in a world full of other isolated objects. As such, any experience of a connection is impossible.

So… Coincidence: the one word that kills all magic.

It would have to be a coincidence, right? Otherwise, what is the alternative? That everything we've ever learned about the nature of our universe is wrong?

If it wasn't a coincidence, then this means there must not only be some kind of invisible connection between our thoughts and events, but through this connection outside events could cause inner thoughts or, even more weird, *our thoughts can cause outside events*.

That sounds like a pretty deep rabbit hole – something so complicated that it's easier to call it a coincidence and stop thinking about it. That's pretty much what we've been doing for thousands of years.

Better not to ask too many questions that bring us out of our comfort zone, right?

Well, that depends on how comfortable our comfort zone really is.

Let's ask another question: "Is your life completely *devoid* of magic?"

You live life the way you're supposed to. You don't believe in all this magic mumbo-jumbo, and just focus on getting a good job, buying a nice house and a nice car, and getting the kids through college.

Well done.

And are you satisfied? And I mean *fully* satisfied – full of joy every minute of the day?

I bet you don't even believe that's possible. I bet you believe that the emotional rollercoaster of ups and downs we call *life* is "normal".

I can assure you, most people do *not* feel fully satisfied. Even if they live life the way they are supposed to, and have all the material things they want, they still feel that something is missing. They feel there must be *something more*, but don't know what that 'something' is.

So we start looking for "more" in many different ways. Some want more money, more power, more fame, others want more meaning, more love, more happiness, more spirituality…No matter how much we have, we all seem to want more.

Meanwhile our intellect tells us we're being foolish. We should be happy with what we have. After all, so many others have much less than we do. But our inner desire for more can't be silenced so easily....And so the fight between our feelings and our intellect begins, a fight that can lead even extremely wealthy people into severe depressions.

This book will hopefully help you end this fight, because you'll realize that *the feeling is right, and the intellect is wrong*. It's our *nature* to desire more, it's our *education* that has been leading us in the wrong direction by making us believe we are far more limited than we really are.

We have been educated to see ourselves as material objects, limited to our bodies, all separated from each other. In reality, we are far bigger, far more beautiful, and far more powerful than we could ever imagine in our wildest dreams.

In Part 1 of this book I'll present a simple hypothesis that will allow us to understand how our mind (or our consciousness, to be more exact) can be both connected to our bodies and, at the same time, be much larger than our bodies and be connected to everyone else through a *field of consciousness*.

We'll then see in Part 2 of this book that physics is now confirming that this same field of consciousness is also at the source of all material events. Einstein called this the "Unified Field". Thought and matter all come from the same source and are, in fact, connected.

This is our rabbit hole, and we'll be jumping right in. You'll see that it's actually a lot less complicated than you'd expect, and that there is actually far more scientific evidence to confirm this hypothesis than you'd think.

For example, any kind of "magical" experiences we have are just glimpses of this connection between us and our environment, through this field. For some, such experiences are more obvious than for others, but most of us have them, and it's relatively easy to research them. A survey found that 67% of the population has had clear experiences of a connection between their inner thoughts and something outside of them (usually described as "psychic experiences").

If two out of three people have had these experiences, do you really still believe they're all just coincidences?

I personally always felt that one of the most beautiful ways to describe this universal field of consciousness comes from the 1980 Star Wars movie *The Empire Strikes Back,* where Yoda describes the "Force" (before he did his own little magic trick, moving a spaceship with just a gesture of his hand) :

> *For my ally...is the Force*
> *And a powerful ally it is*
> *Life creates it...makes it grow*
> *Its energy surrounds us...and binds us*
> *Luminous beings are we, not this crude matter*
> *You must feel the Force, around you*
> *Between you, me, the tree, the rock, everywhere*

Even though this is obviously science fiction (we won't be moving spaceships anytime soon), you'll see that as a description of what we'll discuss in this book, it's actually surprisingly accurate.

This brings us to the next question: If this "Force" is real, does that mean it is also possible to "feel the Force"? Is it possible to *experience* this connection to everyone and everything?

And here's an even more important question: What if this experience of being connected to everything is the mind's true nature, and the real reason the mind is always looking for more is because the mind is looking for the experience of being *everything*? What if the mind won't ever be fully satisfied until it has this experience (no matter how much "stuff" we have)?

There was a time when we did have this experience. In ancient times, people actually had techniques to experience this Force but, over time, these techniques have been forgotten.

This loss has been the greatest tragedy that has ever happened to mankind.

Bold statement, I know, that's why I put it in bold...just wait until you see what happens when people remember.

This is what this book is essentially all about.

You'll be surprised.

About 60 years ago, the technique to bring the mind to experience this field was rediscovered and was again taught around the world. Very likely you've already heard about it - it's now one of the most widely practiced mental techniques in the world.

Very likely you also have no idea what it's really all about because it's also one of the most *misunderstood* technique in the world.

Let's test this. What comes to your mind when you read: "Transcendental Meditation"?

If you're like most others, you'll think it's a meditation technique.

It's not.

In fact, in almost every respect it's exactly the *opposite* what most people assume meditation is all about.

When people think about "meditation" today, they think about controlling the mind, usually through some form of concentration (on the breath, a sound, or "observing your thoughts").

It's because of this *misunderstanding* about meditation that the technique to experience the Force, the unity with everything, got lost.

Concentration, or any kind of control, suppresses the natural tendency of the mind for more by forcefully keeping it on one point of attention. True meditation, on the other hand, will *use* this tendency. If meditation is practiced correctly (which means learning to properly direct the mind, but with *no* concentration and *no* control), the mind will go to this experience of the Force by itself.

According to what we'll see in this book, this Force is indeed the source of everything. Maharishi Mahesh Yogi, the founder of the Transcendental Meditation technique (or TM, for short), described this field as "more than the most". If we use the mind's desire for more and direct it in the correct way, *the desire for more will cause the mind to go to this field by itself,* as naturally and effortlessly as an iron filing is drawn to a magnet.

We'll call the process of experiencing this field *transcending* and, with the right technique, it becomes the easiest thing anyone has ever done. Anyone can learn to do it. Yet the results of this experience are spectacular.

We'll discuss those in Part 3 of this book.

Once that inner anxiety and insatiable desire for more is replaced by an inner satisfaction, all aspects of life start to change. We'll see how our self-confidence improves, how stress disappears and a wide variety of chronic problems (anxiety, depression, insomnia, addictions, hypertension, obesity, diabetes, etc.) spontaneously start to heal.

If you thought that sounds good, how about this one: We'll also learn that our brain develops based on the experiences we have. When people experience this state of unity with everything, their brain also starts to develop in more holistic ways. We'll see how this has remarkable effects on anything from IQ, EQ, creativity, concentration, memory, emotional stability, ADHD, Alzheimer's, autism, etc.

Finally we'll see how the mind eventually comes into a state which most of us consider impossible, a state of 24/7 spontaneous inner happiness, independent of outside circumstances.

Most people, believe it or not, start to get some first glimpses of all these changes within the first week after learning to transcend.

Yet even among the 6 million people who already learned TM, few realize that *feeling the Force* is only the beginning. Once people are trained to feel the Force there are advanced techniques (called the TM-Sidhi program) to learn to *use the Force*.

This is where the true magic starts. I was fortunate enough to be able to take this training at a young age and I could only describe it as the closest thing in real life to a Jedi Knight training (or attending Hogwarts, if Harry Potter is more your thing). Fair enough, no light sabers or magic wands, that's the fiction part, but the essence of the training is real: learning to have a desire in your mind and watching it manifest in the world around you.

All I can say is that it really worked for me. As an example, I started a video-game trading network at age 19 with only a $100 startup investment and zero business experience. The only thing I had was several years of this training and quite a lot of magic as a result (a sharp intuition, the right thought at the right time, desiring something and watching it happen, etc.). By the time I was 22 I had turned it into a $5 million company*.

That is just one example. We'll see far more spectacular ones: such as high-school students who learn to transcend from a young age as part of their school routine, and win one world championship in creative problem-solving after another, beating hundreds of thousands of other students around the world.

Or Ray Dalio, who describes how TM has helped him rise from a below-average student to become one of the most successful Wall Street traders in the world, managing a $160 billion hedge fund. (Dalio is one of the most

---

* I also learned, the hard way, that this training requires constant practice, just like competing in sports requires constant practice to stay at the top of your game.

generous donors to the David Lynch Foundation, which has already given more than 500,000 children the chance to learn TM.)

But even this is just the beginning. The real story of this book is about far more than understanding how "magic" works, or how to use it to bring more success and satisfaction in life.

> **This book is about the discovery of an extremely powerful way to change the entire destiny of mankind.**

The way it works is simple: if only a few people learn to experience this connection to everyone and everything, and learn to use this connection through the advanced TM-Sidhi techniques, they spontaneously start to enliven the connection between those around them as well. Suddenly *everyone* starts to feel more connected to each other, and spontaneously starts to think and behave differently.

Just for a second, imagine we'd be living in a world where everybody felt so connected to each other that the thought of hurting another person wouldn't even arise. In this world, *hurting somebody else would feel as stupid as taking a hammer with your left hand to hit your right hand.* You wouldn't even consider it.

Imagine we'd be living in a world where people would feel so connected to nature that everybody would spontaneously move away from polluting technologies. You wouldn't need to impose government regulations to combat global warming, everyone would insist on them.

Wouldn't such a world be magical?

Well, you'll discover soon enough that it's not only possible to create such a world, but that it's, in fact, ridiculously easy. We could do it in a few weeks if we wanted to, at a cost that is so low that our governments would start saving so much money they could even reduce our taxes.

And we'll see that this is not just some fancy new theory but that the "technology" to create this new world *has already been used*, through 20 spectacular scientific experiments that have played a significant role in some of the most positive events of last century, like the ending of several wars and even the fall of the Berlin Wall.

I'm willing to bet that the story of how these experiments happened will be one of the most fascinating stories you'll ever read (a story that *very* few people know about…and it's high time we changed that).

Not only are these 20 experiments *the most consistently successful scientific experiments in the entire history of social sciences*, but, even more important, they also form the most solid body of evidence to date that there is indeed a Field between us through which we influence each other, and that this influence can be used for the good of mankind.

You're about to find out that "magic" can actually be very scientific.

All it takes is the right paradigm.

> The technologies that are presented in this book could the larges positive transformation we've ever seen for our world...in a matter of weeks. *All it takes* is that enough people realize there is a better way, and understand how it works.
>
> This is why, even though this book took me 15 years of research, writing and rewriting (until it was all as simple as possible), I decided to give the entire book away for free. Anyone can simply download the PDF on www.fieldparadigm.com.
>
> I can only hope we'll reach enough people this way to create the change that is possible...but I'll need your help to reach those people.

Part 1: The Field Paradigm at a glance

Meeting the President 10

The Field Paradigm: How it Works, How it was Forgotten, and How it was Rediscovered 13
    1. We are Far Bigger Than We Think 13
    2. We are Far More Beautiful Than We Think 16
    3. We are Far More Powerful Than We Think.................................. 17
    4. Losing the Ability to Transcend: How Our True Nature Became Hidden 18
    5. The Field Paradigm Rediscovered 21

Rediscovering our True Selves 22

The Field Effect of Transcending 26

> Part 1 Overview
>
> In this part, we'll explore a new hypothesis about the nature of human consciousness. This new hypothesis will allow us to understand that we are far bigger, far more beautiful, and far more powerful than we ever dared to believe.
>
> We'll see how, from this new perspective, some fundamental questions about life suddenly get simple answers.
>
> We'll also get a first glimpse of how experiencing our true nature can create profound changes, both for ourselves and the world as a whole.

Meeting the President

It's 7 p.m. on a dark January night in 2006. 'Why me?' is the only thought that keeps racing through my mind as my car races down the highway.

An hour ago, I received a call. "We're flying to Africa to meet the president of Guinea-Bissau to present our technologies to end their civil war. We chartered a private jet, which is leaving in two hours. Maharishi said you should come, if you like."

"Would I like? Sure – private jets and meeting presidents always sound like fun." But I still couldn't help but wonder, 'Why me?' Most of the top managers and scientists of Maharishi's organisation would be there, but I wasn't a scientist and definitely not a top manager. I didn't even have an official position. I did some volunteer work for them now and then, but that was it.

8.15 p.m. When I arrive, the plane is already on the runway, ready to go. The rest of the group isn't there yet, though, and the airport will close in a few minutes. If the others don't come soon, we won't be able to take off.

8.30 p.m. The rest of the group arrives at the last possible moment. Eight people jump out of the car and I help unload the luggage. When I ask what's in the big reinforced suitcases, one of the assistants casually says, "Oh, that's a satellite uplink video conferencing set. There probably isn't an internet connection where we're going."

They're all very warm, welcoming me as part of the delegation, even though I'm sure some are wondering why I'm there as well.

We all get on the plane and I'm surprised how relaxed everyone seems. For most of them, this is far from their biggest adventure. They had already met several other presidents, including President Chissano of Mozambique. Chissano had already used their technology to end a 17-year civil war in a matter of weeks and turn his country into *the* African success story, creating the world's fastest growing economy in the process. I'm assuming Chissano played a role in organizing this meeting.

8.40 p.m. The plane takes off. I'm sitting in a comfortable seat in the back, thinking how surreal everything feels. Are these people even aware of the role they're playing in the history of mankind?

If this were a fiction story, it would go something like this:

From the texts of the most ancient civilization known to mankind, a group of scientists discovered a secret method for the human mind to directly access an invisible energy field that connects everyone and everything. The texts claimed this experience was essential to develop our full potential as human beings.

The scientists began researching what effects this experience had on people...and saw results they had never seen before. All aspects of life seemed to be positively influenced at the same time: from full brain development, improved IQ and creativity, to increased happiness hormones, reduced stress and mental problems, improved health and self-confidence, and even reduced ADHD.

In almost every case, the improvements were far bigger than those from any currently known treatment, so it didn't take the scientists long to realize that if this were a drug, everybody would want it...and all the other pharmaceutical companies would be in big trouble.

But that was just the start. They soon discovered an even more remarkable side-effect: when people experienced this energy field they appeared to stir it, like a light bulb stirs the electromagnetic field to radiate light. This side-effect caused people around them to suddenly feel more connected to each other. People started to think and behave differently. They found that the effect was so strong that a relatively small group of a few hundred people stirring this field could stop nearly all crime, corruption, terrorism, and even war.

The scientists start organizing several experiments to demonstrate this technology and use it to stop several wars in the process. Eventually, they played a crucial role in ending the Cold War and the fall of the Berlin Wall.

They also discovered, however, that not everybody wants things to change...

Does that sound like a good story? Hey, all I'd have to do is to add a few Da Vinci paintings and I'd have a guaranteed bestseller ;o).

But this isn't fiction. Everything you're about to read here is 100% true. It happened. It is happening right now, and somehow I'm a part of it.

...and now you are too.

However, there is one downside to this technology, and this is the main reason why not everybody in the world is using it yet:

> It simply doesn't make sense from our current understanding of who we are.

There are no known technologies to heal ourselves or develop our full brain potential, let alone to radiate peace. If there were, everybody would be using them, *right*?

Wrong.

Scientists at more than 200 universities, including several of the most prestigious institutions in the world, have confirmed that this technology works. In fact, we'll see throughout this book that there is no other solution available with as much scientific evidence, documenting such a wide range of improvements on so many different areas of life at the same time.

And still very few people are even aware that it exists, for a very simple reason: if the technology itself doesn't make sense, no amount of research will convince people.

For this technology to make sense, we require a paradigm shift – a completely new understanding of who we are...and how powerful we are.

Here's how I would explain this new paradigm.

The Field Paradigm: How it Works, How it was Forgotten, and How it was Rediscovered

1. We are Far Bigger Than We Think

A paradigm is like a set of glasses that we forget we're wearing. It's a collection of our most fundamental beliefs, that define how we see the world.

If the glasses are pink, our world is pink.

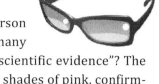

What would happen if you tried to convince a person wearing pink glasses that the world consists of many different colors? What if you held a color chart as "scientific evidence"? The person wearing the glasses would only see different shades of pink, confirming their belief that the world is, in fact, pink, and that it is *you* who are mistaken.

But if suddenly, through some kind of shock, the person's glasses fell off, then they'd see everything differently. Now they could see things as they really are. Suddenly that color chart appears to be legitimate scientific proof of how it really is.

Likewise, we have our own glasses through which we see the world. We think we see things clearly but our glasses actually blind us from seeing 90% of the true reality.

Here's how we see the world with our current glasses:

When we look around us, we see many distinct objects, separate from each other. There's a chair, a table, and nothing in between. Likewise, we see ourselves as separate from each other. I am here, you are there, and there is nothing connecting us.

Because our bodies are separate, and our minds are linked to our bodies, we naturally believe that our minds are separate as well.

This is how we see the world, but that is not how it really is.

The texts from the most ancient tradition in the world, the Vedic Tradition, describe civilizations where people had a very different set of glasses. They believed they were a part of a larger interconnected whole, an invisible force that connects everyone and everything. They described this force as a field of universal life, universal consciousness.

They also described how our individual minds are individual expressions on this field, just like many different waves can come from one single ocean at the same time.

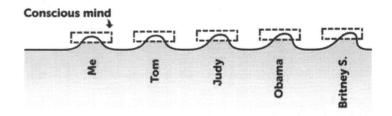

The ancient texts described this "ocean" as having qualities of pure love, omnipresence, omniscience, and omnipotence: the qualities that are usually associated with a divine being. They didn't see this divine being as an individual person however (old man with a long beard sitting on some clouds somewhere), but rather as an omnipresent, impersonal force of which they - were all a part.

As romantic as it may sound to be *part of some higher force*, it can't be possible, right? Our consciousness is clearly restricted to our bodies, and our bodies are clearly separate from each other, right?

Well, yes and no. It all depends on how we see it.

Dr. Tony Nader, an MIT and Harvard educated neuroscientist (who was later appointed as Maharishi's successor), described it as follows: we often compare the relationship of the body and mind to a computer, where the hardware (the brain) creates the software (the mind).

This feels like a logical analogy. Turn the hardware off (sleep), and the software stops working. Damaging the hardware (brain damage) will affect the quality of the software. And if the computer is permanently broken (death), it's "game over".

From this perspective, *we would have to be* separate from each other. We all have our own hardware, each running its own software.

But what if, Dr Nader says, we use the analogy of a radio instead?

In this case, the music clearly connects to the hardware, just like software to a computer. Turn the radio off, and the music stops. Mess around with the hardware of the radio and the quality of the music is affected. And if the hardware is permanently broken, the music is gone.

Well...no. The local expression of the music through the radio stops, but the music itself continues.

In the case of the radio, the music is *expressed through* the hardware, but it's not *coming from* the hardware. The music itself is a vibration of the electromagnetic field, which we call radio waves. We all know that this field can vibrate in many different ways at the same time, just as an ocean can rise in many different waves.

- 97.1 FM: Classical
- 101.7 FM: Rock
- 103.5 FM: Pop
- 106.4 FM: Dance

In this analogy, each human body would be like a radio tuned into a unique frequency, allowing each person to have their own thoughts. But at the source of our thoughts we are all connected.

The radio analogy allows us to understand how we can all have our individual identity while at the same time being part of a larger field of consciousness.

Now here's the interesting part. In ancient time, this being part of a larger whole wasn't just a belief system, it was people's direct experience. They had a way to bring their minds to a state where they were completely silent, while remaining fully conscious and alert at the same time. A silent wave becomes the ocean itself. If they could

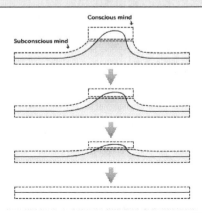

15

consciously experience this, this means they had a conscious experience of their unity with everything and everyone.

> We call this experience *transcending* because they transcended the boundaries of their individual minds, which brought them to an unbounded state.

We'll describe transcending as diving into the ocean. It's creating a splash and enlivening the surface of the water. In terms of this field, its qualities simply became lively in their awareness.

2. We are Far More Beautiful Than We Think

One quality of the Unified Field that became lively in people's awareness is *omnipresence*. Omnipresent means that it is everywhere, and connects every single point in creation to every other single point. It's because of the omnipresent quality of fields that it is possible to broadcast a radio signal at one single point, and pick it up at any other point around it, even at the other side of the universe if the signal is strong enough.

We can all directly experience this quality of omnipresence in our lives every single day, and we have a name for this experience: Love.

What is love?

When we love somebody, we feel connected to them, right? *Love is an experience of feeling connected*, even if there's nothing physical connecting us. The only reason we *can* have this experience is because we are in fact all connected through this omnipresent field at the source of our minds.

Another word for this experience of connectedness is compassion. Sometimes people send money to help people on the other side of the world after a natural disaster strikes there. These are people that we don't know and will probably never meet, but still we feel connected to them. We know they need help, and we feel compelled to do something.

16

> One of the oldest questions of humanity, "Why do we love?" suddenly has a very simple answer. Love doesn't make sense from a paradigm of separation. Computers don't love. From a paradigm of connectedness, on the other hand, love is simply an experience of our true human nature, an *experience* that we are all, in fact, connected.

To distinguish this kind of connection from the experience of love we feel towards a limited selection of people, we will call this "Primal Love", a universal higher love that connects everything.

If this Primal Love is at the source of our consciousness, then everybody's true nature would be pure love. It would mean we are far more beautiful than we think.

In ancient times, when people transcended regularly, they enlivened and strengthened this unity of love in their own awareness, and started experiencing this connection on a permanent basis. For them, the concept of "unconditional love" was not some dogmatic ideal. It was an everyday reality.

3. We are Far More Powerful Than We Think

Transcending also had an even more interesting side-effect. When people dive into the ocean, they don't just create a splash where they dive in, but also create waves that spread out around them. This means the quality of

connectedness was not only enlivened within the person doing the transcending, but also with the people around them.

As a result, when one person took a dive into the transcendent, all the people around them spontaneously changed their behaviour as well. Yesterday they didn't feel anything was wrong with hurting their neighbour to get something for themselves. Today *it just doesn't feel right anymore*. They can't explain why they changed their minds, they just did.

> The technique to transcend was essentially a technique to "radiate positivity", or "radiate love", just like a light bulb radiates light.

This would mean that we are far more powerful than we think. A small percentage of people who learn to transcend can change the world.

4. Losing the Ability to Transcend: How Our True Nature Became Hidden

Over time, people forgot the technique to transcend, and as such, their experience of reality changed as well.

> When people no longer had the ability to experience the deeper layers of their minds – where the wave meets the ocean – it was as if the mind split into two parts, what psychologists now call the conscious and subconscious mind.

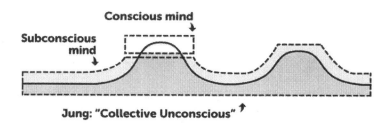

They could only consciously experience the top part of the wave, where they experienced themselves as separate, while the ocean, the part where we're all connected, became hidden in the subconscious mind. (Carl Jung called this the "collective unconscious", a part of our unconscious mind that we share collectively.) People were no longer able to experience their connection to nature and to each other and forgot it existed in the first place.

This caused their paradigm to change. They still believed that there was some kind of higher omnipresent, omniscient, and omnipotent being that controlled everything in the universe, but they started to see this being as a personal deity, separate from them, rather than something of which they were all a part.

We will call this the *God Paradigm*, a belief that there is a higher being but we are separate from it.

As a result our relationship with this divine entity changed, from inner experience of a part of ourselves to outer worship of something external.

The way how this process of worship happened became different in different cultures, and became the most important part of our cultural identity. We started calling ourselves Christians, Jews, Muslims, Hindus, etc.

By itself a strong cultural identity is a good thing, as it creates a feeling of being part of something larger and an integration in society. The problem was that this identity eventually became like a set of paradigm glasses. Suddenly it was no longer a matter of one deity, and different ways to worship and celebrate this deity, but we started believing in different deities. We were the only ones who saw things correctly, and the only ones who had the right deity. All other religions were wrong, and it was our responsibility to bring them back on the right path or, if they were not able to see the light, simply remove them from the equation.

This illustrated how losing our connection to each other lead to a far bigger problem still. Not only did our worldview and our view on the divine change, but also the way we started treating each other changed. Our religions may preach compassion and unconditional love, but it's a lot harder to put this in practice with beings that are separate from you and your culture and beliefs than with those who are a part of you.

> We still believed that 'God is love' but our behavior towards each other became a whole lot less loving, as we no longer experienced we were *part* of this universal love.

And this was only the first paradigm change. A far more fundamental shift in our paradigms was about to come...from the scientists.

As their understanding of the forces in nature grew, scientists started to explain more and more phenomena as material processes: our universe was made up of little balls, called atoms, interacting with each other through invisible, omnipresent force fields like gravity and electromagnetism.

Eventually, it was no longer necessary to include a higher being to explain why the Sun came up, why weather patterns changed, or why we got sick. Suddenly they had far more logical, and far more reliable, explanations. As a result, people started to believe there might be nothing higher at all. The universe might just function as one big predictable machine.

We will call this the *Machine Paradigm*, a belief that there *is no higher being*, and that our entire universe is material, mechanical.

The more we were able to understand the laws of nature, the more the resulting technologies brought material comfort to our lives. As a result, we started to see the Machine Paradigm as the ultimate reality – it all works, so it must be true – until *we started to believe that even life itself was an expression of material processes*. We started to believe, in other words, that the hardware creates the software.

> In essence, this reduced us to sophisticated walking robots. It wasn't very romantic, but at least the technologies seemed to work. If we knew how the hardware worked, we could also fix it when it broke down.

The Machine Paradigm brought us amazing technologies: brain scanners, airplanes, instant communication with people at the other side of the world, etc. But did it help us improve our behavior towards each other?

Not really. In fact, the opposite happened. When people started to believe that the material reality was the only true reality, they also started to see the fulfillment of life as *gathering as many material things as they could.*

Under the God Paradigm people were at least hesitant about hurting their neighbours because, oh boy, were they going to pay for that one in the afterlife. In the Machine Paradigm, there was no God and no afterlife, just the not-so-pleasant smell of our decaying bodies. When the computer breaks down, the game is over. Finished. It's as simple as that.

So it doesn't matter if you hurt others. Just get as much stuff as you can for yourself while you can still play.

But something wasn't quite right with this picture. How many people do you know who on their deathbed said, '*You know, I really wish I had gotten a bigger car*'? How many super-wealthy people still have to deal with anxiety or depression?

At some point in our lives, we all realize that there has to be more than just material things.

In some ways, the Machine Paradigm made things a lot worse. In the God Paradigm, when people started behaving inhumanely to each other (because they lost their connection to their own source of humanity) the maximum damage they could do to each other was pretty much limited to whatever damage they could inflict with a sword or an arrow.

In the Machine Paradigm, we gained almost full mastery over the laws of nature, allowing us to build ever more powerful destructive devices: explosives, tanks, missiles, and nuclear bombs or bioweapons that could fit inside a suitcase yet could wipe out an entire city.

At the height of the Machine Paradigm we built a nuclear arsenal big enough to destroy the entire world many times over. At the same time, we moved even further away from our own humanity, allowing ourselves to *actually use some of these weapons*.

Fortunately, things eventually started to turn around.

5. The Field Paradigm Rediscovered

> Most of us live either in the God Paradigm, the belief that there is something higher from which we're separate, or in the Machine Paradigm, the belief that there's nothing higher at all.
>
> Both the latest scientific discoveries and the experiments that we'll discuss later are now revealing that *neither is true*.

In the end, the very science that started the Machine Paradigm – physics – also resulted in its undoing.

Throughout this book we'll see how:

- Quantum physics revealed that our idea of a universe built out of tiny separate material balls called atoms was an illusion. Subatomic particles are themselves waves of omnipresent fields, waves that only appear as separate material objects.
- Einstein predicted, and physicists later mathematically defined, one "Unified Field" that creates all the different phenomena in the universe by vibrating in many different ways.
- With a few simple steps of logic, we can demonstrate that this one field, by definition, must be a field of consciousness.

> We'll see how the latest discoveries in physics are confirming exactly what some of the oldest texts in human history already claimed 5000 years ago: consciousness is a field.

We will call this the *Field Paradigm*: the reality that there is only one field of consciousness and everything – both our subjective inner world and our objective outer world – is a part of this field.

In Part 2 of this book, we'll discover that the Field Paradigm appears to be a scientific reality, rather than just a philosophy. We'll discover that the universe is not a dead material machine, but something that is alive, breathing life into every subatomic particle we see around us. (We'll see later how physics is now discovering how even the smallest subatomic particles show properties of consciousness). We'll see that we are part of this living entity, like waves are a part of the ocean.

Once we change our glasses and start to see ourselves as a part of this larger whole, we'll see that a lot more things start to make sense. We'll also find that there is a solid body of scientific evidence showing that 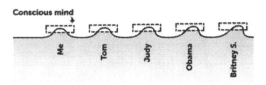 we are far more powerful than we believe. Through this field, we can change our reality just with the power of our thoughts.

This is where the "magic" comes in to our story.

Rediscovering our True Selves

If we are part of a field that has the divine qualities of omnipresence (love), omniscience, and omnipotence then this means *we must have these qualities as well*, even if they are hidden deep inside our subconscious minds.

> Most of us intuitively feel there must be more to life than what we are experiencing. We all feel that we're good, wise, and loving people deep inside, but we somehow forget this in our behaviour. We seem to have lost

> something along the way.
>
> We can't even begin to imagine what would be possible if we could only remember to be our true selves.

We've already seen that if we really are like waves on an ocean, and if we could bring our minds into a state of complete silence while remaining conscious, we could theoretically experience the ocean itself.

But how do you make the mind silent? Have you ever tried this? It almost sounds impossible. The more you *try* to make your mind silent, the more you keep it active.

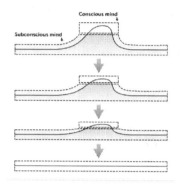

The process of silencing the mind was commonly understood as "meditation". Over time, however, the natural process of meditation got lost when people started *trying* to meditate (usually through some form of concentration on one's breath or a sound, or in monitoring one's thoughts).

This *misinterpretation* that meditation involves some kind of control of the mind resulted in the loss of the ability to transcend. Trying only keeps the mind active, preventing it from transcending. *Even the slightest activity* from the wave will prevent it from becoming silent and merging with the ocean.

As a result, the best thing people could hope for when they meditated was some relaxation. The real goal of meditation – to come back in touch with our true essence, a complete unity with this higher force in the universe – was lost.

Or rather, it was *almost* lost. There was still a group of masters in the Himalayas, completely secluded from the rest of mankind, who had the proper techniques to transcend. They kept this knowledge in its pure form for thousands of years, but the only way to learn it was to give up pretty much your entire life and go live in a cave in the mountains near these teachers.

In the early 20th century, a young physics student did exactly that. He joined this tradition and spent 13 years as a student of one of its last great masters. Eventually, the student became a great teacher himself and was given the title *Maharishi Mahesh Yogi*.

In 1958, Maharishi began teaching a simple message around the world:

We don't have to force the mind to be silent. With the right technique, it will happen naturally. Meditation, if practiced correctly, is the easiest thing you've ever done, and anyone can learn to do it... yet, at the same time it will develop your full potential.

To distinguish his technique from all the hundreds of other forms of meditation he called it Transcendental Meditation. This was not another technique to meditate. This was *a technique to transcend*.

As soon as he started teaching his technique, commonly referred to as "TM", people felt that this was something different, something authentic. They felt that transcending was indeed easy to do, yet at the same time it was extremely effective. Most people felt the effects from the first few sittings, and more often than not, these effects were life transforming.

The rest is history. Over the next 50 years, the Transcendental Meditation technique became the most practiced "relaxation" technique in the world, with over six million people learning it.

However, given what transcending really is, six million sounds rather disappointing.

> Few people understand how powerful transcending is, or that it has effects ordinary relaxation could never create.

Let's come back to the quality of omnipresence we experience as love. The ancient texts described this field as the "pure good". When people experience this, negativity simply cannot continue to exist, just as darkness cannot continue to exist when we turn on the light.

The true nature of everyone is pure love, pure good, but most of us have forgotten this. Even if the music itself is beautiful, if the radio playing it is distorted enough something rather unpleasing can come out.

As soon as we can remove the distortions, however, *everything* starts to change.

It wasn't very hard to objectively verify this. Transcendental Meditation quickly became the most researched relaxation technique in the world, with over 350 scientific publications from 250 universities and research institutions.

The results were spectacular.

Here's a list of some of the many benefits they confirmed, all happening at the same time...and in almost every case we're talking about far more profound changes than what can be achieved through medication or other current treatments:

Improved health: decreased anxiety, depression, insomnia, PTSD, nicotine addiction, alcoholism, drug addiction, hypertension, cholesterol, diabetes, cardiovascular disease, obesity, fibromyalgia, asthma, ADHD, reversal of the detrimental effects of aging, etc.

Improved brain functioning: improved IQ, creativity, concentration, memory, EQ, learning ability, field independence, emotional stability, increased serotonin (happiness).

Being yourself: improved self-confidence, self-acceptance, spontaneity, job performance, and a greater capacity for warm, interpersonal relationships.

Spiritual growth: improved intuition, more spiritual experiences of unity with nature, more love, more in touch with one's deepest desires, more spontaneous fulfillment of desires, and...more magic.

> The research shows that transcending, going back to the core of who we really are, has a profound influence on pretty much all areas of life.

In Part 3 of this book we'll examine how transcending creates all these effects, and how the scientific research that confirms this is of an extraordinary high quality (one reason why more and more governments are already supporting TM...though not nearly enough).

However, the best part is yet to come. As we mentioned before, the effect of transcending is so powerful that *not even everybody has to learn*. Whenever a person transcends, they also create a ripple effect throughout their environment, just like a diver creating waves across the surface of the water.

It is mainly this effect that our delegation was going to present to the president of Guinea-Bissau.

The Field Effect of Transcending

6 a.m. The plane lands in Guinea-Bissau. A motorcade comes to pick us up and bring us to the hotel (there's only one hotel in the entire country that is suitable for international guests), so we can rest and freshen up a bit.

11 a.m. The motorcade drives us to the presidential palace. This is supposed to be the nicest neighbourhood in the country but there's still poverty everywhere we look. Guards with big machine guns surround the presidential palace. They look menacing, but I guess that is their job. After years of violence and civil war, they've gotten pretty good at it.

We are invited to the presidential suite. Everybody sits down and the scientists make their presentations.

I was impressed by the dignified manner of the presentation, with the scientists making it clear that they were there to offer something rather than to ask for anything. The President seems to enjoy this. I'm sure he isn't used to this kind of exchange.

The essence of their presentation focused on the TM Field Effect as the quickest proven way to solve the civil conflict.

Essentially, this is how it can be explained:

The TM Field Effect works like a light bulb. A small light bulb can light up an entire big room because the bulb *is connected to the whole room* through an invisible field called the electromagnetic field. It will excite this field with vibrations – creating light waves – that will spread in all directions and light up the room.

Now, what happens if we turn off the light? The electromagnetic field doesn't disappear. It's still there, but it's no longer enlivened. We experience this as darkness.

Likewise, the Unified Field of consciousness that connects all of us is always present. But when humans forgot how to transcend, it's like they forgot how to turn on the light.

Light, in terms of the Unified Field, is Primal Love, the pure good we all have inside of us. When this fundamental aspect of our humanity is no longer enlivened, the resulting darkness will start to result in inhuman behaviour: crime, corruption, terrorism, wars, etc.

> Negativity is just the absence of positivity, the absence of our true human nature; just as darkness is only the absence of light.

Just as it only takes a few streetlights to light up a whole city, it's not necessary for everyone to transcend to remove the darkness in everybody's minds. Just a few people can radiate it for everyone else.

This is why Maharishi always used to say, *"Don't fight the darkness, just turn on the light."*

The most powerful way to create this effect is if people practice transcending together in big groups, using an advanced meditation technique called the TM-Sidhi program. This allows people to stay in the transcendental state for much longer and allows them to "coordinate their transcending" with each other. Then something really special happens.

Let's use our diving analogy one more time.

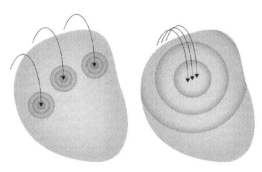

If three people dive separately, they will create three waves that will affect the surface around them. But if they jump together, the three waves will add up to one single much bigger wave, which will influence a much larger area still. This

27

way a small group of even as few as a hundred participants could create a wave that is powerful enough to influence an entire country.

The most relevant experiment that the scientists could propose to the President of Guinea-Bissau was the one that had already transformed the destiny of Mozambique.

In 1992, a similar delegation from the TM organisation met with the president of Mozambique, Dr. Alberto Joaquin Chissano.

Chissano was impressed by the scientific research on the TM Field Effect and decided to give it a try.

He learned the TM technique and its advance techniques himself and had the entire army learn and practice it daily as a group. From that moment, the civil war that had been raging for 17 years came to an abrupt end, and never started again. Over the next 10 years Mozambique – once the world's poorest country – became the world's fastest growing economy.

This was the biggest success story of a government-sponsored TM Field Effect experiment so far; yet it was only one of many.

The other experiments that have taken place during the past 40 years, several of them with precise results predicted in advance, range from:

- creating record decreases in crime rate and car accidents
- stopping wars in more than a dozen other countries around world
- reducing global terrorism by 72%
- playing a crucial role in the ending of the Cold War and the fall of the Berlin wall.

All at a cost easily *1000 times lower* than conventional methods of dealing with these issues, while being both far more effective and far more reliable by all scientific standards.

The scientists presented several leading scientific journals that had already published the research confirming these effects. Generally speaking, research is only taken seriously if a journal examines and approves it through a process called peer-review. If the reviewers feel the research is correct, and the journal is willing to link its reputation to the study, the journal will publish. Our delegation could show more than 20 such publications, several of which were published in the most prestigious social science journals in the world.

Taken together, these publications now form the most solid body of scientific evidence to date that *the Field Paradigm is real*. (The TM field effect is only possible if there is, in fact, a field that connects us at the source of our consciousness.) Not only that, they showed that there is now an extremely powerful, practical technology to use the field properties of consciousness. It really is just a matter of "using the Force".

When all this data was presented to the president of Guinea-Bissau, you could see from his expression that he was interested. So were all the other ministers with whom our delegation met afterward. You could see on their faces that they all started to realize something I figured a while ago:

> If this is all true, it must be one of the best-kept secrets in the world. This could change the destiny of mankind.

After our meetings, they asked us to wait in the hotel while they would deliberate how to move forward with the proposal.

So, while we wait, let's dive into the Field Paradigm a little deeper.

In the next few chapters, we'll become more familiar with the Field Paradigm. We'll discuss the evolution of physics as it has now discovered that the Field Paradigm can be taken seriously as a scientific reality.

Next, we'll show how a lot of phenomena in nature and personal experiences (especially the ones that we call "paranormal") start to make sense when we look at them through our Field Paradigm glasses.

In Part 3 of this book, we'll then dive into the research on the changes that are possible when we can actually learn to *experience* the Field. These are the 20 experiments that will truly change the world.

Part 1 Summary

By using the analogy of a radio rather than a computer to describe the relationship between our body and mind/consciousness, we can see ourselves as both individual beings linked to our bodies and part of a universal field of consciousness.

This field connects everyone and everything, a connection we experience as love. In our true natures, we are far more beautiful than we can imagine.

The technique to experience our true nature was lost over time but has been recently rediscovered. When people practice this technique they find healing effects on almost all levels of life, and they also create a positive effect for their environment.

Part 2: The Field Paradigm as a Scientific Reality

A human being is part of a whole, called by us the 'Universe'— a part limited in time and space. He experiences himself, his thoughts, and feelings, as something separated from the rest— a kind of optical delusion of his consciousness.

- Albert Einstein

The Field Paradigm Rediscovered in Science 34
   Subatomic Particles with Consciousness?... 34
   A bit of Physics History 36
   How Einstein killed the Machine Paradigm (and nobody knows about it) 39
   From Diversity to Unity: How Things Appear Different at Different Scales 47
   Why the Unified Field Must be a Field of Consciousness..................... 50
   Man in the Image of God, or God in the Image of man?...................... 52

Examples of Connectedness in Nature 56
   Telepathic Plants 56
   Birds United... 59
   Collective Memory 60

The Science of Miracles: How Paranormal Phenomena Start to Make Sense... 62
   I'll Believe it When I see it 62
   Memory: The Key to Understanding Psychic Phenomena.................... 66
   The Science of Probability... 69
   I Want to Move It, Move It: Research on Mind-Matter Interactions......... 71
   Do you Mind? Telepathy!... 76
   I see...I see...What You Can't See... Clairvoyance................................... 80
   Eternal Life: The Ultimate Challenge to the Machine Paradigm 85

The Law of Action and Reaction from a Field Paradigm Perspective . 95

Part 2 Overview

In this part, we'll see how research has shown, from many different angles, that the Field Paradigm appears to be a scientific reality rather than just a philosophy. We'll learn that understanding fields and waves requires a completely different logic than understanding material particles. We'll become familiar with this new logic.

We'll see many examples of phenomena in nature and in human behaviour that never made sense from a Machine Paradigm point of view, but make perfect sense in the Field Paradigm.

We'll also discover how, through the field that connects everyone and everything, our thoughts can influence our environment. This influence becomes a lot stronger if it's created from deeper levels of the mind.

My First Footsteps in a World of Magic

Throughout my life I've had many experiences that showed me a very different universe than the one the Machine Paradigm describes. Most people would describe these experiences as "paranormal", though I prefer the word "magical".

The one that still stands out most, though, was my very first experience.

I was 17 and had just finished my TM-Sidhi course. We'll discuss this course in more detail later, but like I said earlier, it's the closest thing in real life to going on a Jedi Knight training course or attending Hogwarts. It's all about bringing more magic in your life.

A few weeks after the course, I had my first clear taste.

I was at home listening to the radio, when the DJ announced a contest. In a few minutes, they would play a song selected from all songs released between 1960 and now. If you could guess the name of the song and the band that played it, you would win a ticket to a rock concert.

As I listened to the announcement, a thought came up that the song would be *Vamos a la Playa*. The strange thing was that this thought came with such clarity, a kind of certainty. I didn't know the band's name, however, so for a second I considered calling my friend who had the CD to ask him.

But then my intellect kicked in: *'Are you crazy? What do you think the odds are of them picking exactly this song? Are you going to waste money on a telephone call for that?'* True, I thought, the odds are indeed pretty slim. Thirty years of music, maybe 1000 new songs released every year: that would put the odds at roughly one in 30,000.

Naturally, I didn't call.

And then, five minutes later, guess what was playing on the radio?

Vamos a la playa, o ohohoho.

Ever since that moment, whenever my intellect tries to interfere, I gently remind it that it still owes me a concert ticket! ;o)

But then the bigger questions come. *"How does this work? How can it be that a thought I have in my mind exactly matches an event in the outside world? Does this mean there is a connection between the two?"*

And then the more important question comes: *"If this connection exists, why don't we have these experiences more often? Why does it only seem to happen now and then, not all the time?"*

Answering these questions is a large part of what this book is about – that and learning how to actually have them much more often.

As for my own experiences, since that moment I have had many more. They may not always have been as spectacular as the radio incident, but they nevertheless often proved extremely practical. Usually, such thoughts come in the form of intuition, a vague feeling that I should go in a particular direction, even if I couldn't intellectually explain why.

I learned to develop and trust this intuition, and it has served me very well in my life. It's what brought me from being a 19-year-old with $100 start-up capital and no business experience starting a network to trade videogames to running a chain of 13 games stores with 30 employees in just three years.

The problem with "magic" is that it requires constant exercise. It's just like competing in sports, which requires constant practice to stay at the top of your game. I had to learn that rule the hard way. I got carried away by my success. I wanted more and more and started to work harder, while neglecting my training. I made the mistake of thinking that success came from what I did, rather than who I was. As a result, the thoughts that started coming up were no longer the right thoughts at the right time anymore.

> So I started making the wrong decisions and in the end lost everything - except the lessons I had learned.
>
> Those put me on a very different path, almost exclusively focused on spiritual growth and developing my full potential. I even lived a monk's life for several years and eventually got to work on projects where I could report to Maharishi directly, often on a daily basis.
>
> Looking back, I can assure you I have zero regrets about losing a $5M company. What I gained instead was far more valuable.

The Field Paradigm Rediscovered in Science

Subatomic Particles with Consciousness?

The $9 billion CERN Large Hadron Collider (LHC) is the most expensive experiment in the history of physics. It's essentially a 27 km-long ring of tubes buried 175 metres below Geneva, Switzerland. Scientists designed the LHC to accelerate subatomic particles in opposite directions to insanely high speeds, close to the speed of light (300,000 km per second). They then smash the particles into each other, releasing an enormous amount of energy.

To imagine the power of these collisions, imagine a particle that weighs less than one billionth of one gram, but when it hits something, it has the power equivalent to a 300-ton train travelling at 100 km/hour. Now imagine two of these trains crashing into each other, and you get an idea of the kind of force we're talking about. The energy released in this collision can recreate conditions similar to those right after the Big Bang. It is enough force to break subatomic particles into even smaller pieces that fly off in all directions, a bit like the debris that flies off when you crash a car into a wall.

By measuring these smaller particles, scientists can look for the high-energy particles that physics models would predict. The most famous discovery so far has been that of the Higgs Boson, a particle that gives all other particles mass.

Yet on September 22, 2010, the BBC News website[1] reported on another LHC discovery that some physicists regarded as far more important still.

CERN researchers noticed that when the particles smash into each other, the resulting debris doesn't fly off in all directions at random but follows certain patterns. "In some sense, it's like the particles talk to each other and they decide which way to go," ex-  plained CERN spokesperson Guido Tonelli. How is this possible? Particles that communicate with each other? "I go this way, you go that way"?

The data was solid. Even though the effect was small, statistical analysis showed phenomena that couldn't be explained by random behavior. The scientists, however, simply didn't know what to do with these phenomena

According to the Machine Paradigm, consciousness arises from the functioning of our brains, but these subatomic particles (which obviously didn't have brains) were showing a form of conscious behavior. It just didn't make sense.

So when the scientists announced it, they called it 'new and interesting effects', without daring to make any further interpretations.

Actually, the CERN scientists were not the first to notice this strange behavior at the subatomic level. The BBC article mentioned that another research lab in the U.S. had already noticed similar results. In fact, more than 60 years earlier, physicist David Bohm had already demonstrated in the 1950s that subatomic particles like electrons often behave as if they know what other electrons are doing and coordinate with each other. They seemed to have a conscious awareness of each other's actions.

So here we have something that is utterly impossible according to the Machine Paradigm, and yet the data shows that it's happening. (We'll get a lot more of those, by the way.)

 But what if we change our glasses and start to think of consciousness as a field, and think of these particles as waves on this field rather than individual lifeless material balls (as quantum physics already discovered 100 years ago, as we'll see in next chapter). Would it make more sense then?

This is where the qualities of omnipresence and omniscience of this field come in.

Omnipresence, as we have already seen, means that the field is in all places at the same time, connecting every single point to every other point.

Omniscience, on the other hand, implies that this field has a conscious awareness of every point of creation. It knows everything that is going on. This could also mean that one part of the field (say, a subatomic particle) can know what is going on with another part of the field.

I know this probably all is a bit of a stretch for your imagination, but that's exactly what we will be doing with this part: stretching your imagination until you feel completely comfortable with a complete new perspective on our reality. We'll go on a journey through the history of physics and see how physics first led us to the assumptions of the Machine Paradigm, only to later prove their own assumptions wrong.

As we go on this journey you'll learn how fields and waves have a different logic than material particles. Becoming familiar with this new logic is the key to understanding the true potential of the Field Paradigm.

A bit of Physics History

Since the early days of the Greek philosophers, there were two schools of thought with very different views on reality.

On the one hand, there was the camp of Democritus, widely regarded as the founding father of the scientific móvement (and the first messenger of the Machine Paradigm). Democritus described that reality was ultimately material, built from tiny small building blocks, which he called atoms (*atom comes from the Greek word atómos,* which means *indivisible* – Democritus used this word to describe the smallest building block of creation). Everything was material and perfectly predictable, like one big machine.

On the other hand, there was the view of Socrates and Plato, who both described that the ultimate reality was spiritual. They claimed that the material world only covers up the true spiritual nature of the universe. Plato was, in essence, one of the first messengers of the Field Paradigm in western civilization.

During the last 300 years, the advancement of science seemed to indicate that Democritus' hypothesis would win, as physicists were able to reduce almost every phenomenon in nature down to predictable mechanical events. That is, until the whole material worldview started crumbling down.

It began with the discovery that these smallest indivisible building blocks, atoms, *were* actually divisible. They were built from even smaller building blocks, an atomic nucleus with protons and neutrons, with electrons orbiting around them.

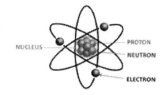

Even more surprising was the minuscule size of these smaller particles compared to the empty space between them. Scientists estimated that if an electron were the size of your fist, the distance to the nucleus would be about from here to the moon.

In other words, it turned out that atoms, those small building blocks from which our entire material universe is constructed, *are mostly empty space*. The actual physical matter within atoms was estimated to take up only one-billionth of the size of the atom. So if I took the desk in front of me and squeezed it together so that all the empty space is squeezed out and only the actual physical matter remains, that desk would be one billion times smaller than it is now.

That's a small desk.

Now that brings up an interesting question. If the desk in front of me is mostly empty space and my hand is mostly empty space, why can't I move my hand through my desk? I can't because this empty space is not completely empty. It is empty in a material sense, but it is filled with energy, force fields.

Since the early 19th century, physicists knew of the existence of the electromagnetic field. The electromagnetic force keeps electrons with a negative charge circling around the positively-charged nucleus. Through this electromagnetic "glue" all atoms and molecules are kept intact.

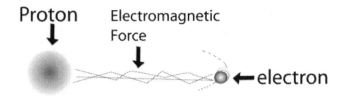

If the electromagnetic field disappeared, our entire physical universe would collapse immediately.

So let's come back to our question: why doesn't my hand go through the table?

Not because the physical matter in my hand repels the physical matter in the desk, but because the electromagnetic forces in between the particles of the table repel the electromagnetic forces between particles in my hand. Can forces really repel material substances? Anyone who has ever tried bringing the same poles of two magnets close to each other knows the answer to this question.

The result is that the physical material in the table appears to repel my hand, giving our illusion of a material world a rather realistic feel.

Of course, it all depends on exactly how much force you apply when you try to move your hand through that table. If you want to play *Karate Kid* and apply a force that's strong enough, stronger than the electromagnetic "glue" between the molecules of the table, you might break the bonds, and break the table. In this case, your hand will actually go through...or you might break some bones in your hand. Perhaps better not to try this one.

In other cases, depending on the chemical composition of the material you are touching, you might be able to bend the material. Some materials feel soft, some hard. Some are in solid states, others are liquids, and others still are gasses. It all depends on how the atoms and electromagnetic bonds between them are structured. But what repels our hand is energy, not matter.

Don't we live in a wonderful illusion?

Physicists discovered that matter... doesn't matter, so to speak. In reality, it is 99.9999999% empty space.

Or at least that was what physicists assumed.

This was only the beginning of the end for the Machine Paradigm.

The real undoing came from a particular scientist whose name you may have heard mentioned once or twice before: Albert Einstein.

How Einstein killed the Machine Paradigm (and nobody knows about it)

Einstein is probably the most famous scientist in history. Voted the most important person of the 20th century by *Time* magazine, Einstein's name is almost synonymous with the word "genius".

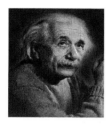

And I'm willing to bet you have no idea of what his most important contribution to physics was... the fact that he almost singlehandedly killed the Machine Paradigm.

Few people are aware that when Einstein got his Nobel Prize, it wasn't for his famous e=mc² formula, which ultimately resulted in atomic energy, or for his General Theory of Relativity (which almost nobody understands, but everybody seems to be pretty impressed by). Instead, he got his Nobel Prize for a paper he wrote in 1905 where he created a theory to explain some phenomena his colleague Max Planck had found. This paper ultimately led to an even more important event in physics: the quantum revolution.

Quantum physics revealed that even the one-billionth part of our atom that was still considered to be physical matter, wasn't material at all. It only *appeared* that way.

> Even the most basic building blocks of nature, like electrons, were in reality vibrations of fields, like waves on an ocean. The only difference between matter and empty space is that wherever there's matter, the field – in this case, an electron field – vibrates, whereas in empty space it doesn't.

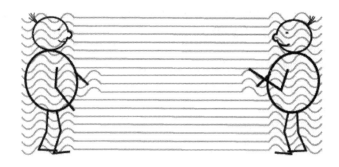

It's kind of like light and darkness. The electromagnetic field in a room with the light on is the same as in a room where it's dark. The only difference is that in a lighted room, the field vibrates, and in a dark room, it doesn't. Like that, matter "appears" where the field vibrates, and there's empty space where it's silent.

So the entire idea of our universe as a dead material machine was just one big illusion. There is no matter, only energy.

Niels Bohr, one of the founding fathers of quantum physics once famously said:

> *"If quantum mechanics hasn't profoundly shocked you, you haven't understood it yet."*

Given how many people are still frantically collecting material things as if their lives depend on it, more than 100 years after it was revealed that all material things are just illusions, it seems like few people understood it so far. At least they don't seem to be very shocked.

The breakdown of the matter illusion was just the beginning, however. It was about to get a lot weirder still.

It seemed electrons were sometimes behaving as waves, and sometimes as particles.

Before we get into this, we first have to explain a fundamental difference between a wave and a particle.

Let's use an example:

Imagine you ask your friend to run circles around you. Can you see him running? Good. Now if you tried to throw a ball at him, you'd better throw more or less in the right direction. Otherwise, he won't be able to catch it. On the other hand, if you shouted at him, he will hear you no matter where on the circle he is running.

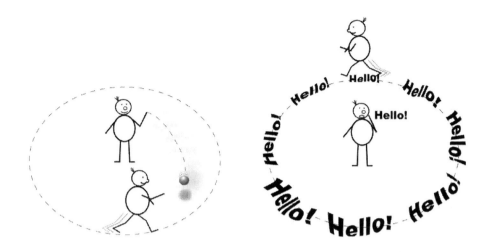

The ball, a particle, can only be at one location, whereas the sound waves are everywhere at the same time.

Do you get the difference? Okay, then please tell your friend to stop running his circles, he's probably getting dizzy by now.

The strange thing about electrons was that sometimes they behaved as particles, being in one specific place, at other times they behaved as waves, being at many places at the same time.

But here's the weirdest thing about it. Whether it appeared as a wave or as a particle seemed to *depend on whether it was being observed or not.*

When unobserved, the electron is a waveform, a state of all possibilities. It will not be in one particular place in its orbit around the nucleus, but at all places at once. However, when the scientist puts his conscious attention to it, the waveform collapses and becomes a particle, localized in one particular place*.

---

* There is a continuous debate up until today whether it is really conscious attention that collapses the waveform into a particle. Like with all paradigm-shifts this radically new idea is very controversial in contemporary science, and by no means is generally accepted. For our purpose, we will make the assumption that it does, and show how it perfectly fits in and fully supports the paradigm that is proposed.

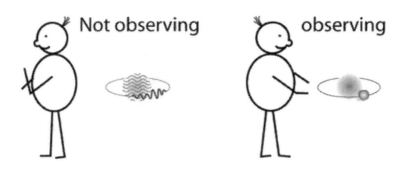

Do you remember the game kids play where one kid stands with her back to all the other ones, who are running towards her, but the moment she turns around, they all have to freeze?

It seems the physicists were playing this game with the electrons…or the electrons with them.

So how is it possible that we can influence the behaviour of subatomic particles?

This is the kind of influence-at-a-distance phenomenon that is usually associated with fields, but that means there must be a field between human consciousness and the material world.

Let's dig into the concept of fields a bit deeper.

A field is an energetic medium that allows objects to influence each other at a distance, without anything physical between them. A magnet can attract iron through its magnetic field. The Earth can cause an apple to fall without anything physical between the apple and the Earth, through a field called gravity.

Funny things can happen when apples fall; just ask Newton.

Similarly, there would have to be some kind of field between the conscious awareness of the scientist and the electron wave/particle for this influence to take place.

Basically, this phenomenon *just didn't make sense*, especially from the Machine Paradigm point of view.

Eventually, most scientists just stopped asking questions about it. Niels Bohr famously put a sign on his door that said *'Philosophers keep out. Work in progress'* – and everyone just focused on the mathematical equations rather than interpretations.

The math worked and the results created a 'quantum' leap in our technologies, becoming the basis to devise a wide range of new high tech toys, from lasers to computer chips. In fact, it's estimated that today roughly about 30% of the US GNP consists of products that would not be possible without the findings of our quantum forefathers.

But what about the philosophical implications? In fact, surprisingly little has happened, given the fact that these discoveries were made almost 100 years ago.

In the end, it was Erwin Schrödinger who was both at the forefront of the mathematical equations and the philosophical side of things. Schrödinger was probably most suited for that task, after all, since he originally started his degree in philosophy and only later switched to physics, where he became one of the most brilliant physicists of our time. (The Schrödinger equation became the basis of quantum theory.)

Nevertheless, throughout his career as a quantum physicist and professor of physics at the University of Vienna, he kept looking for answers to his questions. In the end, it seems he found them... in some of history's oldest texts, the Vedas, the manuscripts from the same tradition from where the techniques to transcend originated.

He published several books on the subject, and collected all of his conclusions on the topic in *Mind and Matter,* published by Cambridge University in 1958. His conclusion was as radical as it was simple.

> *There is no separation between subject and object, between ourselves and others and the world around us. There is only an illusory division that our minds create for ourselves. In truth, the mind is the source of everything.*
>
> *The mind has created the objective outside world of the physicists from its own substance... This is the doctrine of the Upanishads [Vedic texts].*

In other words, he says there is only one field of consciousness, and both our inner subjective world and outer objective world are created from there. Through this field, the inner mind is connected to the outer world.

> The conclusion from the scientist who played the most important role in the development of quantum physics, and most of our modern technologies that are based on it, was basically the central hypothesis of the Field Paradigm. But *because it didn't make sense in 1958,* few people took it seriously. Even if they did, they simply didn't know what to do with it.

We'll investigate later how field effects between the inner mind and the outer world have been researched in detail, as that is what so-called "paranormal" phenomena are all about.

The question we'll focus on now is whether physics itself can also provide some concrete evidence of the Field Paradigm, evidence for the concept of consciousness as a field.

The answer is, "Yes", which brings us back to Einstein.

Quantum physics indicated a randomness in the behaviour of the basic particles of nature, which Einstein strongly resisted. *"God doesn't play dice,"* he famously said. He eventually started to look for a more complete theory, which he called a Unified Field theory.

Einstein got a lot of his inspiration from Spinoza, a famous Dutch philosopher from the mid-17th century. Spinoza used to say, *"All of creation is just a thought of God."* When he referred to God, however, he was not referring to a personal God, but identified it as *Nature*. He proclaimed that both human thought and material creation were just an extension of this impersonal universal force.

Spinoza, in other words, was another messenger of the Field Paradigm.

Spinoza's views were not very popular in his time...and that's putting it mildly. Although he was said to live the life of a saint, Spinoza was exiled from his Jewish community in Amsterdam at the age of 23, out of fear that the powers of the church would retaliate on the entire community if they didn't distance themselves from his views[2].

Einstein, however, believed Spinoza was on to something. When asked about his religion, Einstein answered that he believed in *"Spinoza's God"*[3].

And so Einstein started a quest to find mathematical descriptions of this force in Nature, mathematical equations that described how everything in creation would arise from one single field. This quest would become his life's work, taking almost the entire second half of his life.

Einstein didn't succeed in finding the formulas, but did pave the way for others to continue his work, and eventually, in 1984, in what has become known as the *superstring revolution*, the mathematical formulas were completed. These formulas can describe how all different phenomena in the universe arise as vibrations from one singular field.

To understand how one single field can give rise to the entire diversity of creation we have to examine a second fundamental difference between material particles and fields/waves.

> A material particle or object can only be one thing at a time, while fields can express themselves in many ways at the same time.

This is a rather complicated one, so let's try to illustrate it with a simple example, by looking at what happens with the electromagnetic field.

The electromagnetic field can create many different phenomena in nature. Depending on the wavelength, it can manifest as radio waves, microwaves, light, X-rays, etc.

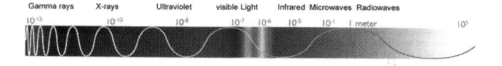

The cool thing about fields is that they can vibrate at all these different frequencies *at the same time*.

Let's do a simple experiment to demonstrate this.

Turn on the light. Now turn on the radio. Next, put your spaghetti in your microwave oven. As you can see, they are all working at the same time.

Few people stop to consider what a miracle this is: *the same field is creating many different phenomena simultaneously*. Even when we just look at radio waves, we could have 20 radios in the room, each playing their own music, yet it's all the same field vibrating in 20 different ways at the same time.

So how can one field create all these different phenomena? It's actually really simple. The individual waves simply add up.

We can have the field vibrate at a small wavelength (light) and at a much larger wavelength (radio), and the field will just vibrate in a complex waveform where the ups and the downs of the individual waves all add up to each other, but where the memory of the individual waveforms is still present.

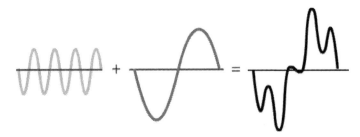

Likewise, Einstein predicted that one day, physicists would find that there is only one field. If this field vibrates in a certain way, it will give rise to protons. Vibrating in another way, it will give rise to electrons, in yet another way it will create the electromagnetic field, gravity, nuclear forces, etc. And it can create all these different vibrations at the same time, in every single point in creation.

This prediction came true in 1984, when physicists formulated the superstring formulas that could indeed explain every single phenomenon in nature as different vibrations of one single underlying Unified Field.

One physicist who played a crucial role in this field, as he developed "one of the more successful Unified Field theories[4]", is Dr. John Hagelin.

As a teenager, Hagelin already had an IQ that was off the charts and used his intelligence to dive deep into the mysteries of physics. He eventually obtained a Ph.D. in physics from Harvard, and worked with the top researchers in the world at the Stanford Linear Accelerator Center and CERN.

Still, Hagelin saw the world differently from most of his colleagues. He had learned the Transcendental Meditation technique at a young age, allowing him to experience the unity of everything. Like Einstein, he was already wearing the Field Paradigm glasses and simply started looking for the formulas to describe his intuitive feeling of unity mathematically.

Even though his publications on Unified Field theories remain some of the most quoted publications to date, most of his colleagues appeared to be too stuck in the Machine Paradigm way of thinking to really appreciate his more spiritual views on physics. So Hagelin eventually left his stellar career in the world of physics to work more closely with Maharishi, the greatest expert on Vedic Science in the world at the time. Somehow, he felt this was where he would find the true answers to his questions. Hagelin is currently the leader of the US TM organisation and President of Maharishi University of Management.

Even though the Unified Field formulas are more than 30 years old, we are now in the most exciting time since these discoveries. The Large Hadron Collider in CERN is now powerful enough to prove several aspects of the formulas experimentally.

The Higgs-Boson discovery was a big step forward, although the Unified Field theories actually predict that researchers will find several of them. They already found signals that could indicate that there are in fact multiple Higgs-Bosons, but more data is needed to claim a statistically significant discovery. The feeling is now that it's a matter of weeks or months, rather than years, before they'll expect to find much more experimental evidence for the Unified Field theories.

Meanwhile, however, there are many other ways to verify this theory that don't require billion dollar particle accelerators, just some simple logic.

From Diversity to Unity: How Things Appear Different at Different Scales

To understand the concept of unity at the basis of diversity, we have to understand that reality looks different depending on the scale of our observation.

If we walk around anywhere on this beautiful planet of ours, we observe Earth as a (largely) flat disk. This is what we clearly see everywhere around us, flatness everywhere (less so if you're walking in the Grand Canyon or the Swiss Alps, but you get my point). For a long time, people believed that Earth was, in fact, a flat disk. After all, that was what they saw.

Yet if we'd change our perspective and zoom out, we'd see very clearly that the flatness is only an illusion. At a larger scale, we can clearly see that the Earth is a sphere.

Likewise, if we look at the objects around us, they all look very different and separate from each other. A wooden desk, a picture of grandpa and grandma in a metal frame (they looked so happy in their days), a whole bunch of paper bills that really need to be paid someday, about 200 post-it notes of very urgent things to do sticking on the glass screen of our monitor, etc. All these are clearly different materials with clearly different properties.

But what would happen if we changed our perspective and zoom in? Then the differences would disappear rather quickly.

At the molecular level, millions of varied structures make up all the stuff we see around us. Zoom in on the atomic level, however, and we'll see that all these structures are just different arrangements of the same building blocks, the 118 different elements of the periodic table.

If we zoom in more, even these 118 different elements start to look surprisingly similar. They are actually just different arrangements made from the same subatomic building blocks: protons, electrons, and neutrons. The only difference between them is the quantity. Hydrogen has one proton and one electron; helium two of each, oxygen has eight, etc.

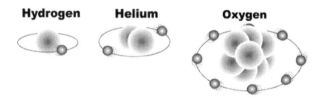

On the subatomic scale, our diverse universe is suddenly looking a lot less diverse than on the molecular scale.

Originally, physicists thought that's where the unification would stop. They concluded that there were four matter fields in nature creating the elementary particles; two types of quarks, which combine to create protons and neutrons; electrons (charged leptons); and neutrinos.

They also discovered four force fields interacting with matter. They had already discovered that both electricity and magnetism were two different manifestations of the same force field, now called electromagnetism. In addition, they found three other forces: gravity, and two types of nuclear forces, the strong force, and the weak force.

Physicists could basically explain every phenomenon in nature as an interaction of these four force fields and four matter fields.

But physicists soon found that unification continues at scales even smaller than the subatomic level. At scales 100 times smaller than the atomic scale, it was found that there is no more difference between electromagnetism and the weak force, between the two types of quarks or between electrons and neutrinos.

At still smaller scales (about 1 trillion times smaller) they found that there isn't a difference between any of the particles, or between three of the four forces. They are all just different vibrations of the same field that appear as different things on larger scales.

And at the smallest scale we know of, called the Planck Scale, there is no longer any difference between any of the forces and material particles. They are all just different vibrations of the same field.

Unified Field Theory

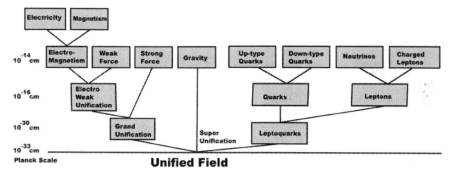

> Our idea that we live in a world of many distinct objects is just as big of an illusion as the idea that we live on a flat Earth. We just have to change the scale to see the true reality.

This is why we call it a uni-verse.

Get it?

Isn't it brilliant?

Unity as the basis of diversity.

But now comes the million-dollar question: *"Does this make any practical difference in my life?"* "Why should I care about what's happening at scales a billion, billion, billion times smaller than my small pinky?"

For practical purposes, we shouldn't care. Just like we don't take the curvature of the Earth into account when we plan a bike ride. We still live in our world where the classical laws of physics apply. As long as we take into account those laws, and don't go jumping off buildings (thinking that gravity is just an illusion anyway), we should be fine.

But where it *is* important is regarding the philosophical implications, as these show we should change our paradigm through which we see the world and change what we define as *reality*. These implications have been ignored for far too long.

Why the Unified Field *Must* be a Field of Consciousness

We've already seen two fundamental differences between particles and fields:

1. A particle is always localized (in one place at the same time), while fields are unlocalized (waves can be in many places at the same time).
2. A particle can only be one thing at the same time, while fields can express themselves as many things at the same time.

In this chapter, we'll discuss a third fundamental difference.

> A particle or material object can exist independently of its creator, or source, while waves cannot.

If I make a chair, and then I disappear, the chair will happily continue to exist. Once it's created, it doesn't need me.

But what if I create a sound wave? The *moment* I stop creating it, the sound will disappear. Similarly, the moment I turn off a light bulb, it stops creating vibrations on the electromagnetic field and the light will go out.

The whole Machine Paradigm way of thinking arose from the idea that we were living in a universe built of tiny material balls. In this case, no creator was needed. Everything started with the Big Bang and evolved from there, according to specific laws of physics and chemistry, into the universe we know today. Everything functions like one big machine.

From the moment quantum physicists demonstrated that these little balls aren't the whole story, but are themselves just fluctuations of different fields, the creator *must* also return to the picture, because *something must be continuously creating those waves*, all the time.

And when it turned out that all the different waves in the universe are all different fluctuations of one single field, then the *only way* this picture can make sense is if this field itself is the creator.

Let's explain this in a bit more detail.

In our example of the electromagnetic field, the field can vibrate in many different ways at the same time, but the vibrations are all created by external forces (a light bulb, a radio broadcaster, etc.).

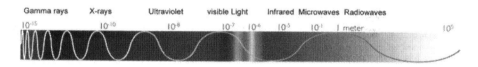

When we are talking about the Unified Field, *there can't be any external force creating these waves on the field, because the field itself is the source of all the forces in nature*. This means it *must* create all these vibrations within itself.

If this field creates every possible vibration in nature within itself then, by definition, this field must have some specific qualities. Without these qualities, it wouldn't be possible for this field to create anything. These qualities are:

1. <u>Omnipresence: being everywhere</u>
If this field creates every single grain of creation, it must also be present in every grain of creation.

2. <u>Omniscience: knowing everything</u>
Not only is this field creating everything as vibrations within itself, but it also has to coordinate every particle in creation, from the smallest atom to the largest galaxies. This means it has to *know* what is going on everywhere, which would require an enormous, almost infinite, amount of intelligence.

3. <u>Omnipotence: the ability to create anything</u>

This speaks for itself. If this field is creating everything, it must have an unlimited creativity, and obviously have the *ability* to create anything.

> Awareness, intelligence, and creativity are the core qualities of consciousness. At the same time it's generally assumed that omnipresence, omniscience, and omnipotence are the core qualities of a divine being.
>
> If the Unified Field is real, and all the latest discoveries in physics are indicating that it is, it must by definition be a field of "divine" consciousness.

If this may still all sound a bit abstract at this stage, don't worry. The more you'll become familiar with the Field Paradigm, when we observe more and more phenomena in nature and our own experiences, the more you'll start to feel at ease with it.

Man in the Image of God, or God in the Image of man?

According to the hypothesis of this book, the cutting-edge discoveries in physics only appear to be confirming what the ancient Vedic texts claimed several thousand years ago: consciousness is a Field.

Basically this means that rather than assuming, as we have, that material processes creates consciousness, now we're turning it around, consciousness creates matter. Can we say this with 100% certainty? No, we can't. The Field Paradigm is still a hypothesis. But then again, *The Machine Paradigm is also just a hypothesis.* This is difficult to hear for most scientists. After 300 years of seeing that it all (or almost all) seems to work, the Machine Paradigm glasses are so fixed that many view the Machine Paradigm as the absolute certainty. It's not even to be questioned.

So if we have two hypotheses, which one will win? Usually there are two condition for a new paradigm to replace an old one.

1. The new paradigm can explain both the normal things and the things that doesn't make sense in the old paradigm in a better and more logical way
2. The new paradigm offers better practical solutions than the old paradigm

This was definitely the case when the Machine Paradigm replaced the God Paradigm, and as we become more and more familiar with the Field Paradigm, we'll see it will also be the case here. (Well, at least I believe that to be the case. All I can do is present the facts and let people make their own conclusion.)

The phenomena that subatomic particles appeared to be having a conscious awareness of what other particles were doing is a good example. It just didn't make sense from the Machine Paradigm point of view, where these particles would be isolated dead individual balls, but once we start seeing them as part of an omnipresent omniscient field it starts to become more logical. If the ocean displays certain qualities, it would make sense that the waves on this ocean have them as well.

In living beings, consciousness gets an even more complete expression, through the being's nervous systems. The more advanced the nervous system, the more advanced the expressions and the clearer the properties of consciousness in life will be, as we'll see in next chapter.

And while we discuss nervous systems, here's another side hypothesis that we'll discuss in this chapter.

The most highly advanced nervous system is the human nervous system. According to the ancient text it is possible for human beings to get a full expression. Basically this means that even right now the expression is already pretty advanced with most people (that's where all our creativity, intelligence, love, etc. comes from, the core qualities that make us uniquely human) it could be far more advanced still: experiencing unity with everyone and everything.

This, however, can only happen on the condition that:

1. <u>The nervous system is pure</u>: Just like a radio that is not tuned in properly will not give a clear expression of the music, so will a nervous system where stress, tensions and other impurities have accumulated also not work properly. The qualities of the Field might be

pure good and pure love ("God is love") but if enough stress accumulates, those qualities might not always show.
2. <u>We learn to develop our full potential</u>: This, it turns out, is just a simple matter of fitness for the brain. We need to learn how to develop our brain properly.

In part 3 we'll see that transcending will do both. It both removes the impurities and will provide the development that our brain requires. That's why the ancient texts always claimed that this experience is essential for our full development.

But first I wanted to discuss a famous quote from our religious texts: "Man is made in the image of God", because there have been some discoveries which indicate that there might be a lot more truth to this than we previously imagined.

The ancient Vedic Rishis (Rishi means "See-er", people who were able to see the true reality of life) were not only able to perceive and describe this field at the source of all creation and all life, but they were also able to *cognize it's structure*. It is said that they cognized this in the forms of sounds that came to their awareness deep in their meditations, which were recorded as the Vedic texts.

These texts kind of served as a series of guidelines on how to live life in harmony with Nature and develop our full human potential. There are many branches of these texts, like the Upanishads (knowledge of the unity of all life), Ayur Veda (a form of natural medicine that is mostly focused on activating the inner power of the body to heal itself), Sthaphatya Veda (an ancient system of architecture that promotes health and happiness of the inhabitants), etc.

But the practical guidelines didn't seem to be the whole story. In the early 1990ies Maharishi spent several year working with the TM organisation's top neuroscientist, Dr. Tony Nader, to show that there was also a deeper value to the structure of these texts.

They found that the very structure of the texts closely matches the structure of different parts of the human nervous system. Maharishi had already described that this field of consciousness needed to have many more qualities than just omnipresent etc. to fully express itself in living beings. (one of the additional qualities we'll discuss later is memory). He found that each of the branches of the Vedic texts describes one of these other qualities. Then it was just a matter of seeing how this quality is expressed in the human nervous system, and see of the structure of the texts matches the structure of that part of the nervous system.

And it did.

Dr. Nader wrote a 600 page book called *Veda in the human physiology* showing incredibly detailed correlations, so detailed that it seemed highly unlikely they could be due to coincidence.

To summarize this discovery as simply as possible I'd say that, if this book presents a hypothesis that human consciousness is part of an omnipresent field, then Dr. Nader's book presents a more elaborate theory on *how* this field can actually manifest itself through the human nervous system to create our experience of consciousness.

A radio can give a local expression of vibrations of the Electromagnetic field, in the form of music, *because of its specific structure that allows this expression*. Likewise, a human nervous system can give a local expression of the qualities of the Unified Field because of its specific structure that allows this expression. It would mean that human beings *did not mysteriously come into being by a series of random coincidences*, as Darwin would have us believe, but by "divine design".

To go into this in more detail is beyond the scope of this book, as it requires an profound understanding of both neurology and Vedic Knowledge to fully appreciate it – also, I'm probably stretching the limits of your imagination enough already ;o) - but I hope that someday I'll have the chance to write another book about this.

As long as there's no definite scientific proof to Dr. Nader's theories, they are just theories, but at least it's an interesting topic. Maharishi certainly felt it was interesting, because it was largely because of this discovery that he appointed Dr. Nader as his successor as global leader of the TM organization.

Basically, if this discovery proves to be correct, the claims from our ancient religious texts, like "Man is made in the Image of God" might hold a lot more truth and wisdom that we think.

The problem is this: we could say that the ancient texts from almost all religions were written in a kind of code, and you need the proper cypher to decode them and understand their true meaning.

The cypher is the glasses we wear, how we see the world. *If we wear our Machine Paradigm glasses, we will interpret the religious texts very differently than if we wear our Field Paradigm glasses.*

For example, most of us have taken *Man is made in the Image of God* and turned it around. We started imagining a God that is like a man. (The old man with a long beard sitting on some cloud in heaven.)

We still believe our Gods are divine, which means they have the divine qualities of omnipresence, omniscience and omnipotence, but we somehow tried to squeeze these qualities in a man-like being.

Of course, if you think about this for even one minute, you can see that this *simply doesn't make sense.*

Omnipresence means it's everywhere at the same time. This means it must, by definition, be a field, rather than a localized being.

Omniscience means that it knows *everything,* so it must be connected to everything. This means it must, by definition, be a field rather than a localized being.

Omnipotence means it creates everything, which also means it must be connected to everything. This means it must, by definition, be a field rather than a localized being.

So many people have been looking for God everywhere all their lives, while He/She/It was right there in front of their nose all the time, everywhere they looked. They simply didn't have the right glasses on to see it, just like the person wearing pink glasses was not able to see the wide variety of colors.

Once people change their glasses and switch to the Field Paradigm view, the first thing that usually happens is that they start to get a lot more respect for their own religion. They now finally start to understand what their great teachers were trying to tell them all along. They finally have the right cypher.

To examine this in more detail, how the wisdom from the great teachers from all religions starts to make a lot more sense, would also take a book on its own. It's a fascinating subject so I hope I'll someday get a chance to write this book as well.

Meanwhile, I'm sure you'll be able to find plenty of examples on your own. Just look at the ancient religious texts from the perspective of Unity rather than separation. You'll be surprised how quickly a lot of things will start to make a lot more sense.

But even more important than having a lot more respect for their own religion is that people also start to have a lot more respect for the *other* religions around the world.

They start to understand that our Divine source of life is not some personality with typical human qualities, favoring one population over another, but an omnipresent Field of nature that is equally supportive and nourishing to everyone, exactly as Spinoza described it 350 years ago.

They also start to realize that different cultures have different names and descriptions for this Field, according to their own culture and traditions, just like we have different names for gravity, according to different languages.

Once people change their glasses it would never be possible to have any religious wars ever again. It would feel as absurd as starting a war over which is the correct name of gravity.

And finally, once people change their glasses, and start living the Field Paradigm (by learning to transcend and experience the field), they will spontaneously start to behave like our religious leaders would have wanted us to behave.

Unconditional love, anyone? It's a lot easier when you have no more stresses in your nervous system and have developed your brain potential to such a degree that you can actually experience everyone as part of yourself.

> By thinking of the Divine from the Machine paradigm point of view, we've been making our Gods a lot smaller than they really are.
>
> This also means we've been making ourselves a lot smaller than we are.

Examples of Connectedness in Nature

Telepathic Plants

In 1973, Peter Tompkins and Christopher Bird published a book called *The Secret Life of Plants*, which became almost an encyclopedia of *things that don't make sense* in nature. Basically, it described how scientists have been finding that all of nature is far more interconnected than we previously believed.

For example, Tompkins and Bird wrote about experiments that show how plants react to us in conscious ways.

Scientists connected plants to galvanic skin response (GSR) detectors to measure if they would show a reaction when scientists created a stressful situation for them, like setting their leaves on fire. GSR is often used on humans to measure stress reactions, like with lie detectors. To the researchers' surprise, when they created a stressful situation for the plants, the plants showed a clearly measurable response that was similar to humans.

Next, they decided to try another test. They put two plants next to each other, set the leaves of one plant on fire and measured the stress reaction of the other plant. It showed the same reaction as the plant that was burned.

Were these plants communicating?

Next, the scientists went really crazy. They kept two plants standing next to each other for a while, then moved one plant to the other side of town, and set its leaves on fire. The other plant measured the same stress reaction. It *knew* what was going on with the other plant.

This was reminding the scientists a bit of a phenomenon that Einstein called "spooky action at a distance." In physics, scientists had already found that if two entangled particles are separated and the spin of one particle is changed, the other changes as well. The communication between the two particles happened instantly, faster than the speed of light, which violated Einstein's principle that no information can travel faster than the speed of light. The only way to make sense of this is to see these two particles not as separate entities but as a part of one whole.

It seems like the same was happening with plants, which means that these plants' consciousness must be somehow connected.

This doesn't make sense if we think of plants as individual material things, but once we start to think of plants as waves on a self-aware ocean, it starts to become a lot more plausible.

Next, the scientists tried another experiment. Would it also work if the scientists just *thought* about setting the plant's leaves on fire? Yep, the plant showed exactly the same stress reaction, which showed that there was also some kind of connection between plants and humans.

In Russia, scientists conducted similar experiments on plants, with similar results. For example, they used plants to identify a "murderer". They had a person completely destroy a plant while another plant was "witnessing" the whole thing. Next, they measured stress reactions of the witnessing plant when a number of different people walked in the room. As soon as the "murderer" walked in, stress reactions went through the roof.

If only they could use this in our courtrooms to identify criminals, just imagine how many more witnesses we would suddenly have.

Likewise, Tompkins and Bird's book lists hundreds of examples showing that plants are connected to each other and to human beings, through some kind of field of consciousness. They seem to use this connection to communicate telepathically.

It doesn't always have to involve a negative event. Another example lists a chemist who became so attuned to his house plants that they reacted excitedly when he made love to his girlfriend eight miles away.

The Secret Life of Plants was widely criticized by the scientific community for promoting *pseudoscience**. (From this perspective, we can define pseudo-

---

* One criticism was that, in a lot of cases, the experiments that Thompkins and Bird listed could not be replicated in a controlled environment, which is fair. It could very well be that in several cases some of the experiments really deserved the title "pseudoscience", but it's not always black and white. We'll see later that a lot of these type of experiments don't always work because of the human element. For example, studies have found that some telepathic phenomena clearly worked, but the moment a highly skeptical or highly negative researcher came into the room, they immediately stopped working. Perhaps this only shows that *everybody* is creating an influence with their thoughts and that we all see what we believe. If people don't believe it, they create the right circumstance for the effect not to show. The examples here are meant as examples of cases in nature where it did work, inviting people to find more such examples in their own lives, not as definite evidence.

science as "anything that does not fit in the Machine Paradigm and as such cannot be scientific"...we'll see plenty more examples.)

That didn't seem to stop it from becoming an international bestseller though.

Birds United

Animals have a more developed nervous system than plants, and a more highly developed conscious awareness as a result. So can we see signs of a unity of consciousness with them as well?

Absolutely, and there is no more beautiful example than watching a flock of starlings. Starlings are small birds that usually fly together in flocks that range from a few hundred to tens of thousands, yet move *as one unified whole.* You can watch a beautiful example of this on this video: www.fieldparadigm.com/birds-video/

It's just pure magic, but that didn't stop materialists (people who believe that the Machine Paradigm is the ultimate reality) from trying to remove the magic by explaining it as mechanical events.

The first obvious attempt to explain it was that the birds simply see each other and then react to the flight patterns of the other birds, kind of like computers in self-driving cars scanning the road and adjusting their paths.

That may be plausible if we're talking about a few dozen birds; but imagine the processing power required to analyse the flight path of each and every bird if there were tens of thousands of birds, all flying criss-cross through each other. You'd be talking about super-computing power very quickly, and that poses a bit of a problem. Starlings are tiny small birds, with tiny small brains – definitely no room for a supercomputer there.

The other factor is that a bird's visual field is limited, and they simply can't possibly see and react to every other bird.

But here's the most important factor that makes this explanation completely implausible. *Scientists have measured how quickly birds can react to a visual stimulus* and found that these birds reacted far more quickly to each other's movements than they could have possibly done based on their visual reaction time.

> These birds are flying as if they are all communicating telepathically; as if they were are all part of one bigger consciousness. This is clearly visible when you watch them. That is what makes it so magical.

It's the same story as with our "telepathic" plants. It doesn't make sense from the Machine Paradigm but makes perfect sense from when viewed from the Field Paradigm. If the birds' consciousnesses are all like waves on one single field of consciousness, and this field is aware of everything, then it makes sense that every bird could be aware of the movements of every other bird.

Collective Memory

Another beautiful example of connectedness in nature comes from the works of Dr. Rupert Sheldrake, who found that species have a kind of *collective memory.*

In his book *The Presence of the Past,* for example, Sheldrake describes a phenomenon that nobody has been able to explain. When chemists try to synthesize a new crystal molecule, usually the first time it takes a very long time for the structure to crystallize, sometimes even several months. Once it does, however, they find that the second time it crystallizes very quickly, even if that second time happens in a lab on the other side of the world. Somehow, the *memory* of that new structure had to be imprinted in the field first, and once it was, it could guide the next specimen of the same system to develop much more quickly.

It is like when you have to learn a new skill, like riding a bicycle. The first time you try, it might take a while, but once you learned it, it becomes very easy to do it again the next day, because you remember. What Sheldrake is saying is that all beings of the same species share that memory between them, through a process that he called *morphic resonance*. He describes it as, "The influence of like upon like through space and time". The more times a particular action within a species is performed, the more it will be imprinted in the memory, and the stronger the guidelines for a next action will be.

There are countless other intriguing cases of how a new "habit", or a newly learned skill, spreads in nature across the boundaries of space and time.

One of the best-documented cases is the opening of milk bottles by birds. When milk bottles are delivered to the doorsteps in the early morning, birds can open the tin foil caps and drink as much as two inches of milk. The first record of this habit was in Southampton in England in 1921, and its spread was recorded at regular intervals from 1930 to 1947. It has been observed in 11 species, but most frequently in tits. Even though tits only travel a few miles from their birth place, the habit spread across Britain and also appeared in Sweden, Denmark, and Holland. Any time this habit appeared more than 15 miles from where it had been previously recorded, it could be assumed that it was a "new discovery" by an individual bird. The records showed that the spread of the habit *accelerated* over time; the more times it had been done, the faster other tits "discovered" how to open milk bottles.

The records in Holland were particularly interesting. During the Second World War milk bottles all but disappeared, and only became common again in 1947. Tits have a lifespan of three years, and milk bottles were out of use for eight years. No tits familiar with opening bottles before the war could have survived during this period, but nevertheless the attacks on bottles restarted quickly.

Sheldrake formulated his theory when he was in India, studying the concept of unity of consciousness in the Vedic literature. He simply was brave enough to change his paradigm glasses, and then started studying nature from this new perspective, only to find that a lot of things, including a collective memory, *started to make a lot more sense.*

There are countless examples of connectedness in nature like these. Rather than listing them all here, the main purpose of this book is to give a glimpse of how connectedness suddenly makes a lot more sense from the Field Paradigm point of view and then invite you to find your own examples. You'll be surprised how many you'll find.

It's very simple. Just change your glasses and start to see everything as waves on an omnipresent interconnected field rather than as individual entities, and see how much more magical everything becomes.

Our Machine Paradigm glasses are a bit like watching an ocean, but with the bottom half of your visual field covered by holding a book. You only see the top of the waves, which then appear as separate entities.

So GET RID OF THOSE GLASSES. They've been making your life miserable. They managed to turn a truly magical universe full of interconnected life into a boring machine.

Let's see if the beings that have the most highly developed nervous system of all – humans – can have experiences of unity.

The Science of Miracles: How Paranormal Phenomena Start to Make Sense

I'll Believe it When I see it

Obviously, you are aware that more than 130 years of research has established, *beyond a shadow of a doubt*, that paranormal phenomena, like telepathy, telekinesis, premonition, etc. are real, and that everyone can experience them.

Wait, you're telling me you *didn't* know this?

This might have something to do with the fact that a large part of the scientific community has been rather busy either ignoring or actively trying to discredit the research, branding it as *pseudoscience*. As we already said, everything that can't be explained by the Machine Paradigm cannot be scientific because it's impossible. Since no true scientific experiment can prove something that is impossible, something must be wrong with the science.

So we behave like the person with his pink glasses when he sees a colour chart. We put a label on it calling it "not real science", and the problem is solved. Everything discredited... let's not talk about it anymore.

Well, in this chapter we are *going* to talk about it because this collection of studies can give us more clues about our true potential as human beings than just about anything else (other than the 20 experiments which we'll discuss in Part 3, at least).

You can see that this chapter is going to get rather serious, so let's lighten things up a bit and start with a joke:

> Jesus, Moses, and an old man are playing golf. Moses is on first strike. He hits the ball but hits too soft. It flies right into the lake. No problem. Moses just makes a grand gesture with his arms and parts the water. He walks up to the ball and strikes it onto the green.
>
> Next, Jesus is up. He also hits too soft and again the ball flies right into the water. No problem, he just walks across the water to where the ball is and strikes it towards the green.
>
> The old man is up next. He casually hits the ball, and it flies off in a totally wrong direction, again straight towards the water. Right before it hits the water a fish jumps out of the lake and catches the ball in its mouth. Next, a seagull flies down from the sky and catches the fish. When the seagull flies over the green, the gull is hit by a lightning bolt. The seagull drops the fish on the green, the fish drops the ball which then rolls nicely into the hole. A hole-in-one.
>
> Moses gives Jesus a dry look and says, "I hate playing with your Dad!"

We would usually associate this kind of scenario with the "divine", right? This is omnipotence, where everything in nature is under one's control. It probably classifies as the most magical and extreme psychic experience possible, yet many people have experienced that it *is* possible, even if usually not as extreme as in the golf joke. They just have a desire in the deep silence of their mind (usually in the form of prayer to some higher power) and then see all the circumstances in nature cooperate to fulfil it (which they interpret as the higher power answering their prayers).

But this still means there must be a connection between the thoughts people have in their minds and the events that happen in the outer world, unless it was a *coincidence*.

You'd be amazed how many people reason away the magic in their lives with the word "coincidence".

> We all have far more potential than we could imagine in our wildest dreams, but most of us never realize this potential... and it usually all comes down to one little sentence:
>
> *"I'll believe it when I see it."*

So let's get to the bottom of this. Let's analyse what we're seeing in the first place. We see millions of things every day, and I bet you never ever stood still and wondered what it is you really see.

Why do we see another person standing in front of us? We used to think that a light source emits little balls of light called photons that are then reflected by the person and registered in the retina of our eye.

In reality, we now know that these photons are light waves, vibrations of the electromagnetic field.

What happens when we turn off the light? Did the other person disappear? No, of course not – the person is still there (probably shouting at you to turn the damn light back on).

So we don't really see the other person, do we? What we really see is the light waves, vibrations on the Electromagnetic field that is between you and the other person.

The only reason we see the other person is because there is a field that connects us to the other person, *but the field that connects us itself is invisible.*

> This is another fundamental difference between fields and particles: particles are visible, while fields are invisible. The real essence of our existence, fields, is something we can't see.

So now what happens when we say, "I'll believe it when I see it"?

The rather messy state our world is currently in, that's what happens.

We only see the things that are separate from us, and so we live in this delusion that we are all separate from each other. Einstein called this an "optical delusion of [our] consciousness."

If we see our bodies as separate, and our minds are created by our bodies, then our minds must be separate from each other as well... and then psychic phenomena are impossible.

The truth with psychic phenomena, or actually with most paradigm shifts, is that *I believe it when I see it* in reality usually works the other way around. *I see it when I believe it.*

In that sense, It's actually surprising how many people still have psychic experiences (two-thirds of the population, according to the survey mentioned before), given how thoroughly we were educated not to see them.

<u>Who is primitive here?</u>

I once heard a lecture from a missionary stationed near a small tribe in Africa. He related an experience that had made a deep impression on him. One day he was talking to a woman who was nursing her newborn baby, but also had to work almost all day in the fields. When the missionary asked how she could manage these two responsibilities, she looked at him amused. "Very simple," she said, "I go to the fields, and when the child is hungry I come back to feed it."

"But how do you know when your baby is hungry?" the missionary asked.

Now she looked at him as if he had completely lost his mind. "How do you know when *you* are hungry?"

We have spent the last 130 years bickering over whether or not the scientific data around psychic phenomena like telepathy (feeling at a distance) are real, while people in primitive tribes appear to be simply *using* these abilities, almost like we use mobile phones. Perhaps we should ask who is really primitive and who is advanced here.

Throughout these chapters, we'll go over many different types of "paranormal" experiences and show how they are only paranormal when viewed from the Machine Paradigm. From the Field Paradigm perspective, they start to look a lot more *normal*.

Understanding how such phenomena can work is the first step to help us recognize them when they happen (I see it when I believe it), rather than dismissing them as *coincidences*. More importantly, it's also the first step in understanding how we can develop them, but we'll discuss this in more detail in Part 3.

Memory: The Key to Understanding Psychic Phenomena

We have seen that a fundamental difference between particles and waves is that material objects (particles) can exist independent of what created them, while waves cannot.

This means that our universe cannot be the material machine created at the Big Bang and then left on its own as we once imagined. It means that the "Creator" (the omnipresent Field) is continuously creating and recreating it. If the Creator decided to take a break for even one split second, everything would instantly collapse, like light instantly disappears the moment the bulb is turned off.

This all sounds logical, but how can we make sense of it?

Here's where five years of playing video games as a profession comes in handy, as video games allow us to illustrate how this works in a very simple way.

Imagine you're playing a racing game. What you see on the screen is a continuous flow that looks and feels very real. You could almost imagine being in a real racing car.

But what happens on the level of the computer to create this illusion of reality? The computer calculates a new screen about 60 times per second based on three factors:

- memory of the previous screen
- programmed laws of physics, and
- input from the player.

So let's say that you are driving at 200 miles per hour and you decide to turn the car left. Based upon the memory of the previous screen, the computer calculates the car's movement and momentum using the laws of physics described in the game's code, and then generates the new screen with car now turning left.

Ninety-nine percent of the new screen, however, will be the memory of the previous screen. It's pretty much the same as it was before, just with the car now turned slightly more left.

Now imagine that nature works the same way. In other words, a new reality is created every moment, but mostly from the memory of how reality existed before. This is exactly what the ancient Vedic Texts claimed several thousand years ago.

This is how we get the illusion of one continuous flow in nature, just like in a video game.

From this perspective, Dr. Sheldrake's research indicating that species appear to have a collective, transcendental memory may just be the tip of the iceberg. The ancient texts described the *whole* field of consciousness as pure memory.

> Imagine we'd forget every split second what happened the previous split second... Life wouldn't be much fun, would it? Imagine if the *Creator* would forget what happened every previous moment. Our creation wouldn't be much fun, either.
>
> Consciousness and memory are closely intertwined because we need memory to make sense of any conscious experience.

Are you still with me? I know this is all getting a bit abstract, but I promise this is really leading to something practical.

Now let's come back to the second element in the video game: programmed laws.

Just as certain laws are programmed in the video game, there are laws "programmed" in nature, like gravity. As with memory, these laws are elements in nature that give us stability and continuity. If everything were a collection of random events, life wouldn't be all that much fun either, would it?

That's how computer games work. Programmers don't program every possibility of where the car can go, they just program some laws, let the player move within them, and the computer calculates the new world accordingly.

The third element is the input from the player. In real life there isn't one player, but many billions of them. Massively multiplayer online games (MMOGs) sometimes have tens of thousands of players connected to the same game, playing in the same virtual environment together. Every instant an individual player makes a move, the entire virtual world is recalculated, and the new updated reality is shown to every other player.

This is kind of how it works in real life.

In terms of doing a physical action, this makes perfect sense. If I move my chair to the left, the entire universe will be different for everyone else in it. It is now a universe where the chair is in a different spot.

Where it becomes unfamiliar is that we also change the entire universe with every thought we have.

Everything is ultimately vibrations on the ocean of consciousness, including our thoughts. Every time we have a thought we will create a ripple in the field of consciousness, and that ripple influences the entire universe and everything in it.

These ripples are usually small, and the effect is negligible, but if enough people create the same ripple together (like many millions of people in a city having stressful thoughts) sooner or later the effect will begin to show (like a rising crime rate).

> Every thought one has is imprinted in the memory of the Unified Field, and if enough people imprint similar thoughts, or if one person imprints the same thought long enough, the influence eventually can become strong enough to manifest.

This is why so many people buy all these books on the power of positive thinking. It does appear to make a difference in people's lives, even if that difference is small and often barely noticeable.

But what if we could learn to create far more powerful ripples?

What if everybody was using a dial-up connection to the server running the video game, and everyone was suddenly able to upgrade to a high-speed fibre optics connection?

Even better, what if we could access the *source code* of the game on the server, and even change it if we wanted to?

Having been an avid video game player for most (probably too much) of my life, I can assure you that a large part of the fun of playing computer games is bending or breaking laws that one wouldn't be able to break in real life (without getting into serious trouble, at least).

So what if we could do the same in real life? Go to the field where all the laws of nature are programmed, and where everything is connected to everything else, and then have some fun with it?

This is where the science of miracles begins.

> In a strictly material universe that was created once and then evolved according to physical laws of nature, paranormal phenomena aren't possible.
>
> In a universe that consists of pure vibration and that is created again and again, every split second, based on memory, programmed laws *and* the input from the players, paranormal phenomena not only become possible.
>
> They become logical.

Let's go over all the different types of psychic experiences and some of the research done on them, commonly grouped as "PSI research", and how they make a lot more sense from the Field Paradigm perspective. We'll limit ourselves to an overview of the most important studies and some of their interpretations. If you want to read more, I'd suggest reading *The Field* by Lynne McTaggart, or *Conscious Universe* by Dr. Dean Radin.

The Science of Probability

Before we dive into the science of psychic phenomena, we have to examine the concept of probability, as understanding this will be crucial to see the phenomena for what they really are.

As we already illustrated with the radio story at the beginning of this chapter, phenomena of extrasensory perception only happen once in a while, and for most people such events are outside of their control. This makes the phenomena notoriously difficult to study.

By comparison, it is relatively easy to study new sports shoes. We tell people to jump, which they can do at will, and we can measure the impact when they land. Asking a person to telepathically feel what color of playing card the person in the other room is holding is not nearly as straightforward. Sometimes it might work, most of the times it won't.

It's important to understand here that *it's actually designed not to work*. Just imagine if you could feel every thought every single person on Earth would have. You'd go crazy.

So we can take the radio analogy one step further. A radio doesn't just express one particular type of music, it also acts as a filter, making sure it doesn't express any of the other vibrations. This is a good thing, right? If all the music channels were playing at the same time, the result wouldn't sound very harmonious.

Research on extrasensory perception and other phenomena is mostly research on whether there really is a field that connects our minds to our environment. At the same time, it investigates the degree to which people can actually turn off the filter at will and tune into a particular frequency of another person or some physical event. Given the amount of frequencies there are, it's to be expected that this won't always work perfectly.

In other words, researchers have not been studying whether it works 100% or not, but whether over a large number of inquiries there is a deviation from what we would expect from chance. They can then determine whether this deviation was due to a coincidence or whether something more was going on, revealing a (largely hidden) potential of human beings.

This is where *probability* comes in. Probability is the statistical calculation to what degree a result could happen due to chance. This is actually a crucial factor to take into account in all research that involves human beings.

When we research a physical event, we can usually predict with near certainty that a specific cause will result in a specific effect. With human beings, on the other hand, such accurate predictions are impossible, because researchers can't isolate one single cause from all the other factors that influence their subject's lives every day.

If a company develops a drug that makes people happy, and they test it on *one* person for *one* day, and the person does feel happier, can they say for certain: "The drug works, let's go make a billion dollars"? No, because it could have been due to chance or another factor. Perhaps the person just got a promotion at work, perhaps they fell in love, or just had a good night's sleep. Let's say that in this case the *probability* that it was due to chance was

50%. This means the research is worthless (or "insignificant", as it's called in scientific terms).

However, if we give the drug to 1000 people over a period of three months and every single person *on average* feels happier than they've ever felt before, the probability that this happened by chance will be a lot lower, probably low enough to conclude that the drug works.

> The calculations behind probability are simple: the larger the effect (deviation from normal patterns) and the more consistent the effect over a large group of people, the lower the chance that it could be a coincidence.

What we see in research on psychic phenomena are generally small deviations from chance, but so highly consistent over a large number of trials that we can still say with a very high level of confidence that they weren't due to chance. This means that these researches provide some compelling evidence that there is, in fact, a field that connects humans to physical events in their outside world and to other humans.

Let's look at some of the research.

I Want to Move It, Move It: Research on Mind-Matter Interactions

Nina Kulagina from Russia was famous for her remarkable telekinetic abilities. Among other abilities, Kulagina could mentally move small objects several feet away, and could direct a compass needle at will. The material she was influencing didn't matter (it worked just as well on wood as on metal) and her abilities worked just as well in a highly controlled laboratory environment, where researchers could be sure she wasn't faking it.

Kulagina drew the attention of Soviet scientists and was involved in studies for the last 20 years of her life.

One of her strangest experiments, which was filmed, demonstrated the effect of her psychic powers on a raw egg floating in a tank of saline solution two metres away from her. With intense concentration she separated the yolk from the white of the egg and moved the two apart and then put the egg back together again. Her focus was so strong during these experiments that her pulse reached 240 beats per minute, and she lost almost 2 pounds during such a session[5].

If our intention can create a measurable influence on an object then this would demonstrate that there is a field that connects mind and matter. Otherwise, such influence-at-a-distance would not be possible.

But how does one measure this? As it was impractical to start testing whether people could create bread out of thin air (as nobody has really done that for the past 2000 years), and there weren't too many Nina Kulaginas around either, the mind-matter researchers set goals that were slightly less ambitious.

They simply had a machine that did something similar to flipping coins and tested whether human intention could influence the result, creating a deviation from the 50% heads and 50% tails scenario we would expect.

At first, researchers like Helmut Schmidt worked with known gifted psychics who were able to create an influence. They were creating an average 4% deviation from chance, so 54% heads and 46% tails. Not a huge difference, but consistent over a large enough number of trials to know that it could not have been a coincidence.

The research really took off in 1979, when Princeton University decided to dedicate a whole lab to it. They called it the Princeton Engineering Anomalies Research, or PEAR. The lead researchers, Robert Jahn and Brenda Dunne, purposely chose to work with normal people rather than gifted psychics, as they wanted to research if a latent power was present with *all* humans, rather than just a few individuals. This was what the research was all about, after all: finding evidence that the Field Paradigm is correct.

Jahn and Dunne found that there was a big variation between people in terms of how much they could influence matter with their minds but, as expected, overall the influence was much smaller than with gifted psychics. They generally found only 1% deviation from chance, so 51-49 instead of 50-50.

Did this prove mind could influence matter, or did it prove it made no difference? After all, a 1% difference could easily be due to chance, right?

Well, yes and no. It all depends on the number of trials.

If you do 100 coin tosses and you get 51 heads and 49 tails, then the deviation could be easily due to chance. However, if you do 10,000 tosses and get 51% heads, then this means that on 100 occasions there were more heads than expected by chance. The *probability* of this happening will be a lot lower already. In one million trials, a 1% difference would mean that on 10,000 occasions, there would be consistently more heads than expected by chance. The probability of this happening by coincidence is close to zero.

Basically, whatever effect was showing would have to be consistent over a *very* large number of trials if the researchers wanted to prove anything.

Fortunately, this became possible with the advent of computers. Rather than the traditional mechanical coin-flipping machine, Jahn and Dunne were able to use Random Event Generators, (REGs) – computers that would randomly generate either a zero or a one. They then asked the subjects to desire more ones than zeros.

The REGs allowed them to generate 10,000 "coin flipping" in a half hour session – resulting in more events in one afternoon than most researchers could generate in their entire career. Over such a high number of events any influence, however small, should be clear in the statistics.

Over the next few years, they created 2.5 million such events, with the average 1% deviation from chance remaining consistent. The probability that such a consistent change could have happened by coincidence throughout all the trials from the PEAR lab (plus another 800 studies from other labs around the world, which showed similar results) was smaller than one in a trillion. In other words, if they repeated the sum of these experiments one trillion times (which would take about as long as the existence of our universe multiplied by one thousand), only once would this consistent deviation have taken place by chance.

> Something was going on. However small, human thoughts were having an influence on their environment – the changes could not be due to coincidence.

The people at Princeton University certainly felt there was something worthwhile going on, as they kept funding the lab for the next 25 years.

The influence was still very small, though – too small to make any noticeable difference in daily life. If we look at what it takes to create a real change in the environment, such as separating the yolk from egg white by mental power, we'd need to create a change in the waveforms of billions of particles. Theoretically, this is possible, as Kulagina had shown. However, to go back to our massively multiplayer online game, you'd need to have a pretty fast fibre optic connection to the central server to create a change like this. Based on these results from the Princeton labs, it appears most people only have an old dial-up modem connection.

A 1% difference was also too small to convince any of the Machine Paradigm believers to change their minds. Mind-matter interaction isn't possible according to the Machine Paradigm; it's as simple as that. The fact that there was almost no change convinced them they were correct more than anything else. Most sceptics conveniently never bothered to study the statistics behind it.

It was like when Galileo made his claims about the sun being at the center of our solar system rather than the earth, and said: "Just look in the telescope and observe for yourself." The answer from the religious authorities was: "Anything that cannot be observed by the naked eye doesn't count as evidence."

Here it's the same story in a different form. If people don't want to see evidence, it's very easy to find a reason not to see it.

Jahn and Dunne discovered, however, that thoughts generated from deeper levels of the mind appeared to have far more power than thoughts from superficial levels. Lynne McTaggart's book *The Field* describes how they discovered this when one of their experiments failed in an interesting way.

They had subjects look at a number of images that were randomly selected by a computer. For example, if there were 20 images, each image should show up 5% of the times as predicted by chance. Then they asked their subjects to desire for one image to show up more than the other ones.

The experiment didn't work. The image that was desired did not appear more times with any statistical significance.

However, when they looked at the results in detail they found there were a number of other images that *did* show up a lot more often than they should have by chance. They examined those particular images and found that all of them fell into a similar category: the archetypal, ritualistic or religiously iconographic; the kind of pictures Jung would put in the domain of dreams and the subconscious world. All these images were designed to engage the unconscious mind.

75

> It appeared that the subconscious mind had more to say in the outcome of these tests than what the subjects were consciously desiring. The deeper levels of the mind created a much stronger influence than the more superficial ones.

From the perspective of our wave analogy, this would make sense, as the subconscious mind is a lot closer to the ocean than the conscious mind.

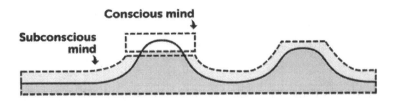

We could compare creating an influence on the Field with one's thoughts to throwing a rock in the water. If you have to throw it from a great distance, the rock you can throw will be small, and the waves the rock creates will be small as well.

But if you can move closer to the lake you'd be able to throw a much bigger rock and create much bigger waves.

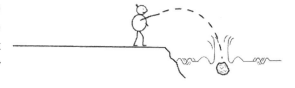

This is an important topic we'll come back to later in this book when we talk about the TM-Sidhi techniques – this is where the secret lies to develop our full human potential and start to create a *real* difference with the power of our thoughts. This is where the magic resides.

However, trying to actively create an influence from the subconscious mind is tricky, as this requires a conscious intention and the subconscious mind is, by definition, out of our conscious control. *Receiving* influences, on the other hand, is much easier from a deeper level of the mind, and that's where we also start to see far more impressive research.

Do you Mind? Telepathy!

The bridge is moving! A monitor in Charles Honorton's lab is showing a video clip of a collapsing suspension bridge taken from a 1940 newsreel. The film shows the bridge swaying back and forth and bending up and down. Light posts are swaying, suspension cables are dangling. The bridge finally collapses from the center and falls into the water.

Someone is watching the video over and over again and is trying to mentally send it to another person in a different room down the hall. The receiving person has his eyes covered, has a red light shining on his face, and is wearing earphones playing static noise. This way all of the subject's sensory inputs are blocked as much as possible and the receiver can pay closer attention to whatever comes up in his mind. The receiver is asked to talk about any impressions he has. Here's what he had to say:

> *Something, some vertical object bending or swaying, almost something swaying in the wind... Some thin, vertical object, bending to the left... Some kind of ladder-like structure but it seems to be almost blowing in the wind. Almost like a ladder-like bridge over some kind of chasm that's waving in the wind. This is not vertical, this is horizontal... A bridge, a drawbridge over something. It's like one of those old English type bridges that open up from either side. The middle part opens up. I see it opening. It's opening...*

Telepathy experiments examine the degree to which somebody can pick up a vibration created by someone else on the Field. Again, this would only be possible if there were a kind of field between the conscious minds of two people, which would give more credibility to the Field Paradigm.

For telepathy and most of the other psychic phenomena to make sense we need to discuss one more difference between particles and fields:

> Particles/material things are isolated, unconnected to anything (outside of their molecular structure), while on the level of fields, every point is connected to every other point.
>
> We have been thinking of ourselves as *particles*, while we need to start thinking of ourselves as *fields*, with all the fun omnipresent, omniscient, and omnipotent qualities that come with it.

During the first telepathy experiments, people sat in a room with a deck of cards that had five symbols on them (circle, square, triangle, etc.). Each time a person picked a card they tried to mentally send the symbol to a person in another room, who then had to guess which card the sender was holding. From 1882 to 1939 over 4,000,000 such trials were reported in 186 scientific publications. The deviation from chance, however, was similar to the REG experiments, only 1%. (So 21% correct guesses compared to only 20% expected by chance.)

As with the REG trials, Machine Paradigm believers would use this as an argument that it *doesn't* work, and all these psychic researchers are just wasting their time on pseudoscience and should get a *real* job instead.

But when scientists looked at the probability of a 1% deviation from chance over such a large amount of trials they found it was less than one in one billion trillion[6], a billion times better than the REG trials still.

This was just the start, however.

> In contrast to the REG experiments, simply receiving impulses from the Field rather than sending them was a lot easier to research when the subjects were in altered states of consciousness. The results then also became a lot more impressive.

For example, a comparative study showed that when the subjects were hypnotized, the results on extra sensory perception tests were around three times better than in the normal waking state of consciousness[7].

When researchers started blocking out the sensory inputs to minimize distraction, like in the bridge video experiment earlier, the probability of successful telepathic communication became higher still.

In the video experiments, one person is trying to mentally send the content of a videotape to the receiver. Next, they show the receiver four videos afterward, and ask him to guess which video was playing during the experiment.

By 1997, 2549 such experiments were reported in 40 publications around the world. A meta-analysis of all this research combined showed an average 8% deviation from chance (eight times better than the earlier card experiments), with a probability smaller than one in a million billion.

My guess is that the subject in the collapsing bridge experiment was one of the people who guessed correctly. ;o)

The most impressive telepathy results, however, appeared to happen during the dream state.

Most natural telepathic experiences that were reported throughout time appeared to happen during the dream state, so it was natural that scientists wanted to research this.

Researchers in the Maimonides Medical Center in Brooklyn set up their experiment so that when EEG measurements showed a sleeping subject started dreaming, a subject in another room would mentally send the dreamer a particular image randomly chosen from a pool of images. Next, the person was awakened and had to guess which image the sender chose. The average deviation from chance was 13% - 13 times higher than the standard telepathy studies. 450 dream studies were reported in journal articles between 1966 and 1973. The chance that such a high deviation from chance could be consistent over 450 studies by coincidence was one in 75 million.

Dream telepathy experiences

Even though my father hadn't talked to his parents for a while, one night he dreamt that something had happened to his mother, so the next day he called her. It turned out she had fallen down the stairs and broken her wrist. It could have been a coincidence, but he had already had so many experiences like this that he knew better.
I've had many of these experiences as well.
Two friends of mine, whom I've known for more than 20 years, got married 17 years ago. As I spent most of my time abroad I hadn't been in touch with them for 2 years, but suddenly I had a dream that their marriage was in trouble. The next day I found out they were getting divorced.

So why is it that impulses from the Field seem to come through more clearly in the dream state or altered states of consciousness?

To examine this, let's compare a thought to a bubble of air in an ocean. The bubble originates from the bottom of the ocean, then grows and grows as it goes up and until it reaches the surface of the ocean, where it pops. This popping of the air bubble is what we experience as a thought, the moment when the bubble reaches our conscious minds.

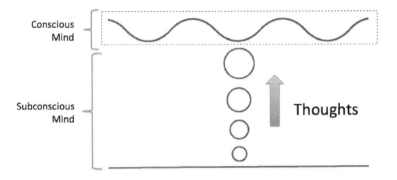

But have you ever thought: *"Where does a thought come from before I think it?"*

It comes from somewhere, right? A thought is an expression of who you are; only in this case we're saying that who you really are is a local expression of the Field.

Any thought has to go through all the layers of the subconscious mind before it reaches our conscious mind. It's kind of like music that has to go through the different parts of the radio (transistors, amplifier, etc.) before it reaches the speakers. During that process the music can get filtered, distorted, or both.

If the radio isn't tuned properly, or one of the parts aren't working properly, the music will be distorted.

In terms of the mind, we could compare this to a game of golf. Even if the putt is perfectly in the right direction, the ball can still deviate if there are some bumps on the green.

In terms of our nervous system, these bumps are impurities, things that disturb the natural functioning of mind and body, usually as a result of accumulated stress.

So even if every thought that originates from the source is perfect (perfectly loving, or perfectly in tune with what the sender is trying to send, in the case of our telepathy experiments), by the time it reaches our conscious minds, it might have deviated enough so that something different arrives.

But if we can expand our conscious minds, allowing us to go deeper in the areas of our subconscious, we can learn to pick up a thought from a deeper level. In this case, it would be logical that it will be more reliable if it is closer to how it was originally formed.

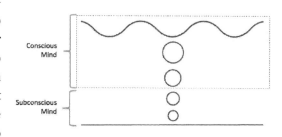

Basically, all we did is move the goal of the golf game a bit closer.

By now it probably won't surprise you that recent research by Dr. Dean Radin shows that meditators have consistently better results at PSI (parapsychological psychic phenomena or power) experiments than non-meditators[8]. This is an area that is now under full investigation.

I see...I see...What You Can't See... Clairvoyance

For a long time, psychic researchers were getting seriously frustrated.

> From the outside, their work was ridiculed as pseudoscience. At the same time they knew what was really going on but weren't allowed to talk about it because they were involved in secret government-sponsored projects.

In 1995, several of these secret psychic research projects were declassified, which already revealed quite a few interesting stories. In Jan 2017 the CIA decided to put a wide selection of their classified records online: 11 million pages detailing, among other things, thousands of records of their psychic research projects.

These records show that the CIA has actually been very busy with these projects, investing over $20 million to subsidize them throughout the 1980s (the equivalent of $50 million today).

While they researched different phenomena, they were especially interested in the ones on remote viewing, which could provide a strategic advantage over the bad guys at the time.

Basically, if remote viewing was shown to be reliable, they could create the perfect spy: someone who could have a look around in an enemy military base without endangering their life having to go there. All they needed was a set of coordinates. That information seemed to be enough for the clairvoyants to let their mind travel to the actual place and have a look around.

It didn't always work. Like all psychic phenomena, clairvoyance is not an exact science. You can't tell for sure whether an impression is really coming through in pure form from the Unified Field, the big memory storage unit where all information about anything is contained, or whether it got distorted along the way.

Still, there were a few individuals who had impressive track records of accurate remote viewings, and when conventional intelligence techniques were at a loss to provide critical information, sometimes remote viewing was used to provide the missing link so badly needed.

For example, here is a story from PSI researcher Dean Radin's *The Conscious Universe*:

> *In September 1979 the National Security Council asked one of the most consistently accurate army remote viewers, a chief warrant officer named Joe McMoneagle, to "see" inside a large building somewhere in northern Russia.*
>
> *A spy-satellite photo had shown some suspicious heavy-construction activity around the building, which was about a hundred yards from a large body of water. But the National Security Council had no idea what was going on inside, and it wanted to know.*
>
> *Without showing McMoneagle the photo, and giving him only the map coordinates of the building, the officers in charge asked for his impressions. McMoneagle described a cold location, with large buildings and smokestacks near a large body of water.*
>
> *This was roughly correct, so he was shown the spy photo and asked what was inside the building. McMoneagle sensed that the interior was a very large, noisy, active working area, full of scaffolding, girders and blue flashes reminiscent of arc welding lights.*

In a later session, he sensed that a huge submarine was apparently under construction in one part of the building. But it was too big, much larger than any submarine that either the Americans or Russians had ever built. McMoneagle drew a sketch of what he "saw": a long, flat deck; strangely angled missile tubes with room for eighteen to twenty missiles; a new type of drive mechanism; and a double hull.

When these results were described to members of the National Security Council, they figured that McMoneagle must be wrong, because he would be describing the largest, strangest submarine in existence, and it was supposedly being constructed in a building a hundred yards from the water. Furthermore, other intelligence sources knew absolutely nothing about it.

Still, because McMoneagle had gained a reputation for accuracy in previous tasks, they asked him to view the future to find out when this supposed submarine would be launched. McMoneagle scanned the future, month-by-month, "watching" the future construction via remote viewing, and sensed that about four months later the Russians would blast a channel from the building to the water and launch the sub.

Sure enough, about four months later, in January 1980, spy-satellite photos showed that the largest submarine ever observed was traveling through an artificial channel from the building to the body of water. The picture showed that it had twenty missile tubes and a large, flat deck. It was eventually named a Typhoon class submarine.

Experiences from clairvoyance are related to the omnipresence and omniscience qualities of the Unified Field. If one part of the Field is affected, then the entire Field is affected. This stir is imprinted in its memory allowing the Field to know everything about everywhere. A clairvoyant is someone who has developed a skill to tap into this Field and obtain information.

In 1995, the CIA commissioned a review of all the government-sponsored remote-viewing research. Their conclusions were that although extra sensory perception seemed to be present with everyone, a small group of select individuals showed far better results than the rest. Mass screenings to find talented remote viewers revealed that about 1% of all those tested were consistently successful. Just like with music or sports, everybody seems to have some basic ability to do it, but some people have more talent for it than others.

At the PEAR research center, Jahn and Dunne did their own research on remote viewing but like with the REG experiments, they preferred to work with normal everyday people rather than talented clairvoyants.

They picked a target destination from a pool of sites, anywhere from 5 to 6000 miles away from the lab, had somebody go there and fill out a standardized checklist. Meanwhile, the person inside the lab would try to describe the site and fill out the same checklist. This was an objective way to measure any correspondence. Even though they weren't working with gifted psychics, they still found that nearly two-thirds were more accurate than could be accounted for by chance, with a probability of less than one in a billion[9].

Through what medium do psychic phenomena take place?

This was one of the questions that puzzled scientists from the very beginning.

The first thought was that it would be through the electromagnetic field, that the brain somehow sends out and receives signals similar to a radio. It was discovered soon after that this could not be the case. When a subject was in an electromagnetically shielded room telepathic experiments worked just as well as when they were sitting outside of it.

Later on, the Russians formulated theories that psychic phenomena happened through ultra-low frequencies. Hal Putoff, a researcher at Stanford Research Institute (one of the CIA funded PSI research labs), put this theory to the test.

In two studies, he had his most consistently successful clairvoyant sit in a small submarine 170 metres under water. Meanwhile he himself, in the presence of an independent government official, randomly picked out a target from a pool of destinations in the San Francisco area, 500 miles away from where the sub was diving, and went there. The clairvoyant then had to try to "see" where they were. In both cases, he correctly identified the target sites, a hilltop in Portola Valley and a shopping mall in Mountain View.

A few hundred metres of salt water is known to filter out nearly all frequencies, even the lowest ones. According to Putoff, the only vibrations that weren't disrupted by 170 metres of water were the ones on a quantum level, the level of the Unified Field. So that appeared to be the only plausible explanation that was left.

Does distance affect PSI experiments?

Another question that PSI researchers were wondering was to what degree distance influences the results of PSI experiments. This is again related to a way of thinking that there must be a medium through which PSI effects take place, like the electromagnetic field. In this case, any influence that is created will become weaker over greater distances.

But that did not seem to be the case. In the earlier PEAR remote viewing experiments it didn't make any difference whether the target site was 6 or 6000 miles away, and the CIA experiments had remote viewers scan areas all around the world, and it didn't make any difference.

Still, Dr. Edgar Mitchell tried an even bolder experiment, at a far greater distance still: would telepathy work from 150,000 miles away in outer space?

Edgar Mitchell was an astronaut on Apollo 14, and the sixth man to walk on the Moon. He certainly did not fit the typical profile of a PSI researcher, having a bachelor's degree in industrial management and a doctorate in astronautics from MIT. Still, all the PSI experiments, which were so easily ridiculed by his Machine-Paradigm-educated colleagues, somehow inspired him.

So while he was in outer space, Mitchell did his experiment. (He didn't tell the other astronauts.) He transmitted a telepathic message to four individuals on Earth, 150,000 miles below. At specific times, he wrote down sets of numbers and symbols of a particular card deck and asked four subjects down on earth to try to guess which numbers and symbols he picked.

The experiment was a success. Although the subjects didn't get all the sequences right, the results were significant: the chance that they were due to coincidence was 1 in 3000.

Distance did not seem to make a difference.

This is another confirmation that PSI doesn't happen at any level where we are separate from each other, because any kind of vibrations would decrease over greater distances (like radio signals decreasing over distance) Instead, PSI happens at the level of the Unified Field, where everything is united and any concept of distance disappears.

Eternal Life: The Ultimate Challenge to the Machine Paradigm

If you want to know if you are challenging someone's core beliefs, just look at their reaction: the more uncomfortable they become, the more you know you're hitting something profound.

Few things make materialists (who believe that consciousness is created by material processes) more uncomfortable than the topic of near-death experiences and reincarnation.

They are either very quick to dismiss it with "I don't believe in reincarnation", or you can just feel the atmosphere change as soon as the topic is brought up.

> If you want to measure to what degree somebody is hanging on to the Machine Paradigm, bring up the topic of reincarnation, and see how they react.

People don't know *why* reincarnation makes them so uncomfortable because most people aren't consciously aware of their core belief systems.

Basically, it all comes down to the computer vs. radio analogy.

If a computer breaks down, it's "game over". *There is no other possibility*. The software can't function if the hardware is broken. As such, any after-life events are impossible.

If a radio breaks down, on the other hand, the music itself simply continues, until either the radio starts functioning again (near-death experience, or NDE) or a new radio tunes into the same frequency (new birth or reincarnation).

If scientific research showed that NDEs and reincarnation are real, it would be the strongest indication yet that the radio analogy is the better way to describe consciousness.

You can probably imagine that, if the reaction from the scientific community towards all the "pseudoscience nonsense" like telepathy or remote-viewing hasn't been very supportive, the reaction towards NDEs and reincarnation research has been negative still.

Don't try to convince me of something that is impossible. It's impossible – end of story.

Well, research is showing that it is not only possible, but that it simply appears to be the reality of life. Michael Talbot's book *Holographic Universe* gives a good overview of the research on NDEs and reincarnation. We'll just summarize some of the research here.

Let's start with the least controversial one.

Research on near-death experiences

In 1976, an art student named Elane Durham had a stroke caused by a brain tumor. As she was brought to the hospital she experienced being next to her body, rather than inside it. What follows was an experience which she later stated was the "most singular and most important thing that has ever happened to her."

Here's how she described it:

> The next thing that I can remember is running across the fields of grass. There were maybe five or seven people that were there waiting for me. And I realized that one of them was my grandmother who died when I was nine years old. The other one was my husband's friend Virginia and she had just died the previous February.
>
> There was sound in the air that completely defies description. It was as if there were a multitude of voices, and a multitude of instruments, blended and playing soft music. The twittering of birds, and other beautiful sounds, were all melodically instrumented into the music which wafted through the air. The sounds just flowed into me in a soft, soft manner.
>
> Looking about me, I turned toward the right, and I saw a distant light that resembled a bright star. The light began to move toward me at an incredible rate of speed; at the same time, I had a sense of moving toward the light.
>
> As the light got closer to me, I realized that it had a personality to it. Love and understanding were emanating from the light. It was the most intense amount of love that you can imagine. It was as though you were in the presence of the one person in your life who had loved you beyond anything, despite what you might have done, and that love was magnified many times. That's how it was, in a way...
>
> Then I was back in my body with a body slam and the defibrillators were above me getting ready to jolt me again.

You can find countless testimonies like Elane's on www.neardeath.com.

> ### The loving light, an everyday meditation experience
>
> Throughout the ages, the experience of the higher divine reality has been consistently described as an experience of "the Light of God", similar to Elane's description.
>
> This experience is an everyday experience for me. I experience this light during almost every single TM session I do. (Though not as intensely as described here, it's more a soft feeling of coming home.) It didn't happen that way immediately, only after I started learning the advanced TM techniques, which are meant to refine the experience of the path to transcending.
>
> From this experience, it's very clear why transcending often has such miraculous healing effects (as we'll see in Part 3). Whether people have a very clear experience of the "presence of the one person in your life who had loved you beyond anything" or have a vague subtle experience of it, the healing effects are very obvious. The more this presence of love had been lacking in a person's life, the stronger the healing effects of transcending usually are.

People with experiences like Elane's generally report that the experiences feel very real; more real than anything else, in fact. For a lot of people, NDEs have been life-transforming. People report becoming more loving, their senses become sharper, they start thinking differently, and most of them no longer have any fear of death.

Now here's the interesting part about NDEs, and what makes it relatively easy to research them: people who are about to die are often lying in the hospital connected to measuring equipment, like an EEG machine measuring the electrical activity of the brain. When a person dies, there is no activity whatsoever. In fact, a flat EEG (complete halting of any brain activity) is one of the criteria to pronounce a person clinically dead. If the computer is switched off, the software cannot run. Even hallucinations aren't possible.

And yet the software is running!

The materialists have tried to find mechanical explanations to explain this situation. Recently they found a spike in brain activities in rats right before the rats died, and proclaimed that this was the explanation for near-death experiences.

This has just been one of the many explanations that have been offered, but they all come down to hallucinations created by some part of the brain that generates a last spike of activity.

When other scientists who are less attached to the Machine Paradigm point of view hear such a "traditional" explanation, few are convinced. It sounds much more like a desperate attempt to keep holding on to the Machine Paradigm in the face of overwhelming evidence to the contrary.

First of all, human brains are quite different from those in rats. Secondly, what happens in the brain as someone dies is different in almost every case, yet the experiences during NDE's are often very similar.

The biggest blow to any attempt to keep holding on to mechanical explanations of NDE's probably came from Dr. Eben Alexander. His experience, which he described in his book *Proof of Heaven* was probably the perfect storm of NDE's. He was a neuroscientist himself who was very much in the materialist camp. During the 15 years he worked at Harvard Medical School he had encountered several of NDE's among his patients but used the same materialist arguments all his colleagues used to explain them...until he had one himself.

He got a rare bacteriological brain infection that affected his neocortex, and ended up in a coma, while having a near death experience. The difference was that while most NDE's lasted only a few minutes, his lasted for *seven days*. What was especially interesting about his experience was that when the neocortex is down, it's not possible to experience dreams or hallucinations. It's not possible to experience *anything*.

After seven days in a coma with that kind of infection, chances of mortality were 97% and, even if he'd survive, chances of a full recovery and a normal life after the damage that had been done to his brain by the infection were virtually zero. Yet he made a full recovery to tell his story of his NDE (which contained a lot of the elements commonly described, though some unique ones as well) but also offer his perspective as a neuroscientist on why all the traditional materialist explanations for his experience completely failed.

His book, published in 2012, became a #1 New York Times bestseller.

Here are some of the most commonly experienced elements of an NDE, as an article in *The Atlantic* on NDEs reports:

> Though details and descriptions vary across cultures, the overall tenor of the experience is remarkably similar… Many of these stories relate the sensation of floating up and viewing the scene around one's unconscious body; spending time in a beautiful, otherworldly realm; meeting spiritual beings (some call them angels) and a loving presence that some call God; encountering long-lost relatives or friends; recalling scenes from one's life [the life review]; feeling a sense of connectedness to all creation as well as a sense of overwhelming, transcendent love; and finally being called, reluctantly, away from the magical realm and back into one's own body.[10]

Some of these elements, like meeting recently deceased friends or relatives or the life review, have already been described in ancient texts thousands of years ago. It is described, among others, in the *Tibetan Book of the Dead*, the Egyptian *Book of the Dead*, Plato's writings, and the Vedic texts.

Let's have a look at all these experiences in more detail. They are rather interesting by themselves, as each of them challenges the Machine Paradigm on their own.

<u>An out-of-body experience (OBE)</u>. OBEs, like floating above the body, are evidence that consciousness might exist independent of the body, just like music can exists independent of the radio.

Michael B. Sabom, a cardiologist and professor of medicine at Emory University, got so tired of hearing his cardiac arrest patients recount their so-called 'OBE fantasies' that he decided to settle the matter once and for all.

He selected two groups of patients, one of 32 patients that had reported OBEs during their heart attacks and another one of 25 patients that have never experienced out-of-body travel. He asked the OBE+ group to describe how they had witnessed their own resuscitation from their out-of-body state and asked the control group to describe what they imagine must have happened.

Out of the 25 non-experiencers, 20 made major mistakes, three gave correct but general descriptions, and two had no idea at all what had happened. From the 32 OBE+ group, 25 gave correct but general descriptions, six gave highly detailed and accurate descriptions, and one was able to give an accounting so accurate in every possible detail that Sabom was stunned. He is now an ardent believer and lectures widely on the subject[11].

<u>Greeted by deceased friends and relatives</u>. This would be a rather tricky one in the Machine Paradigm. Software from a broken computer is now being

greeted by software from other broken computers? (In most cases where the hardware has probably already largely disintegrated.)

Try to make that one fit within the Machine Paradigm.

Oh, wait... yes, of course... everybody has been hallucinating for the past 5000 years... we know the answer: *it's impossible.*

<u>Life-review</u>. Remembering every major event in your life. If the body is the computer and the mind the software, the memory would be the hard drive. Most people think their memory is stored inside their brain. But the brain has stopped working; no brain activity is shown by the EEG. If the power of the computer is off, it's not possible to retrieve anything from the hard drive, right? So where are the memories coming from? Wherever memories are coming from, it is definitely not *from the brain.*

Of course, if our memories are stored physically, then people shouldn't be able to remember anything from an OBE, or from the entire NDE, as a computer that isn't functioning can't write new memories. Yet they do remember, which also indicates that their memories are not stored in their brains. Perhaps the brain is not a mechanism to store memories locally, but a mechanism to retrieve memories that are stored in "the cloud". We've already seen earlier that the field of consciousness appears to be one giant universal memory databank, so perhaps our own memories are stored there as well.

From this perspective, it starts to become more feasible that memories could be transferred from one body to another, as we go from one life to the next.

Which brings us to our next topic, the one that makes the materialists even more uncomfortable.

<u>Reincarnation.</u>
How can reincarnation be objectively studied? It's rather simple: by invoking memories that people have of their past lives and testing whether these memories correspond to actual events.

Most of us are capable of remembering past lives, but these memories are usually hidden in our subconscious minds. We don't remember them clearly, but sometimes experience strange sensations when we meet certain persons and immediately like (or dislike) them, or even feel we know this person, even if we can't explain why. Or perhaps we go somewhere and immediately feel at home and have a feeling of having been there before, even though we haven't. Most people will attribute these experiences to coincidence and won't think about it much further.

But maybe these aren't coincidences. Maybe you do already know that person. Maybe you have already been at that place before.

So, if past life memories are hidden in our subconscious minds, is there a way to bring them to our *conscious* awareness, analyze them more clearly, and thereby provide a more solid scientific basis for the existence of past lives?

Yes, it appears this is possible. There appear to be two ways.

Hypnosis is one way that seems to work as a research method (even if we would advise against it as a practice, see below).

Dr. Joel Whitton, professor of psychiatry at the University of Toronto Medical School, spent decades using his hypnosis skills to find out what exactly people unconsciously knew about their past lives. He spent thousands of hours with his hypnotized subjects, recording everything they had to say about their past lives.

> Whitton found that 90% of people who are hypnotizable had clear memories of past lives, memories that were often verifiable.

The first thing he found was that there was a striking correspondence between the different experiences. For example, all reported having lived numerous past lives – some could remember as many as 20 to 25 – and that gender was not specific to the soul. Many had at least lived one life as the opposite sex. All reported that the purpose of life was to evolve and learn and that multiple existences facilitated this process[12].

Subjects were also able to give very detailed historical titbits about the time in which they lived, which could often be verified. Some of these things were incredibly fine details they had no way of knowing otherwise, like clothing and shoes, foods eaten, or particular habits of the time. Nevertheless, when the memories were double-checked with historians, the reports in many cases turned out to match the timeframe during which the life was supposed to be lived. For example, researchers found that when people remembered living in the 1700s, they described eating their meals with forks with three prongs, but after 1790 they described their forks as having four prongs. Historians verified that this correctly reflects the evolution of the fork[13].

Whitton had a few cases where, after hearing his subject's testimony, a lot of seemingly unrelated experiences and events in his current life started to make a lot more sense.

One striking example was a psychologist born and raised in Canada who as a child had an inexplicable British accent. He also had an irrational fear of breaking his leg, a phobia of air travel, a terrible nail-biting problem, an obsessive fascination with torture, and as a teenager had a brief and enigmatic vision of being in a room with a Nazi officer, shortly after operating the pedals of a car during a driving test. Under hypnosis, the man recalled being a British pilot during World War II. While on a mission over Germany, his plane was hit by a shower of bullets, one of which penetrated the fuselage and broke his leg. This in turn caused him to lose control of the plane's foot pedals, forcing him to crash-land. He was captured by the Nazis, tortured for information by having his nails pulled out, and died a short time after[14].

Some subjects were even able to speak languages they couldn't possibly know. One man, while reliving an apparent past life as a Viking, suddenly started shouting words that were later identified to be Old Norse. That same man, after being regressed to an ancient Persian lifetime, began to write in an Arabic-style script, later identified by an expert in Near Eastern languages as an authentic representation of Sassanid Pahlavi, a long-extinct Mesopotamian language that flourished between A.D. 226 and 651.

When the subjects are awakened from their hypnosis, they don't remember anything they've said or written.

Hypnosis generally disrupts the normal functioning of the mind, however, and is not something most psychiatrists would condone. Whereas transcending integrates brain functioning (as we'll see in next chapter), hypnosis appears to disrupt it and could potentially have negative long-term effects*. Don't try this at home, in other words. Also, even though some of the individual case studies yielded some really spectacular results, there is some debate about whether the whole body of hypnosis research is really all that statistically impressive as scientific proof that past life memories are real.

So I'd rather focus on the second way to verify past life experiences, which yielded far more impressive results from a scientific perspective: past life memories that spontaneously come up with young children.

---

* Maharishi also advised strongly against using hypnosis. And, even though he said: "reincarnation is a fact, whether you believe in it or not", he also advised against digging up memories of past lives. If there is a good reason for memories to come up in this life, they will come naturally. If not, there is a reason why they are hidden.

Dr. Ian Stevenson, professor of psychiatry at the University of Virginia Medical School, noticed that young children, usually between age two and four, often appeared to have clear memories from past lives. So he asked anyone who had children with such memories to contact him, so he could investigate these memories and see if they match to actual events. Stevenson felt that if this was the case, this approach would give far more reliable results than hypnosis.

He got so many replies from parents that his staff couldn't possibly follow up on all of them. As a result, during the past 30 years, Dr. Stevenson had the chance to examine thousands of such cases.

He quickly discovered that children often remember their past lives *in great detail*, including their former names, names of family members and friends, where they lived, what they did for a living, and what their house looked like. Those memories were often so detailed that Stevenson was able to track down the identity of their previous personality and objectively verify nearly every detail the child described.

In a number of such cases he took the children to the area of their previous incarnation and saw them navigate effortlessly through neighbourhoods they've never been before and correctly identify their former house, belongings, and past-life relatives and friends.[15]

In some cases, where the children remembered an injury or deformity, Stevenson was able to obtain hospital and autopsy reports of the deceased personality. He found that the injury or deformity had indeed occurred exactly as the children described it.

In other cases, he also found that the children had birthmarks or deformities in their present life on the exact place on their current bodies where an injury happened in their previous incarnation. As one rather spooky example, one boy remembered committing suicide by shooting himself in the head in his past life. When the boy's past life identity was found, they could look in the hospital records to see where exactly he had shot himself. They found that in his current life the boy had birthmarks on his head, one precisely where the bullet had entered and another precisely where it had exited.

Stevenson has published six volumes to date on his research studies, and his thorough investigations have gained him a reputation of a respectable scientific researcher, with publications in many distinguished scientific journals. In a review of one of his works, the prestigious *Journal of the American Medical Association* stated that Stevenson has "Painstakingly and unemotionally collected a detailed series of cases in which the evidence for reincarnation is difficult to understand on any other grounds... he has placed on record a large amount of data that cannot be ignored"[16].

And yet it mostly *has* been ignored, because *it just doesn't make sense*. Again, that's what people do when data doesn't make sense according to their paradigm. They don't change their paradigm, they just ignore the data.

But what is the cost of ignoring this data, which appears to show that life continues even if the body dies? The cost is huge. Most people live with a constant fear of dying, or have to live with a great pain in their hearts when a loved one has passed. But would you feel sorry for the music if the local radio breaks down? No. You might miss the music right there in your life, but you know that the music itself can never die. At some point, some new radio will tune into this particular frequency, and the music simply continues.

> People only suffer because they have been living in an *illusion* that we are machines rather than immortal souls who occasionally need a new vehicle, just like we sometimes need to replace our car.

If one of your loved ones decides to get a new car because the old one has just been worn down, would we feel sorry? Quite the opposite, we'd be excited. No more endless repairs and maintenance and worrying that the car might break down at any moment. A fresh new car!

But what if the car crashes while it's still relatively new, long before it's meant to be replaced? Should we feel sad when somebody dies at a young age, before his time has come? It feels so unfair. How to make sense of this?

That's probably one of the toughest questions a lot of people have to deal with. Let's take this one as the last example of how things start to make a lot more sense from the Field Paradigm perspective where everything is connected, before we start to explore what happens when we can actually experience the Field in Part 3.

The Law of Action and Reaction from a Field Paradigm Perspective

Let's play a little game. I'd like you to imagine you are the Divine Creator of the universe.

The first privilege that comes with the job is that you get to decide *everything*, including the fate of all people.

So here you go:

- This person gets to be born in a wealthy family with wonderful loving parents.
- This other person gets to be born in a poor family in a war-torn country in Africa...and his parents will be killed in the war soon afterward.
- This one will win the lottery next week.
- This one is about to find the love of her life.
- This person, sorry, you're going to die in a car crash at a young age.
- This one, oooh, I like this one. She's a keeper. She will get to live till 110.

In the beginning, it's all pretty exciting to display your omnipotent powers. Though after a while it becomes a little boring.

My God, it's a lot of paperwork, isn't it? So many people, so many decisions to make.

And then come all the *appeals*. For some bizarre reason, people often seem to disagree with your decision. Too bad. *You're* the omnipotent one. *They're* just going to have to live with it.

Still, they don't seem very happy. They even start cursing you. How unfair, when you're only doing your job.

After a while, you've had enough. There must be a better way.

Suddenly a brilliant idea pops up. What if you program the universe in a way that you don't have to decide *anything*, and everything is decided automatically, in a way that *guarantees* 100% fairness for everyone?

Being omnipotent and all, programming the universe is definitely one of the things you could pull off, so off you go. First, you program a huge memory databank where every action and thought of every single individual gets stored. Then you program one simple law:

> Every action will have an equal and opposite reaction.

It's basically exactly the same law that you programmed for all physical events.

Remember how it was before you programmed the physical laws? My God, it was so exhausting to decide on every event.

Even with a simple toy, where you had a bunch of balls on wires next to each other, it was so much work.

Every time somebody played with this toy, you had to decide, how many balls are we going to move: one, two, or three?

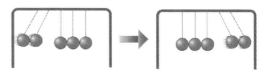

But now life is so easy. You just programmed that *every action has an equal reaction,* so if they play with two balls, exactly two balls will bounce off at the other side. Meanwhile, *you* could go on a well-deserved holiday.

So why not do exactly the same with human action? What a brilliant idea, how come you didn't think of this before?

Now the universe becomes simple: *everything* is just action and reaction. You decided to give human beings complete free will, but they *are* bound by this single law. Every action they do, even every thought they have, will be stored in the universal memory bank and someday the effect will come back to them. As you sow, so shall you reap.

So if somebody decides to steal from someone else, he might actually be smart enough to avoid getting caught (or get a smart enough lawyer if he does) and escape prison in his lifetime. When it comes to cosmic justice, however, there's no escape. *The entire omnipotent universe will arrange for the effect to come back sooner or later.* This phenomena was already described in the Vedic texts thousands of years ago, and they called it "karma" (did you know that the literal translation of the word "karma" is simply "action"...action and reaction). So in a future lifetime the thief might become a jeweler... and guess what happens.

There are still two problems, however.

The first one is that the time between the action and reaction is often so long (sometimes even spanning several lifetimes) that people don't make the connection, and they *still* feel like you're randomly deciding everything, and are still cursing you if they don't like the outcome.

Oh well, now it's really their problem. At least you have a lot less work and, from your omniscient perspective, everything is fair, even if people don't always think it is.

The other problem is a tougher nut to crack. You notice that *very few people actually have free will,* or at least use their gift of free will. People just seem to be getting stuck in endless cycles of action and reaction.

Here's what happens. People did something bad in some past life, which comes back as a negative experience in this life. As a result of this, they accumulate stress, which will result in them again acting impulsively at a later stage (under stress people often lose control, and lose their free will to objectively decide, as we'll see in more detail in next chapter), and they again repeat the negative action. This means that then again they have to receive it back, etc. Remember these stories of people who were abused as children…and then end up abusing children themselves as adults later? It appears to be an endless vicious circle.

Fortunately, there's a way out of the vicious circle. That's what we'll discuss in Part 3.

Part 2 Summary
In this part we've seen that the Field Paradigm appears to be a scientific reality, and that a lot of phenomena in nature, including so-called paranormal human experiences, start to make sense from the perspective of connectedness.

They didn't make sense before because we thought of ourselves as particles, isolated in time and space, rather than a part of an omnipresent, omniscient and omnipotent field.

We have also been thinking about events in our lives as random coincidences, rather than perfectly orchestrated events of an infinitely intelligent, and completely fair universe.

Either we live in a universe where *everything* is a coincidence, or in one where *nothing* is.

In which universe would you prefer to live?

Part 3: Using the Field Paradigm

*At any time, Infinity says:
"I am with you...don't worry."*

Maharishi Mahesh Yogi

The power of true silence 101
The Too-Good-To-Be-True Problem 127
Changing Lives: The long-term effects of transcending 133
   Reduced Stress *133*
   Improved health *135*
   Improved Brain Functioning *138*
   Transforming Education *140*
So Why Aren't We Using This? 147
Spiritual Growth 152
So How Does it Feel to Transcend? 161
Transcending is just the start: The TM-Sidhi program 163
Twenty Experiments that Will Change the World 175
   Research on the TM Field Effect (the 1% effect) *176*
   Did the TM Organisation Gain Anything from This Research? ... *185*
   Research on the Square Root of 1% Effect *188*
   So What Did the Government of Guinea-Bissau Decide? *268*
Five Ways to make it happen...At Virtually No Cost 270
Why We Have Good Reason to Hope: More and more governments are responding 275

Part 3 Overview

In this part we'll see what happens when we start to experience the Field as our true inner nature. We'll see that research has shown powerful (and sometimes miraculous) healing effects in all areas of life. In fact, we'll see that one of the reasons why not everybody is transcending yet is that it sounds almost too good to be true.

Next we'll see how researchers have discovered that when people transcend it also creates a powerful ripple effect on the people around them, which causes a positive change in their behaviour. We'll see the story of how increasing disbelief in the scientific community was answered by increasingly impressive research: the 20 experiments that can change the world.

We'll also discover the story how some of these experiments were purposely designed to play a crucial role in some of the most remarkable positive changes we have seen during last century, including the ending of several wars and the fall of the Berlin Wall.

The regular miracle

"I want to learn TM again...I need it."

That was the message I got on Facebook from an old friend I hadn't seen for more than 20 years.

He was my best friend when we were kids. We learned the Transcendental Meditation technique together when we were ten years old. His family didn't support it as much as mine, however, and he didn't stay regular in his practice.

He eventually moved to another town and we drifted apart. I later heard through some mutual friends that he had fallen into depression and developed a severe alcohol addiction.

One day, he contacted me out of the blue saying that he was tired of his life and needed to change, and he was convinced TM was going to help him.

It was not a smooth case. I went to visit him in his home town three times to discuss how we'd start his course to refresh his TM practice, in his case for free, (anyone who takes the TM course once can retake it for free at any time during the rest of their lives) yet three times he didn't even show up. He had either forgotten or was too drunk.

I decided to be patient, if only for the sake of an old friend.

A few months later, my patience was rewarded. He called me to schedule another appointment, and this time he did show up.

What happened next I can only describe as a miracle.

After his *first* TM session, when he opened his eyes, I could see that something had clearly changed in his face. A tension was gone. He felt it as well.

The next day he came back and asked: *"Joachim, what did you do to me?* I feel happy! I haven't felt like this in years."

That same day he stopped drinking. He didn't feel the need for it anymore. It's now two years later and he hasn't touched a drop of alcohol since and never misses a single meditation.

These kinds of experiences happen with almost every Transcendental Meditation course I give. Out of the typical 8 to 10 people that take the course together there is always at least one case of a profound change within the first few days. People who for years have had trouble sleeping suddenly sleep like babies; addicts stop drinking or using drugs from the first day; people who have been running around with a muscle pain for years find that the pain spontaneously disappears.

Even though I should be getting used to it, it still blows me away every time.

How can such a simple technique create such miraculous results?

This is what we're going to investigate in this chapter.

The power of true silence

In the previous part we saw how both the latest developments in physics and research on paranormal abilities point to the existence of an invisible field that connects everything...and unites everything.

So what would happen if we could *experience* this unity with everything?

If we are just waves on this ocean of unity, experiencing the ocean itself is just a matter of bringing the wave to a state of complete silence. We make our minds quiet while remaining completely conscious and alert.

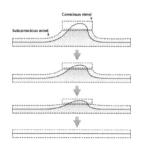

Simple, right? Except that it doesn't appear to be that simple. Have you ever tried to make your mind completely quiet? It sounds almost impossible. The more you try, the more you only seem to keep the mind active.

This is exactly why the technique to transcend got lost, because people started *trying*. They started to invent hundreds of ways to control the mind (concentration on your breath, a sound, some visual point, contemplation, or just "monitoring your thoughts"). Usually, this only results in frustration, and the feeling that "meditation" was difficult.

But should it really be difficult? Let's use some simple logic. According to the ancient texts, regular experience of transcending is absolutely essential to develop our full human potential (and we'll see exactly how this full development happens in the next few chapters). If this is indeed the case, do you think the creator would be so cruel to make it *difficult* for human beings to transcend or, on the contrary, would he design things in such a way that it would be natural and easy?

Transcending was designed to be a completely effortless and natural process.

It's *humanity* that made it much more difficult than it should be, by misinterpreting the technique to transcend.

With the right technique transcending is the easiest thing anyone could ever do.

This was exactly the experience of a rather famous Hollywood actress when she learned TM.

"I have tried meditations but I could not do it. I concluded that I'm apparently incapable of meditating... when I learned TM it was the easiest thing I've ever done, not the easiest meditation I've ever done, the easiest THING I've ever done... I got my entire family to learn." **Cameron Diaz**

Watch Cameron Diaz's full testimony about TM (5 min video) on www.fieldparadigm.com/cameron-diaz

---

If a child with ADHD can do it...

The main obstacle that prevents people from learning to transcend technique is not so much that they don't believe the effects of TM, but a fear that they won't be able to do it. They are afraid that they won't succeed in quietening their minds. More often than not, this fear is confirmed when they already tried some meditation technique and it didn't work.

So they think it's their fault. They're just not good at meditating.

I usually tell them of my experience teaching TM to children with severe ADHD. It's impossible to let a child like that even sit still for 15 minutes, let alone make their minds quiet. But when I give them this technique they can not only successfully practice it, usually from the very first meditation, but they absolutely love it.

That usually shuts everybody up. Well, if *they* can do it...

The reason why people started misinterpreting the true technique to a form of control was because the formula to activate the natural process of meditation was forgotten over time.

As we already mentioned, there was still one tradition of masters who still had the proper technique, This tradition was secluded from the rest of mankind, however, somewhere far away in the Himalayan mountains. At a certain point a young physics student joined this tradition and spent 13 years as the closest disciple of one of the last remaining teachers, until his teacher asked him to go back out in the world and teach it to others. This student was called Maharishi Mahesh Yogi, and his teaching couldn't be more different that what other meditation teachers were teaching. In fact, almost everything a "meditation" teacher would tell you to do, Maharishi would teach you *not to do*. That's why we keep saying TM is *not* meditation.

For those who are interested to learn more about how exactly the technique to transcend works, and how and why it was forgotten., there's a chapter in the appendix that discusses this in more detail

Here we'll focus on how the simple (re)discovery of the proper technique to transcend could change the world in ways we can't even imagine yet.

So what exactly happens when we learn to transcend?

In short whenever we experience the ocean, some memory of this will remain even when we get back into activity. Some part that was hidden in what psychology calls our subconscious minds, starts to become a more conscious part of our experience, until we can consciously experience the unity with everyone and everything all the time.

This doesn't happen overnight, obviously, just like when you start playing tennis today, you won't be competing in Wimbledon or the US open tomorrow. It takes practice, lot's of practice.

But the effects of this growth towards unity consciousness do start to show immediately, usually from the first time people transcend, and even in a very early stage this already changes everything.

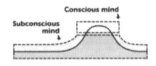

If I'd have to summarize everything we'll see in the next 50 pages in one paragraph, I'd say that when we can only experience the top part of the wave, we experience separation. In this state we feel small, vulnerable, isolated. This forms the one single basis of all negative experiences in life: Anxiety, fear, depression, loneliness, dis-ease, errors, lack of energy, egotism, jealousy, corruption, violence, deception, etc.

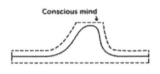

The experience of unity is the opposite. We feel big, powerful, connected, supported. It's the source of everything that is positive in life: Love, compassion, happiness, creativity, intelligence, self-confidence, energy, health, etc.

When the experience of separation starts to be replaced by the experience of unity, all the negative experiences also spontaneously disappear, and are replaced by the good ones.

It's really that simple. It's like darkness that disappears as soon as we turn on the light.

Now let's see how exactly this works, how it's been verified both by scientific research and by personal experience, and how this can transform lives.

By the way, if over the next few pages I'm going to put quite some attention on scientific research, it's not so much to convince you that transcending works... if you made it this far you probably are already convinced and you couldn't care less about scientific research. Still, the research is important to convince governments. The goal of this book is not so much to inspire a few more people to learn TM, but to inspire governments to start supporting it so that *everyone* has a chance to learn.

Ultimately, everything we'll see over the next few pages will lead to one single conclusion: If it's both a lot more effective and a lot cheaper than most current treatments and the scientific research that confirms this is of such high quality (and we'll find that it is) then why aren't governments reimbursing the cost to learn TM as part of our healthcare system? If it has such a unique effect on our brain development, especially with children, then why aren't our governments making it part of our school curriculum?

That's the main question we'll keep asking...until our governments do support it, and the more people will ask this question, the quicker this will happen (many governments already are starting to support it, by the way, but not nearly enough).

So in the next chapters the focus will be on *understanding* why transcending is so powerful, and why the research is so solid.

Ultimately it's all about the power of silence, and we'll discuss what exactly this silence means, from three different angles:
1. Deep rest - activating our own inner healing power and increasing stress resistance
2. Being yourself
3. Developing your full brain potential

1. Deep rest - activating our own inner healing power and increasing stress resistance

Body and mind are like two wheels of a bicycle. Where one goes, the other must follow.

If through the TM technique we let the mind come to a state of complete inner silence, the body will follow and come into a state of deep rest. This rest during the experience of transcending is far deeper than what can be achieved through relaxation, it even appears to be going deeper than the deepest moment of sleep.

This was examined in one of the very first studies that were done on TM, where studies by Dr. Keith Wallace at UCLA and Harvard Medical School measured the state of physical relaxation during TM, and compared it during sleep, by measuring oxygen consumption.

This is what they found.

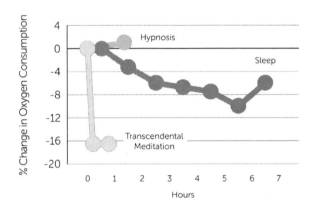

What this research shows is that after 20 minutes of TM practice the body appeared* to be in a state of rest that was deeper than even the deepest moment of sleep.† During hypnosis, on the other hand, there was no decrease at all. So TM is very different from hypnosis‡.

Researchers had seen these kind of results before with monks who had been meditating several hours per day for many years, but never with ordinary westerners who had been meditating for 20 minutes twice per day for only 3-4 months. The study was published in the journals *science* and *scientific American*.

This one chart already explains to a large degree why TM has so many remarkable benefits, especially once we understand what exactly stress is.

We could compare stress to a backpack full of rocks.

---

* There is some discussion about this as in this study the state of rest was compared to starting position, but the oxygen consumption when sitting at the start of TM practice is higher than when lying down at the start of sleep. So we can't conclude from this research alone that during TM the rest is deeper than sleep. Later research, however, measured the change more precisely, second by second, and there it was found that during the actual experience of transcending itself, which usually only lasts for a few seconds, the rest was a lot deeper still than in this research (*Psychosomatic Medicine* 1982 44(2):133-153), and also far deeper than sleep.
† *Science* 27, 167 no. 3926, 1751-1754, 1970, *Scientific American* 226:84-90 1972
‡ Maharishi was not in favor of hypnosis at all. He said it disrupts the mind-body coordination.

Every experience we have leaves an impression that is stored somewhere in the body. If the experience is intense, we can usually feel this clearly. Did you ever have that experience of feeling a knot around the heart, or some other clear stress that remains, after having a fight with someone? This is the kind of impressions that are like rocks that accumulate in our backpack.

Fortunately, the body has a mechanism to remove the accumulated rocks again. And the cool thing is that there's nothing we have to do. It happens completely automatically, as soon as the body is exposed to rest.

> Rest is the best antidote to stress. This is why we sleep at night, to remove all the rocks we've accumulated throughout the day so that the next day we can start with a clean backpack.

This is how it should work in theory...but in practice?

Let's take our knot around the heart after having a fight with someone. When you sleep over it the next morning you feel the knot is a bit less, but it's still there. The rest during sleep didn't seem to go deep enough to remove that particular rock. This is usual what psychologists define as "traumatic stress" which really is their way of saying: "Nothing we can do, you're going to have to live with it". These are the kind of rocks you'll be carrying in your backpack for the rest of your life.

Accumulate enough of these rocks and sooner or later the weight on your shoulders is going to start to seriously disrupt the normal functioning of our nervous system. Depending on the genetic material you got from your parents some people will get an elevated blood pressure, others fall into a depression, others can't sleep. People often blame their problems on genetic factors (thanks dad) but in reality what is genetically defined is only the *weakest link* where the accumulation of rocks is most likely to manifest. The root cause is the rocks.

Stress is now considered to be the main cause (directly or indirectly) of 90% of all health problems.

This means that if now there was an efficient way to remove these rocks, it would also influence almost all areas of health at the same time.

That's exactly what all the TM research shows. The deep rest that we get when we transcend suddenly allows the body to remove even the most deeply rooted stresses (yes, even the traumatic ones). This usually improves all areas of health at the same time. Not only that, but usually we see far better improvements than what can be achieved with regular treatments. Researchers even found that TM practitioners become *younger* the longer they practice TM*. All biological factors that usually deteriorate with age start to improve again.

We'll go into the more detailed research on long-term effects later but here's one study that I'll show you already, because it's such a beautiful illustration of how powerful the effects can be.

Post-traumatic stress disorder (PTSD) results from stresses that are so deep that they are considered incurable, and nowhere are the devastating results of this more visible than with war veterans. War veterans probably carry more rocks in their backpacks than anyone else. As a result, over the last 15 years, *more US soldiers have died from suicide as a result of PTSD than from enemy fire on the battlefield*[17]. There were no treatments and they just didn't see a way out anymore.

In 1985, researchers decided to do a TM study with veterans. If TM worked on them, they reasoned, it would work on *anyone*. A group of Vietnam veterans suffering from PTSD was randomly divided into two subgroups, a group that learned TM and a control group that got the most effective form of psychotherapy that was available. The state of both groups was measured on nine different variables related to stress (anxiety, insomnia, alcoholism, etc.) on a problem scale ranging from *moderate* to *severe.*

At the start of the test both groups were ranking close to severe on all nine variables. After three months there was *virtually no improvement with the psychotherapy group,* as predicted. (everybody knows that PTSD is incurable). But when they looked at the results of the TM group they saw such significant improvements on all nine variables at the same time that 70% of the veterans could go home. They needed no further treatment.†

---

* *International Journal of Neuroscience* 16: 53–58, 1982
† *Journal of Counseling and Development* 64: 212–215, 1985

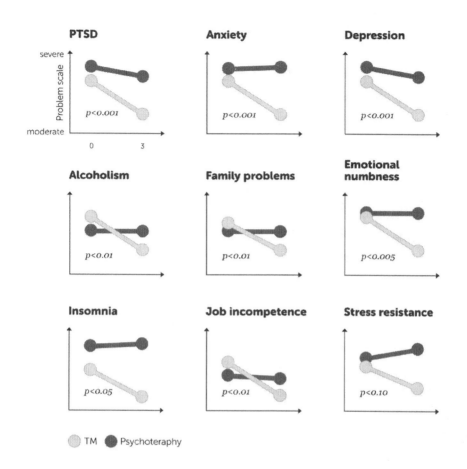

And if you thought that was impressive, you'll be surprised to know that this was the *least* impressive study. Follow-up PTSD studies found that the most significant improvements actually happened *the first 10 days* after learning TM and that PTSD symptoms were almost completely gone after only 30 days.[*]

---

[*] *Journal of Traumatic Stress (Volume 27, Issue 1, 112–115).*

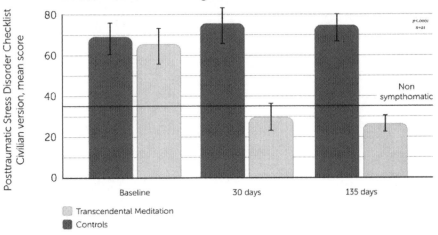

You'd think that a study like this would change the world. How many people are walking around with some serious rocks in their backpack (these days it seems like almost everyone) not knowing that we can teach ourselves to get rid of them. Actually it's only now, 35 years after the study was done, that things are starting to move. One of the big problems was that it simply sounded too good to be true (we'll come back to that one).

So if you're walking around with too much stress, don't waste time. Stop suffering. It's not necessary. Find your nearest TM center on www.fieldparadigm.com/tm and sign up for a free infosession, or contact your teacher to schedule an appointment to learn.

The stress reduction is only 10% of the story, however. There are far more impressive effects still to come. If you thought this one sounds too good to be true, wait until you read about brain development.

Does everybody have the same effects from TM?

Of the 300 people I have taught to transcend over the last three years, I've seen consistently that about 10% have dramatic experiences, even from the first day, like my friend who saw his alcohol addiction disappear from the day he learned TM. Of the other participants, 80% notice a significant change within two weeks (most of them within the first 3 days), and 10% need a bit more patience, but the effects will show within the first three months of practice.

> The time it takes for a noticeable result to manifest often depends on the kind of rocks people carry with them in their backpack.
>
> Some people have a few really big rocks that they're carrying around (usually from some traumatic stress, as in the case of the war veterans) that weigh so heavy on their shoulders that everything is disturbed. Just a few times transcending will allow the body to remove these rocks (the body is usually *very* keen to do so as soon as it has the chance), and then suddenly *everything* becomes different. These people usually see spectacular effects after only a few TM sessions.
>
> The majority of people, on the other hand, just have a bunch of medium rocks. They usually start to notice some subtle changes within the first three days, which develops into a significant improvement within a week or two.
>
> And then there's a minority that may have a layer of small rocks, just from the accumulation of everyday stress, that perhaps covers up some bigger rocks deeper in the backpack. Every time they transcend the body will dissolve some of these smaller rocks, but if there are hundreds of them, they don't notice any miraculous improvement until after some weeks, or even months, of practice. They need a bit more patience, but if they stick with it the noticeable changes always come.
>
> This is why the scientific research on the long-term effects of TM is mostly done over a period of three months. Some people notice immediate effects, with others it takes a bit longer, but after three months the improvement is usually noticeable with everyone.

Is this unique to TM, or do other meditation techniques get the same results?

To answer this question Dr. David-Orme Johnson[*] did a meta-analysis comparing the effect sizes of four published TM PTSD studies to the four studies that were published using mindfulness. An effect size of 0.2 is considered small (not much improvement, barely worthwhile), 0.5 is considered a medium effect, and 0.8 is considered a large effect.

The comparison speaks for itself. On average the effect size of the TM studies was four times as big as the Mindfulness.

---

[*] Dr. Orme-Johnson has for a long time been associated with the TM organization, though not when he did this study. In the case of a meta-analysis, affiliation doesn't really matter, as all he did was calculate the effect sizes of 8 different studies and compared them, so the potential danger of researcher bias wasn't applicable here.

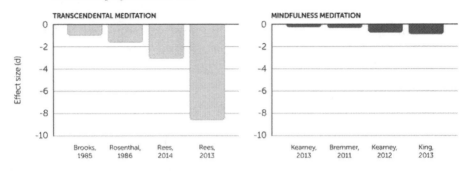

The PTSD study with Vietnam veterans we mentioned earlier (Brooks 1985) was indeed by far the *least* impressive study. The study where PTSD patients saw an improvement within 10 days (Rees 2013) had an effect size of *eight*. Apparently they couldn't even publish the study this way as *nothing* has an effect size of eight (they published it as "an effect size larger than three").

People often say "all meditation techniques produce the same results". Well...not according to the research.

And we're just getting started.

While here we described how the deep rest during transcending allows us to remove the rocks from our backpacks in general terms, there are actually several specific measurable mechanisms that show how transcending activates our own inner healing power. I described three ways how this happens in more detail in the appendix of this book, for those who'd like to understand more how this happens. They're really interesting, as they give a lot more insight into why TM creates such powerful changes on so many areas at the same time. Here's a quick overview.

1. Healing the brain – increased emotional stability: If stress damages our health it has even more damaging effects on our brain, especially on the prefrontal cortex, the "thinking part" or of brains where our free will resides. We'll see how it was designed this way for a good reason (if we are in danger, like when we're crossing the street and see a car coming at us, we don't want to think about it, but want to act quickly and impulsively. So we lose our free will to decide...in order to survive) but it was never designed for the type of chronic stress we face today.

   Scientists can now measure how under chronic stress the blood flow to prefrontal cortex get's permanently shut down, and how during TM practice it get's reactivated. We can now visually see how transcending can heal the damaging effects of stress on our brain. This results in increased calmness and emotional stability, decreased impulsivity, etc.

Remember our story about playing God, and our problem that people didn't seem to have free will to get out of their cycles of action and reaction. This is where we find our solution.

2. <u>Reduced stress hormones – increased stress resistance:</u> Here we explain how stress hormones like cortisol work, and why they are necessary to act quickly in case of a danger (like that car coming at us when we cross the street), but were never designed for the kind of chronic stress situations we face today. We explain the role that chronic high levels of cortisol plays in hypertension, diabetes, obesity, and suppression of our immune system.

Research shows how during TM practice our cortisol levels drop, and we develop more stress resistance.

3. <u>Increased happiness hormones:</u> Under stress the normal functions of our body, including the production of our "happiness hormone" serotonin, get suppressed in favor of the things that need to happen to escape the danger. (You don't need to feel happy when you see a car coming at you, you need to *survive*.) But, again, this was never designed for chronic stress. Chronically low serotonin concentrations has been linked to a wide variety of problems, including depression, insomnia, migraines, emotional instability, eating disorders, addictions, Alzheimer's, and fibromyalgia.

We'll see research how during TM practice serotonin production naturally increases again, again healing the damaging effects of stress. This coincides with a subjective feeling of spontaneous inner happiness that people often report during TM.

Silence = Being yourself

There's one ancient wisdom that all religions and cultures throughout history seem to agree on: *To open the door to a higher spiritual experience you just have to find yourself.*

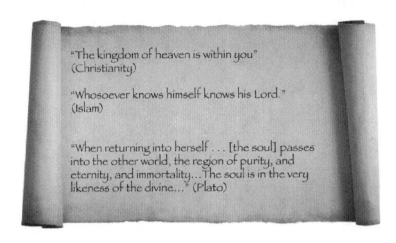

"The kingdom of heaven is within you" (Christianity)

"Whosoever knows himself knows his Lord." (Islam)

"When returning into herself ... [the soul] passes into the other world, the region of purity, and eternity, and immortality...The soul is in the very likeness of the divine..." (Plato)

This statement never quite made sense, however, until we understand what it really means to be your self (or "know your self", which, as we'll see, is the same thing).

Normally our attention is directed outwards, away from "*I am*", towards something we observe, do, or think. This means the attention is directed towards "something" and is no longer on the "I", the knower. We lose ourselves in the world around us.

But when the mind comes into a state of complete silence, a state where we don't observe, do or think anything, there is nothing to draw the mind outward, and the mind comes home. We get to experience our true selves. The knower knows himself.

We have also already seen that if the mind is like a wave on the ocean, then the state of complete silence is also a state where it merges with the ocean, its divine source.

So from the Field Paradigm perspective the ancient wisdom of "know thyself" makes a lot more sense: when the mind becomes completely silent, it is both itself *and* in contact with a higher reality.

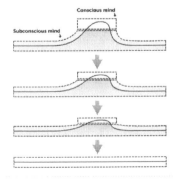

Being yourself is like coming home for the mind. This is why the mind will spontaneously transcend as soon as it gets the chance, because it wants nothing more than to come home.

When we then start to alternate TM practice and activity (we come home, we go outside) something remarkable starts to happen: *we train our nervous system to experience both at the same time.*

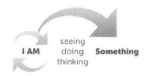

In other words, we maintain the inner silence, inner peace, and inner happiness, the warm feeling of being home, *while we are in activity.*

We train ourselves to be ourselves all the time.

The degree to which you can be yourself all the time can actually be objectively measured through psychological tests that measure self-actualization. These tests, originally developed by American psychologist Abraham Maslow, are one of the best predictors of success in life.

People who could be themselves all the time were highly successful in both their personal and professional lives. They were extremely self-confident and accepted themselves as they were, even if they weren't perfect. They were very creative and problems almost never caused them to lose their inner balance. They saw problems as exciting challenges, opportunities to use their creative power. They also generally followed their own path, rather than being swayed by the opinion of others. They were very spontaneous, went through life with a great sense of humor, had loving personal relationships, a very strong morality, and a deep desire to do good for the world. Basically, they lived life to the fullest extent.

When researchers started using self-actualization tests, they discovered some interesting facts:

- Only 1-2% of the population was fully self-actualized, scoring in the highest scales of his self-actualization tests.
- Self-actualization stops improving around early adolescence. The level you have around that age is usually what you'll be stuck with for the rest of your life.
- There seemed to be one exception to this rule. People sometimes had what Maslow called "peak experiences". This experience seemed to have a strong positive effect on growth of actualization.

Perhaps by now it won't be a surprise if I told you that the description of these peak experiences in a lot of cases closely matches the description of transcending. The problem was that in the past there was no systematic technique to reach this state. Peak experiences just seemed to happen at random to only a few people here and there...until now.

It also won't surprise you, then, that self-actualization strongly improves with TM meditators, even when it's no longer supposed to improve.

Students of Maharishi University of Management (MUM) – who practice TM as part of their curriculum (more about MUM later) – saw such a strong improvement in self-actualization, that no less than 38% was fully self-actualized according to Maslow's scales (compared to normally only 1-2% of the population) after 10 years. The change was so exceptional that it had a chance of 1 in 5 million (p=.0000002) of happening randomly. There was no improvement in the control groups from the other universities[*].

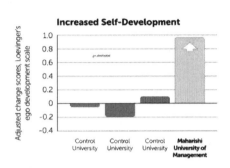

Again, self-actualization only seems to improve when people can actually have the experience of truly being themselves, which means having the experience of complete silence during transcending. Ordinary relaxation doesn't seem to do all that much.

A large meta-analysis comparing the results of 42 meditation studies found that the effect of TM (close to 0.8) was three to four times as large as the effect of other meditation techniques[†].

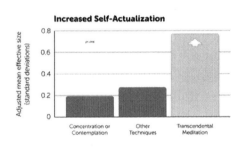

While the effect increased the longer people were practicing TM, the biggest improvement happened during the first three months.

Silence = full brain development
Of all the effects of transcending, the effects on full brain development are by far the most spectacular, but they're also the most difficult to explain in a way that it all makes sense.

Transcending is a state of no thoughts, no activity of the mind at all, yet this state is also the source of everything there is. The flat ocean is nothing, no

---
[*] *Journal of Social Behaviour and Personality 17: 93–121, 2005*
[†] *Journal of Social Behaviour and Personality 6, pp 189-247, 1991*

wave, yet at the same time it has the potential of becoming every possible wave.

Nothing is everything; the ultimate paradox.

Here's one way to explain how this works.

We've already seen that waves can add up, as in our example of the Electromagnetic Field vibrating as light and radio waves at the same time. The individual vibrations add up and the field vibrates in a complex way, but the memory of the individual waves is still there, which is why both light and radio can be there at the same time.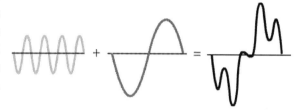

So now let's make another addition of two waves, only this time we add two waves that are perfectly opposite.

The resulting wave is a flat wave, it's nothing, yet it still has the *memory* of the two waves that constitute it. It's both nothing and something.

Now let's expand this analogy and imagine every possible waveform in the universe being added up to each other along with it's opposite waveform. You'd again have a perfectly flat wave, nothing, yet the memory of everything is still there.

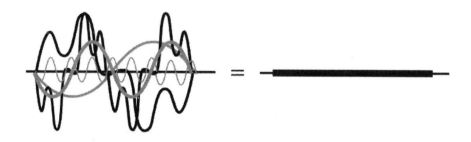

This is how nothing can at the same time be everything.

Now, how is this wonderfully complex paradox relevant to us? Because it allows us to understand why this experience of complete silence, of nothingness, when we transcend, has such powerful effects on our brains.

Our brains are like muscles. Every experience we have will train our brain. If we start playing the violin, the area of the brain that controls the movement of our fingers will start to make millions of new neuronal connections. This area in our brain even physically expands, just like muscles do (though not in the same degree obviously).

This also works the other way around, however. If we don't train our brain, the neuronal connections start to shrivel and die off. If we have an accident and have to stay in bed for several weeks, it will take quiet a while before the muscles in our legs will support normal walking again. Likewise if we'd put a blindfold on for several weeks, and no longer stimulate the neurons in the visual cortex part of our brain, it would take quite a while before we'd be able to see again.

Stimulating all our neurons is especially important when they are in full development. For example researchers have found that when they place lenses with horizontal stripes on young animals during the first days after they are born, the animals can't see any vertical lines for the rest of their lives. If they blindfold them during those first few days, they are blind for life. The neurons weren't stimulated at those crucial times of development of their visual cortex and they were lost, in a way.

And what about humans? It's generally known that we only use a small portion of our full brain potential. Could it be that the reason why we can only consciously experience the top part of the wave, rather than the full ocean, is because *our radio's aren't functioning properly*?

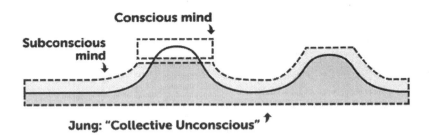

What if it's just a matter of fitness for the brain? What if our brains only function in a limited way, because we never trained our brains to function holistically.

When we grow up we expose our brains to a wide variety of experiences, but they are all localized experiences. We see the mess in our room and our visual cortex is stimulated, we hear mom complain about it and our auditory cortex is stimulated (and perhaps a few cortisol stress hormones as well). We do some mathematics as homework and the part of the brain that is related to mathematics is stimulated. Each local experience stimulates a local part of the brain, but the experience that stimulates the *whole* brain is missing.

By now you already have guessed what that experience is. If we can make the mind completely silent, the brain has the experience of the ocean, the nothingness that is at the same time everything. This experience appears to develop the brain in a holistic way like no other experience can.

This appears to be especially important for children, whose brains are still in full development. Neurologists now know that the amount of neurons in our brains is at a maximum when we're about 10 years old. After that, they start to decrease again. We somehow don't seem to have a way to properly exercise them. Perhaps it's a coincidence that children can start to learn TM from the age of 10, perhaps not.

We'll see what long-term effects TM has on children later, but the first question now is, can any effects on holistic brain development during TM practice be measured?

Yes, it turns out, through fMRI scans and EEG coherence.

Functional Magnetic Resonance Imaging (fMRI)

By the early 1990s Dr. Nicolaï Lyubimov from the Moscow Brain Research Institute had spent 30 years investigating how different experiences create different effects on the brain. The Russian government had provided him with ever more sophisticated equipment, like functional magnetic resonance imaging (fMRI) scanners showing in real time how the brain reacts to different stimuli.

Around this time the Russian government showed a strong interest in bringing TM to the Russian population, so Lyubimov was asked to use his expertise to research the effects of transcending on the brain.

The results were unlike anything Lyubimov had ever seen before.

A sensory stimulus will normally enliven the specific area of the brain associated with it. If we touch something, the area of the brain relating to the sense of touch will become active (dark in the graph).

Lyubimov found that during TM practice, the same sensory stimulus will enliven a far larger area of the brain, including what he called "dormant potentials" of the brain.

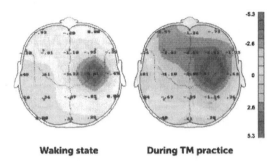

Waking state   **During TM practice**

Here is Lyubimov's conclusion in his own words:

> *The Transcendental Meditation technique taps hidden reserves of the human brain, electrical pathways that are ordinarily not in use. This expansion of the brain's electrical activity may be the physiological counterpart of the experience of unbounded awareness. This is consistent with the reports of people practicing Transcendental Meditation that their consciousness is expanding.*

His research was accepted for publication in Human physiology[*] and Lyubimov himself wrote an official letter to the Ministry of Education recommending that TM immediately becomes a part of the curriculum *in every school in the country*. He was absolutely convinced that this is what the children needed to develop their full potential.

The Soviet government was very interested and they started high-level talks with the TM organisation. However, this was the time when the USSR started to collapse, and the Soviet government became rather busy with other matters. Still, over this period 150,000 Russians learned TM.

<u>EEG coherence</u>

While the fMRI research was impressive, it's a complicated and rather expensive way to study the effects of TM on the brain. fMRI scanners are mil-

---

[*] *Human physiology*, 25: 171–180, 1999

lion dollar machines that are in short supply, not the kind of thing scientists keep on standby somewhere in their garage.

The good news is that there's a much easier way to measure what is going on in the brain during TM practice, something that only requires a laptop (or these days even a smartphone), a few electrodes, and some software.

Whenever a part of the brain is active, there is electrical activity that can be measured, and visualized in the forms of waves, through an electroencephalogram (EEG).

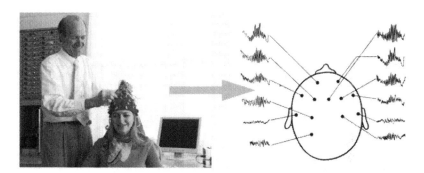

A computer can then mathematically analyze these waves and calculate to what degree the waves of one part of the brain are similar to waves of another part. If the waves are similar – or "phase coherent" as it's technically described – it is an indication that those parts of the brain are working together.

During the normal waking state, the coherence between the different parts of the brain is generally very low (usually only about 20%). This is logical because different parts of the brain are usually involved in different tasks. We see, hear, touch, and smell things, think about the 500 e-mails we still have to answer, etc. Each part of the brain is busy doing its own thing.

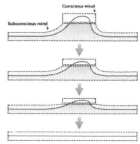

When a person transcends there is no more focus on any specific object of perception, yet the mind remains conscious and alert. Our focused wave settles down and becomes the unified ocean; the stillness where everything is united with everything else.

> When the mind experiences this state of unity, the *entire* brain appears to match this experience, by starting to function as one unified whole.

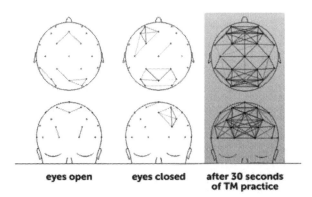

eyes open   eyes closed   after 30 seconds of TM practice

In the image to the left, which represents average EEG results of 50 students[*], a line between two parts of the brain indicates coherence: the thicker the line, the greater the coherence. Within only 30 seconds of TM practice the brain shows almost full coherence.

Modern computers are so powerful these days that EEG coherence can now be calculated and displayed in real time while somebody is practicing TM. There are few things as impressive as watching a live demonstration of somebody practicing TM while their EEG coherence is displayed, and seeing the EEG coherence maximize within seconds after start of the TM practice. You can watch a video (2 min) on www.fieldparadigm.com/EEG.

EEG coherence is a powerful way to dispel the myth that all meditation techniques are the same and give the same results. Nobody who ever put EEG coherence measurements of somebody who transcends next to those of people practicing "meditation" would ever make that claim again.

Now, why is EEG coherence important?

The brain is a flexible organ that will habituate to any experience. The more we regularly (twice a day) create the experience of maximum EEG coherence during TM, the more the brain will change to ultimately maintain a state of high coherence at all time, even outside of meditation.

To give a very simple illustration of why a coherent brain will work better than an incoherent one, imagine a game of rope pulling.

On one side, everybody pulls at random, on the other side they all pull together, in perfect coherence.

---

[*] *Cognitive processing*, 11(1): 21-30, 2010

Which side do you think will win?

How long do you think the contest will even last?

More than 30 years of EEG research has shown that EEG coherence is correlated to a wide range of benefits, with the highest correlations showing with increased creativity (r=.71), IQ (r=.63), moral reasoning ability (r=.63), emotional stability (r=.62) and reflex speed (r=.60).

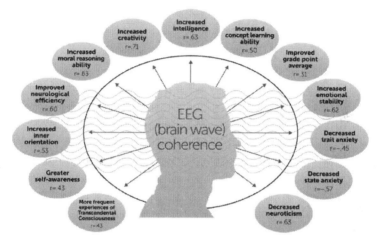

During the last 40 years, more than 40 published studies have examined the effects of TM practice on increased EEG coherence and its effects[18].

Dr. Fred Travis is an EEG researcher who has more TM publications under his belt than anyone else. In one of his studies he followed a group of students for a period of 12 months, to see how EEG coherence changed over time both during and after meditation.

He found that *during* TM practice the EEG coherence increased immediately, from the first few weeks of practice, but then no longer increased over the next 12 months. All this shows is that TM is not something you get better at with practice. It's a natural technique that will bring the mind to the experience of transcendental consciousness from the first few sittings, and the effects on brain coherence will show immediately.

The long-term changes happen *outside* of TM practice, however, showing a habituation of the brain to this experience of high coherence. Here the research shows a continuous increase over the 12 month period.

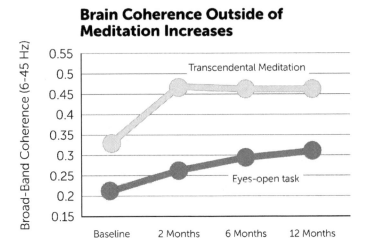

In a long-term study, with people who have been meditating for 9 years, they found almost no difference between EEG coherence during meditation and during activity. The brain had fully habituated to the state of high coherence.

This is of course where it really matters. There's not much of a point to have a fully coherent creative brain while you're sitting with the eyes closed in meditation, is there? It's when you're out in activity that EEG coherence makes a noticeable difference.

So what difference will it make? If we look at the earlier chart with everything that EEG coherence is correlated to (emotional stability, learning ability, IQ, creativity, reflex speed, self awareness, etc.) we could say that EEG coherence is one of the best predictors of success in life.

That's exactly what another research found.

Researchers in Norway compared the scores of average managers to those of top managers on a wider measure of integrated brain functioning, called the Brain Integration Scale (of which EEG coherence forms the most important factor). Top managers had a far higher score than average managers[*].

---

[*] *Management Decision, 47(6), 872 – 894*

Interestingly enough, they then did the same with athletes and found that world-class athletes had a far higher score than average athletes*. Whether management or sports, success seemed to be much more dependent on how well your brain functions than how hard you work.

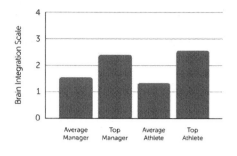

Next they measured the Brain Integration Scale of non-meditators, short-term TM meditators (1 year), and long-term TM meditators (7 years). Here's how there scores look compared to those of the top managers and top athletes.

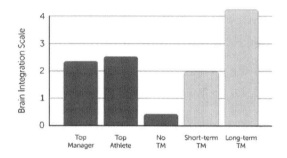

Any questions?

So transcending appears to develop our full brain potential *and* causes the brain to start to function as one unified whole...By now you must be wondering what would happen if children would be able to train the brain like this from a young age. You're about to find out.

As with everything, though, practice makes perfect. The key to really getting the best results from TM is regular practice, twice per day for twenty minutes. This is a significant investment in your time, but if you start to understand what it does (health, happiness, being yourself, intelligence, success) you also understand that going back to the source of life, your true self, is by far the best investment you can make for yourself.

The fact that TM is very enjoyable to do certainly helps. Rather than being perceived as an arduous task, for most people their TM practice is the time of the day they most look forward to.

---

* *Scandinavian Journal of Medicine and Science in Sports, 24, 422-427.*

> People often learn to transcend to reduce their stress, and it certainly does that, but it often happens that once the stress is gone they feel like the goal is achieved and some become less regular in their TM practice.
>
> They don't realize that reducing stress is only 10% of the story.

Even everything we've discussed here in terms of being yourself and brain development is only part of the story. They are all just side-effects of a more holistic transformation that takes place: growth towards a state of consciousness where we can fully experience the whole ocean, the unity with everyone and everything. We'll get some more glimpses of that when we look at the more spiritual experiences that are related to TM practice.

I call my method meditation, but it is, in fact, a technique of self-exploration; it enables a man to dive into the innermost reaches of his being, in which dwell the essence of life and the source of all wisdom, all creativity, all peace, and all happiness...The word meditation is not new, nor are the benefits of meditation new...But for centuries the technique of meditation of this kind has been forgotten.

Maharishi Mahesh Yogi

$250,000 per TM session... and it's worth it?

One person who understood the value of regular TM practice, perhaps better than anyone else, is Ray Dalio. Dalio, founder and CEO of the $160 Billion hedge fund Bridgewater Associates, is one of the most successful Wall Street traders in the world. Over the past five years he's been earning about $1.5 billion per year, which translates into roughly *$750,000 per hour of work*.

He's been practicing TM for 40 years, and has credited most of his success to his TM practice. He says it makes his mind sharp like a ninja.

Now here's the interesting thing: At an income level of $750,000 an hour, *each 20 minute TM session theoretically costs him $250,000*.

But Dalio doesn't count like that, just like he doesn't count the cost of taking a shower, or eating, or brushing his teeth. Some things are just essential in life, and for him transcending is one of them. In an interview he jokes, "I meditate 20 minutes...Except when I've got a busy day. Then I meditate 40 minutes."

Dalio has paid for most of his more than 1,000 employees to learn TM, and inspired a large number of his fellow Wall Street Traders to also learn. (hey, if it helps them feel better *and* make more money, why not?). Dalio is also one of the most generous donors to the David Lynch Foundation, which allowed more than 500,000 school children to learn TM so far.

Here's a video where Dalio and Hollywood director Martin Scorsese (also an enthusiastic TM practitioner) discuss how TM increases creativity: www.field-paradigm.com/dalio

The Too-Good-To-Be-True Problem

> If transcending is what we claim it is - an experience of accessing a universal field of consciousness which develops our full potential – which has been lost for hundreds or even thousands of years...
>
> ...then TM should create effects that we've never seen before.

This is definitely a strong statement, and in science there's a saying:

> *"extraordinary claims require extraordinary evidence."*

In this chapter, we'll show that not only are the effects extraordinary but that the evidence, the research to document these effects, is extraordinary as well. As we mentioned before, research is important for governments to support TM, and that's what we need if we really want to change the world.

We've already seen in the previous chapter how transcending can affect all areas of life: health, happiness, self-confidence, relationships, and brain development.

Now, if there was a pill that would create the effects TM has (make you happier *and* healthier *and* smarter *and* more successful in life), *everybody* would be taking it. In fact, our governments would probably be putting it in our water supply. So then why isn't *everybody* transcending yet? Why have only six million people learned rather than eight billion?

This is an extremely important question. Understanding the answer to this question will hopefully help us to bring the experience of transcending to many more people.

The first answer is obvious: few people know that transcending exists, and even fewer understand how it works, or that it's fundamentally different from "meditation" as it's currently understood. (both much easier and much more effective). This is because transcending doesn't make sense from the Machine Paradigm point of view. We need to understand the Field Paradigm first before we can understand what transcending really is. Hopefully we can achieve this one with this book.

The second and third answers are:
2. The too-good-to-be-true-problem, and
3. "follow the money" (who stands to lose a lot of money if people would suddenly learn to heal themselves?)

This chapter deals with the second answer. The third one will become obvious once you see the long term research.

We all heard the expression: "If something sounds too good to be true, that means it probably is."

What if we have something that improves all areas of life at the same time, at a ridiculously low cost compared to our current healthcare costs and without harmful side effects? Does that sound too good to be true?

What if we claimed, as we'll do later in this book, that a few hundred people transcending together in a group can create a positive influence in an entire country, and significantly reduce crime, corruption, and even stop wars?

For most people, this is so far off the too-good-to-be-true chart it's not even visible anymore.

But what if, in the case of transcending, it *is* true?

How can we know for sure?

Scientific research.

"Yes, but how do we know if *the scientific research itself is reliable*?

That's the real question, isn't it?

These days scientific research has a bit of a bad reputation. People think that anyone can prove anything if they really want to.

Unfortunately, this suspicion is sometimes valid; scientists sometimes do manipulate studies to *prove what they want to prove* rather than objectively measure what is going on, especially if they have something to gain from the outcome. This often happens when universities do research on a drug while being funded by the pharmaceutical company that produced it. (For the same reason we should also be vigilant when research on TM is done by researchers who are connected to the TM organisation).

In this case, the rule is simple:

> The quality and reliability of the research is as important as the results, often even more important.

Even the most impressive results won't matter if there are doubts about the research used to obtain them. This is especially important if the results sound too good to be true.

So what can we say about the TM research? The results are spectacular, but is the research of sufficiently high quality? Is it reliable?

Yes.

In fact, by all scientific standards the quality of TM research is far higher, and the results far more reliable, than almost any other treatment that has ever been researched.

Here are the four main factors that will determine how reliable any result will be:

1. Research design
2. Probability
3. Peer-review and publication by a scientific journal
4. Independent replication

We'll see how TM research scores exceptionally high on all four.

1. Research design

If a certain cause (TM practice) produces a certain result (improved health) how can we be sure that the results are not due to researcher bias, placebo or some other factor?

Some research designs are inherently more reliable than others. For example let's take two designs.

A. Before-after measurements: A group is measured before they learn TM, and again a few months later to see if there is any difference.

B. Randomized controlled trial (RCT): A group of subjects who are all exposed to similar experiences in life are randomly divided into a group that learns TM and control group that doesn't. Researchers who do the measurements don't know who belongs to which group. Both groups are measured before and after.

It's obvious that if the second trial shows a positive result, this result will be considered far more reliable than if the first trial shows a result.

Randomized controlled trials are far more expensive, however. Out of the 600 TM studies that have been performed so far the majority were done in the 70ies and 80ies, mostly by enthusiastic researchers from universities all around the world, but with lower budgets. As such most of them could only do the lower quality studies. Only in the last few years more and more budget became available (including $25M from the National Institute of Health to support TM research). As a result of the 600 TM studies, only about 60 are randomized controlled trials.

But here's the interesting thing. High quality studies will give a more "pure" result, because more of the other interferences are, by design, filtered out. If the results would in any way be influenced by researcher bias, expectation effects or other factors then higher quality designs would give less good results than lower quality studies. With TM research the *opposite* was the case. An analysis of multiple TM trials showed that higher quality TM studies generally showed *better* results than lower quality studies[19].

And, by the way, how many other treatments or medicines do you know that have *sixty* randomized controlled trials confirming its effectiveness. Very few, I can assure you. Probably none.

Very often several trials are combined in what is called a meta-analysis, where the results of these trials are averaged. If then on average still a positive result can be found, it's considered even more reliable. More than 10 such meta-analyses have been done on TM studies, all showing exceptional positive effects.

2. Probability

As we have already discussed, in the social sciences it is never possible to be 100% certain that a cause (like a new drug) is responsible for an effect (improved happiness), because there are many different factors influencing the state of the human mind.

But at least we can try to come as close to 100% certainty as possible. The rule is that the larger the effect size (the improvement), and the larger the group of people where the effect is consistent, the lower the chance that it will be a coincidence.

The standard in science is that we have to be at least 95% certain before we can claim a "significant" effect, which means that the chance of coincidence (or *probability*, as scientists call it) has to be smaller than 5 in 100. This is indicated as $p<.05$.

The lower the probability, the more reliable the result. So $p<.01$ (99% certainty) is 5 times better than $p<.05$, and $p<.001$ (99.9% certainty) is 50 times better than $p<.05$. The smaller the p-value the better.

In many cases, the probability of a study is actually far more important than the effect itself. A 30% improvement is worthless (insignificant) if the chance of coincidence is 50%, but a 10% improvement is considered highly significant if the chance of coincidence is smaller than 1%.

> Most of the TM studies far exceed the $p<.05$ norm, with probability values that range from anywhere between fifty times to one million times lower, far better than most other treatments.

The earlier self-actualization study was a good example, with a p value of 1 in 5 million ($p=.0000002$), 250,000 times better than the norm. Some of the TM field effects studies we'll see later actually have a combined chance of coincidence that is more than *one trillion times* lower than the norm.

All this says is that the effects from transcending are both exceptionally strong *and* consistent over a large group of people, meaning that we can say with a high degree of reliability that everyone can expect these effects.

3. Peer-review and publication by a scientific journal

To protect the scientific community from "anybody proving anything they want to prove", there is a method of reviewing studies before publication by scientific journals. An independent group of scientists is asked by the journal to evaluate the study and see if the research was conducted appropriately. A scientific journal will only publish a study after it has been approved by peer-review. Any journal links their reputation to what they publish. Therefore, the more prestigious the journal, the more stringent the process of peer-review will be before they publish anything.

More than 350 TM studies have gone through this peer-review process and have been published in over 100 scientific journals from around the world, including pretty much all the most prestigious ones.

There are *very few* other methods that have this amount of published research.

Not a single one of all the 350 published studies on the Transcendental Meditation technique found a negative effect of TM.

4. Independent replication

The scientific community would expect that, if the results are truly scientific, they can also be independently reproduced by other researchers. It's the best way to know if a result really stands on its own, rather than being dependent on a specific group of subjects (perhaps from a particular culture) or the researcher who is doing the study.

The fact that there is so much research, from so many universities (more than 250 universities and research institutes have participated in TM research so far) means that most of the results we will see have been independently replicated *dozens of times, all around the world*.

While a lot of the pioneering studies have been done by researchers from institutions connected to the TM organisation (like Maharishi University of Management), there's a consistent trend that independent verification from institutes that are not connected to the TM organization in any way found *exactly the same or often even better results*. Whatever the results, they were not coming from researcher bias.

Conclusion: The results of all the TM research may *seem* too good to be true, but according to all scientific standards the research is of the highest quality, far higher than most, if not all, other treatments upon which our entire system of modern medicine is based.

Let's have a quick look at some of the research.

Changing Lives: The long-term effects of transcending

We've already seen how transcending can heal PTSD, a condition that by all norms is considered incurable. There are many more such cases where TM will significantly improve conditions for which modern medicines really has no solution. All they can do is prescribe drugs to reduce the symptoms, but without solving the actual problem itself.

Here are some of the studies that show the long term effects of TM practice on all areas of life.

Reduced Stress

More than 150 studies have documented the effects of TM on reduction of stress and all the mental problems that arise from it.

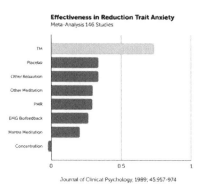

Reduced anxiety: A Stanford University meta-analysis of 146 meditation studies found that the average effect size of 38 TM studies (0.8) was twice as effective in reducing anxiety as any other meditation or relaxation technique ($p<.001$)*. Concentration techniques had a negative effect on anxiety.

Another meta-analysis of only the studies from the highest quality, 16 randomized controlled TM trials with a total of 1296 subjects, found that the effect of TM was the strongest with people who have extreme anxiety. People whose anxiety score was in the 90th percentile (meaning, higher than 90% of the

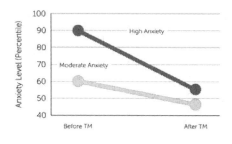

---

* *Journal of Clinical Psychology* 45: 957–974, 1989,

population) saw such a strong improvement after only a few weeks of TM practice that they were only in the 57th percentile (p=0.0000005).

This study was published in the *Journal of Alternative and Complementary Medicine* in 2013, and became one of the journal's most quoted studies of the year[*].

More than 50 studies have confirmed the effects of transcending on anxiety.

Reduced depression: if transcending increases serotonin, we'd expect this to have a strong effect on depression. That is exactly what more than 20 studies on TM and depression have found. Here are two of them.

A meta-analysis of two randomized controlled trials funded by the U.S. National Institutes of Health (NIH) found a 48% reduction in clinical depression within three months of TM practice (p<.001)[†‡].

Another randomized controlled trial, in collaboration with the California West Oakland Health Center and the US government, found a significant decrease of depression with government employees in a (high-stress) high-security institute that had learned TM. By contrast, the control group that took a stress-management course (at the same time the TM group learned TM) showed a significant *increase* in depression.

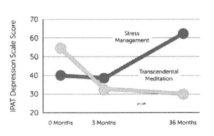

Reduced insomnia: Too low serotonin concentrations are also often related to insomnia, so it's no surprise TM will help there as well.

A study in Canada and another study by the Japanese Ministry of Industrial Health both found significant improvements in time to fall asleep (p<.001) and quality of sleep (p<.01)[§] compared to baseline or controls. More than 20 other studies have confirmed the effects on insomnia.

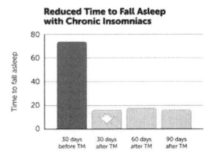

---

[*] *Journal of Alternative and Complementary Medicine* 19(10):1-12, 2013
[†] *Ethnicity & Disease* 17: 72–77, 2007

[‡] *American Journal of Hypertension* 22: 1326–1331, 2009
[§] *Japanese Journal of Public Health* 37 (10 Suppl.): 729

Other research has found: improved emotional stability and stress resistance, decreased burnouts, impulsiveness, OCD, neurosis, behavioral problems, emotional exhaustion

Improved health

More than 200 studies have researched the effects of TM practice on improved health. Here are a few of them.

Reduced hypertension, diabetes, heart disease: The US National Institute of Health (NIH) has a reputation for only supporting the highest quality research with the most promising effects. Over the past 20 years, the NIH spent $25 million to support research on the effects of TM on cardiovascular disease.

One NIH funded randomized controlled trial with 127 subjects found a decrease of 10.7/6.4 mm Hg in blood pressure, compared to no significant change for the control group (p<.0004). The Progressive Muscle Relaxation group also showed a slight decrease, but three times less than the TM group*.

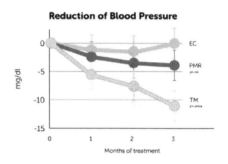

An NIH-funded meta-analysis of nine randomized controlled TM trials on hypertension found that TM was the only alternative method that had a proven effect (p=.0002)†.

The American Heart Association now advises that doctors can prescribe TM as a clinical treatment for hypertension. They advised against prescribing any other meditation technique (including Yoga and Mindfulness) due to lack of consistent results.

Other NIH funded randomized controlled trials also found reduced insulin resistance (type 2 diabetes, p=.01)‡ and reduced arteriosclerosis§. A long-term NIH study where a group of 200 existing heart patients were randomly divided in a TM group and a control group found a 48% reduction in heart

---

Hypertension 26: 820–827, 1995

† *Current Hypertension Reports 9: 520–528, 2007*

‡ *American Medical Association's Archives of Internal Medicine 2006; 166(11):1218-1224*
§ *Stroke 31: 568–573, 2000*

attack, stroke or death with the TM group. Among the regular TM practitioners the decrease was 61%.

Reduced cholesterol: Two randomized controlled trials, one from the Kaiser Permanent Medical Center in Oakland, California, and another one in Tel Aviv University Medical School in Israel, both independently found a 30mg/dl decrease in total cholesterol levels after one year of TM practice ($p<.005$ and $p<.001$) versus no significant change in the control group. The control group were encouraged to change their lifestyle, while the TM group was not asked to make any change, only meditate for 20 minutes twice a day.

Conquering addictions: Addictions are notoriously hard to treat because they involve a brain component (shutting down of the prefrontal cortex which controls our impulses), a physical component, and a mental component (the addict wants to feel good). Because transcending works on all three levels at the same time, it has proven to be an extremely effective way to conquer addictions. In fact, it's so effective that most people who learn TM spontaneously stop smoking, drinking, or using drugs, simply because they start to feel good in their own skin without it and the thought to use them simply doesn't come up anymore.

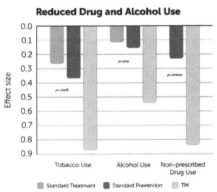

A meta-analysis of 179 addiction studies, including 20 TM studies with more than 4000 subjects, found that the average effect of TM is three to four times more effective in overcoming addiction than any other method that was researched ($p=.0006$ for smoking, $p=.009$ for alcohol and $p=.00009$ for drug addictions)*.

Reduced hospitalizations: Insurance statistics of 2000 TM practitioners were compared to the norm (database of 600,000 other people) over a period of five years. Younger TM practitioners had 50% lower hospitalizations, while older practitioners (>40 years) had 70% lower hospitalizations ($p<.0001$ for both)†.

The older we get, the more the weight of the rocks in our backpack start to influence our health, so it would

---

* Alcoholism Treatment Quarterly 11: 13–87, 1994

† Psychosomatic Medicine 49: 493–507, 1987

seem logical that removing those rocks will make a bigger difference.

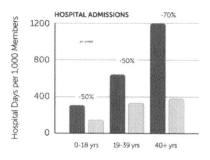
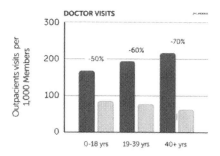

Decreased Hospital Admissions & Doctor Visits per Age Category

When researchers looked at the reason for hospitalizations they found that childbirth (a pretty good reason to go to the hospital) was actually higher in the TM group. But if we look at the other 16 disease categories, hospitalizations were significantly lower in each and every one of them. The biggest decreases were found in stress related problems, including 87% fewer hospitalizations for heart disease and 60% fewer cases of cancer.

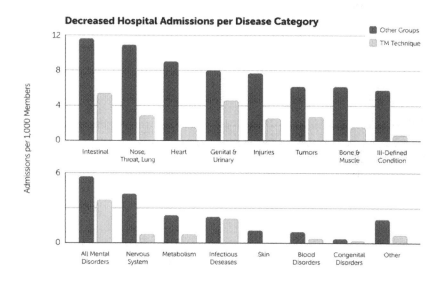

Reduced healthcare costs: To make sure the improved health is due to TM itself, rather than a healthy lifestyle of which TM may be a part, healthcare costs of 1418 Canadian TM meditators were compared to matched controls over a period of 14 years, nine years before they learned TM, five years after.

Before they learned, healthcare costs in the TM group were slightly higher than in the control group. So people who learned TM did not seem to be doing it as part of a healthier lifestyle. After they learned, however, healthcare costs gradually start declining, culminating in 50% lower expenses after five years (p=.006)*.

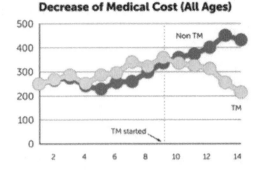

Fybromialgia: Another impressive study found a 97% total reduction in Fybromialgia after 2 years of TM practice† (the biggest reductions were found in the first 3 months). Fybromialgia, characterized by inexplainable muscle pains, is related to too low serotonin concentrations and is often caused by traumatic stress. It's considered incurable according to modern medicine.

Other improvements: Research has found that transcending improves almost all aspects of health that are measurable, including migraines, chronic fatique syndrome, muscle pains, astma, dental health, etc.

Recent research is also showing promising results for Alzheimer's (leading to one of the top experts in the field now using TM as part of his approach to reverse Alzheimer's‡) and Parkinson's.

Improved Brain Functioning

More than 80 studies have confirmed the effects of TM on improved brain functioning.

Improved IQ: The general consensus is that the IQ we have around adolescence is what we'll be stuck with for the rest of our lives. Our brain is fully developed by then and we shouldn't expect any more improvements after this. TM research shows that this understanding is outdated.

Researchers took an IQ test of a group of Maharishi University of Management students who learned TM (and several of them also the advanced TM-

---

* *American Journal of Health Promotion* 14: 284–291, 2000

† *Clinical Rheumatology* Jan, 27th 2012. This is just a first pilot study and more research is needed to confirm it.

‡ http://www.tm.org/bredesen-announcement

Sidhi program, see later) and a control group of students not practicing the TM technique.

When they took another test after two years the control group showed no increase in IQ, as predicted. The TM group, on the other hand increased 5 points, a significant increase that would normally be considered impossible (p<.0001)*

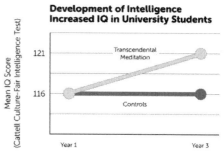

Holistic improvement in intellectual performance: When children practice TM, while their brains are still in development, the results are a lot more impressive still. A meta-analysis of three randomized controlled trials with 360 children found significant improvements in the TM group compared to control groups in fluid intelligence (p=.001), mental efficiency (p=.0003), practical intelligence (p=.00009), field independence (p=.00000004), and creativity (p=.0000000008, about 60 million times better than the norm in science)†.

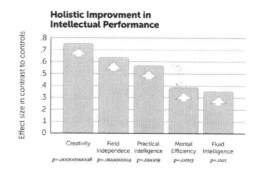

Reduced ADHD: ADHD is related to abnormally low EEG coherence. Adolescents from ages 12 to 14 with severe ADHD were randomly divided into a TM group and a delayed start control group (who learned TM after three months).

The TM group saw a significant increase in EEG coherence and reduction in ADHD symptoms after three months, versus no change in the control group. The researchers saw the same improvement when the control

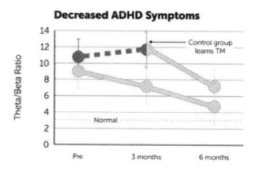

---

* *Personality and Individual Differences* 12: 1105–1116, 1991
† *Intelligence* 29: 419–440, 2001

group also learned TM*. After 6 months their scores were close to normal.

As part of the research the children were asked how much they enjoyed their TM practice. The average answer score was 5.3 on a scale from 0 (not at all) to 7 (very much).

Although this is just a pilot study, and more research is needed to confirm it, it seems like we have found a natural, even enjoyable, cure for ADHD. I'm sure the pharmaceutical industry will love that one.

Other research has found: improved concentration, improved memory, reduced autism, improved academic results, correlation between length of TM practice and improved IQ and academic results.

Transforming Education

More than 60 studies have confirmed the beneficial effects of making TM a part of the school curriculum. All these studies are mostly additional confirmations of the effects we've already seen before, though some also investigate new factors, like reduced burnouts and improved E.Q. with teachers, and improved emotional competency, behavior and mathematics and language skills with students.

The San Francisco Unified School District has been researching the effects of TM practice in their schools for the past eight years, over 17 studies with more than 700 students and teachers. They found that incorporating transcending as part of the school curriculum, just 15 minutes twice per day, created a complete transformation in their schools. For the full research description and references go to www.cwae.org/research_intro.php

With teachers:

---

* *Mind & Brain, The Journal of Psychiatry (2011, Vol 2, No 1, p 78)*

Reduced burnout and emotional exhaustion: A randomized controlled trial with 78 teachers found that teachers who learned TM had significantly reduced burnouts and emotional exhaustion after four months of TM practice compared to the control group.

Improved emotional intelligence: A randomized controlled trial with 98 teachers found that teachers who learned TM had significantly improved emotional intelligence (EQ) after four months of TM practice compared to the control group (p<.001). EQ is correlated with greater leadership ability and work productivity. The TM group also showed improved brain integration, decreased perceived stress, depression, anxiety, and anger.

With students:

Decreased symptoms of stress: A randomized controlled trial with 98 students found decreased psychological stress, anger, fatigue, and increased sleep quality in the TM group compared to controls.

Decreased stress, improved self-esteem: Students experienced improved self-esteem (p<.007), improved strength of character (p<.05), decreased mood disturbances (p<.001), and decreased anxiety (p<.001) after five months of TM practice relative to their own baseline.

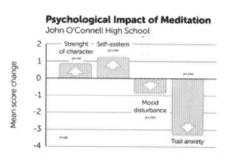

Another study with 333 students found similar results of decreased anxiety (p<.001) and increased self-esteem (p<.001).

Improved emotional competency: 125 students who learned TM saw significant improvements in relationship skills, optimistic thinking, goal-oriented behavior, and decision making after one year, compared to a matched control school.

Improved behavior: Suspensions dropped 63% in the first year and 79% over four years after TM was introduced in Visitacion Valley school. Before the experiment started, Visitacion Valley had the highest suspension rate in San Francisco, after four years it had the lowest. In another school (Burton)

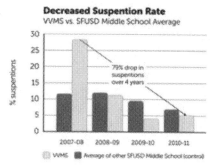

141

suspensions dropped 77% two years after TM was introduced.

Improved mathematics and language skills: 198 students who learned TM improved both their mathematics (p=.001) and language skills (p=.005) compared to control groups

Relationship between regularity of TM practice and improvements: An analysis showed a strong correlation between the regularity of TM practice and improvements in academic scores. This shows that TM gives the best results when practiced regularly.

Do children like TM? A Satisfaction survey

A survey by the San Francisco Unified School District among 600 participating teachers and students found that 95% of them felt that TM was easy to practice, effective to reduce stress and increase clarity of mind, and that is was valuable for them.

A similar survey by the government of Oaxaca in Mexico among 6000 students who learned TM (as part of a government-sponsored school program to bring TM to 450 schools) showed that 97% of the students were satisfactied with their TM practice.

The best example of what TM can do: The Maharishi School
In sports, everybody knows that if you want to become a world champion, you have to start training from a young age.

Imagine what would happen if, instead, children would learn to develop their full brain potential from a young age, while at the same time learning to eliminate their own stress.

Well, we don't have to imagine, because it's already happening.

In the 1980ies a US TM community in Fairfield, Iowa (more about that later) started the Maharishi School, a school with a curriculum like any other, except for the fact that children learn to practice the TM technique from a very young age (a special TM technique for children from the age of 5, the regular TM technique from the age of 10, and the advanced TM-sidhi program from the age of 16), and practice it together in the classroom, as part of the curriculum, twice per day.

The results are mind-blowing.

When children arrive in this school they have an average intelligence, but by the time they graduate they almost all score in the top 1% in the US on standardized academic tests. They have also won more state, national and international championships per capita than any other school in the world, whether in sports, theatre, science, poetry, mathematics, arts or almost any other area they compete in.

But they stand out most in creative problem solving championships. Creative problem solving is pure EEG coherence. It involves analyzing a problem, involving mostly the left analytical part of the brain, and then finding a creative solution, involving mostly the right creative part. The higher the EEG coherence between left and right parts the more they are coordinated and the better our ability to find creative solutions to problems quickly. Children who can learn to develop a coherent brain from a young age simply beat anyone else in these championships.

More than 100,000 of the most creative children in the world participate in the global creativity championships like *Destination Imagination* or *Odyssey of the Mind* every year, so, needless to say, it takes something really extraordinary to win a world championship like this. Students from the Maharishi School appear to have something extraordinary, because they have won the world championships *five* times so far (four in creative problem solving, one in the fine arts category).

No other school in the world even comes close.

The ability to constantly find creative solutions to problems is one of the best predictors of success in life. No matter if you're an engineer, an artist or a housewife, if you can find creative solutions to any problem you face, you'll be more successful.

Where do you keep finding these creative children?

For the past 10 years Dr. Ashley Deans – the former principal of the Maharishi School – has been touring around the world to share the secret of the school's incredible success.

I attended one of his lectures and was so inspired by what he had to say that I begged him to come to Belgium so that I could organize a tour for him. I decided to use Facebook as my main channel to promote his tour, hoping that people would be inspired enough to share it with their friends.

It worked...spectacularly.

In all the cities where we announced the tour we had to upgrade to larger halls two or three times. As soon as we could make more seats available they were booked full. In total we had more than 4600 people attending his presentations. In one city with about 60,000 population we had 600 people attend. The owner of the hall was amazed – he hadn't seen a lecture with that many registrations in years.

During his presentations, Dr. Deans told the story of how one day he ran into the organizers of Destination Imagination, who organize the global creative problem solving championships. "Do you know that you're almost a legend in our organisation?" they said, "There's one thing we always wanted to ask you: where do you keep finding these creative children that keep winning our competitions?" Dr. Deans laughed and replied "Our school is based in *Iowa* – a state that has more *pigs* than human beings. It's not exactly the place where you'll find the world's most creative children. We just take *any* child and teach them how to develop their full creative potential."

As a result of his lectures several schools are now taking the first steps to bring TM to their school curriculum.

One of his lectures in Brussels (a private lecture for a select group of people) was recorded on video and you can watch it online. It's an inspiring lecture that everyone who cares about the future of our education should watch (about two hours). www.fieldparadigm.com/dr-ashley-deans/.

Given the remarkable success of the Maharishi School it's equally remarkable that so few people know about it, though that is changing quickly now:

- Oprah went to visit the school and was so impressed she made an entire documentary about it. She also learned TM herself and was so impressed with the technique that she eventually got almost all 400 employees of her company to learn
- Twin Peaks director David Lynch also visited the school and was so impressed by what these students radiated that he decided to create the David Lynch Foundation, with the purpose of bringing TM to every school in the world. Since then companies like Microsoft and dozens of celebrities (all TM practitioners) have supported his foundation, including Paul McCartney, Clint Eastwood, Ellen DeGeneres, Hugh Jackman, Sting, Katy Perry, Jerry Seinfeld and Tom Hanks. The foundation has already funded TM courses for close to 500,000 students.

The best thing you can do for your child: bring transcending to your local school/university,

The second best: send your child to the Maharishi School as part of their boarding school program, or to Maharishi University of Management.

Every parent wants their child to be successful in life. This is now really simple. There are three skills that, combined, will predict 90% of how successful somebody is going to be: The ability to

1. deal with stressful situations (relationships, clarity of thinking, EQ)
2. always remain yourself (self-actualisation, self-confidence, self-regard)
3. develop your full mental potential (IQ, creativity, concentration, emotional stability, etc.)

As we have seen from the research, transcending develops all three at the same time. All you have to do is make sure that transcending becomes part of the school curriculum where your children attend.

Maharishi School

The best thing you can do for your child is simply inspire your local school to also start incorporating TM in their curriculum. Give the school principal a copy of this book, if you feel that might help.

The general experience is, however, that this will take time. Perhaps by the time they wake up, your child is already graduated.

So the second best option is then to simply send your child to the Maharishi School. Countless of families moved their entire household to Fairfield, Iowa, simply because they wanted their children to go to this school. In case this is not practical, however, the Maharishi school also has a boarding school program that children from all over the world can attend.

For more information visit www.fieldparadigm.com/maharishi-school

Maharishi University of Management (MUM)

Maharishi University of Management ("Management" here stands for "managing all areas of life successfully", not just business) was founded in the same city as the Maharishi School, Fairfield, Iowa. Here's why this small, relatively unknown university (before Jim Carrey's MUM commencement speech went viral, at least) can prepare you for a successful career like no other university can.

The World Economic Forum released a list of skills that are most desired by employers, in 2015 and by 2020. Just think for a moment which of the following skills other universities are developing in its students:

Most important skills according to employers

in 2015
1. Complex Problem Solving
2. Coordinating with Others
3. People Management
4. Critical Thinking
5. Negotiation
6. Quality Control
7. Service Orientation
8. Judgment and Decision Making
9. Active Listening
10. Creativity

in 2020
1. Complex Problem Solving
2. Critical Thinking
3. Creativity
4. People Management
5. Coordinating with Others
6. Emotional Intelligence
7. Judgment and Decision Making
8. Service Orientation
9. Negotiation
10. Cognitive Flexibility

Source: Future of Jobs Report, World Economic Forum

The most honest answer is probably "very few".

Most universities can give you knowledge, but what good is knowledge when just about any information is just one Google search away?

The skills that will truly make you stand out in the job market today are all skills that are considered *talents*, the *you-either-have-them-or-you-don't* kinds of things. The TM research shows this way of thinking is outdated. *All* of the skills listed above are either related to brain coherence (complex problem solving, creativity, emotional stability, learning ability, etc.), to self-actualization (critical thinking, active listening, self-confidence, etc.), or to the ability to remain calm under stress (relationship skills, judgment). Mostly these skills are related to a combination of the three.

TM is an important part of this, but it's not the whole story. You'll truly understand why this university can prepare you for success in life like no other university can once we've discussed the advanced TM techniques and TM field effects.

Jim Carrey's speech actually sums up how this university is so unique pretty nicely. You can see the full speech (26 min) on www.fieldparadigm.com/jim-carrey. It's both hilarious and profound. Jim Carrey has been a devoted TM practitioner for many years.

For more information about attending MUM: www.fieldparadigm.com/mum

So Why Aren't We Using This?

Let's go back to our earlier question. Imagine that a pharmaceutical company released a new drug that could:

- reduce your stress,
- improve your happiness
- heal most chronic health problems (especially the stress-related ones, like anxiety, insomnia, depression, hypertension, etc.)
- improve your health to such a degree that your healthcare costs would drop by 50%
- make you more confident
- make you more intelligent and more creative
- make you more loving and improve your relationships
- and do all of that without *any* negative side-effects.

Would you take this drug?

Now imagine this drug has more solid research showing that it works than pretty much any other drug on the market.

Now imagine that it's also cheaper than almost any other drug in the world because it only requires a one-time investment (for the TM course), rather than people having to continuously buy the prescription.

Do you think our health insurers should reimburse it?

Do you think our governments should support it in our schools so that students from a young age learn to reduce their own stress and develop their full potential?

Then why aren't they?

Fortunately, after more than 45 years of TM research the tide finally appears to be shifting, especially when it comes to governments supporting TM in schools.

- After the success of the experiment in San Francisco, the San Fransisco Unified School District now wants to have TM in every school in the city.
- After the success of the Maharishi School in the UK, the English government is now funding Maharishi Schools as part of their *Free Schools* program.
- The Ministry of Education of Bali decided that they want TM as part of the curriculum in all of their schools.
- In India, more than 200 schools already use TM as part of their curriculum.

- Hundreds of schools are starting to use TM in Nepal.

The most successful programs, however, are happening in Latin America.

- The Brazilian government decided that they'd like to see TM as a part of the curriculum in all 48,000 public schools in the country[20]. The only problem they have is that there are not enough TM teachers. There are currently about 40,000 trained TM teachers in the world. For the Brazil project alone they need 250,000.
- The state of Oaxaca in Mexico already has TM in 450 schools.
- The government of Ecuador already has their entire military (army, navy, and air force) practicing TM and has recently signed an agreement to bring TM to 2000 schools.
- Peru is starting a government-sponsored program to bring TM to their schools.

So while this is all great news, the question remains: why only Latin America and a few other countries? Why isn't *every* government in the world supporting this?

It's definitely not due to lack of scientific evidence.

The absurdity of our healthcare system and how we can change it

If everything about TM sounds almost too good to be true, there is one "downside", if you could call it that. To learn TM properly requires an elaborate training program, which takes about 15 hours to learn the technique, spread over 5-6 evening sessions of 2-3 hours each, plus a follow-up program to ensure correct practice over the next six months.

While the cost of this training varies from country to country, the total cost for the entire course is about the equivalent of two weeks average salary in that country, reflecting the labor costs and other overhead involved in teaching it. This means it's a lot cheaper in developing countries than in most western countries. In my home country, Belgium, for example, a TM course costs 390€ to learn plus 95€ per month for six months for the follow-up course. (follow-up course is an obliged part of learning TM properly).

This may seem like a significant investment, but it's peanuts compared to the savings it could create. For example, the average healthcare expenses in Belgium are 3,800€ per person per year, mostly funded through the taxes we pay.

If you thought that was a lot of money, the U.S. National Academy of Medicine recently released a report showing that the 2016 average U.S. annual healthcare expenses were *$10,000 per person*[21], $3.2 trillion in total.

Now, if all these expenses would lead to real results they would be at least justified, but even that is questionable. Belgium has the highest percentage of children with mental problems in Europe, and the US, in spite of having the highest healthcare costs in the world, is only number 37 on a global ranking in terms of the health of its citizens, behind Costa Rica and Morocco[22].

Now imagine we'd be able to save 50% of these expenses *every year*, while getting much better results, simply by teaching people to transcend (which is essentially teaching them how they can heal themselves). The amount of money governments could save is mind-boggling. They would be able to pass on those savings by reducing our taxes almost overnight.

Yet when we showed the cost-saving potential of the TM technique to health insurers their answer was, *"This doesn't fit in our strategy"*.

I was blown away.

How can saving costs not fit into a health insurer's strategy?

I found the answer to this question a few months later when I taught one of the employees of a major Belgian insurance company to meditate, and he explained how insurers work.

For every healthcare cost they reimburse, they send their bill on to the government, which reimburses the costs to them, plus an extra percentage for their working costs. In other words, *it's to their advantage to keep costs high* because they get more income.

Of course every country is different, and in other countries private insurers might not get as much funding from the government, but there is an undeniable tendency in the healthcare industry to keep costs high. In the US, for example, the same medicine often costs twice as much as in other countries.

Did you know that the total annual global revenue of the pharmaceutical industry is roughly *one trillion dollars*[23], and that profit margins in the pharmaceutical industry are higher than in any other industry[24]?

Keeping costs high is better for everyone, except for the average Joe who has to pay for the party from a large portion of his salary, whether that goes to taxes or to sky-high insurance premiums.

By now it's clear that having scientific proof that something works is by itself insufficient to make a difference. In fact, *without the political desire to do something with it, scientific proof alone appears to be completely useless*, as the past 45 years of TM research have shown.

A politician's decisions are generally guided by two forces of influence:

1. The will of those who vote for them

2. The powerful lobbying from different industries or from donors who funded their election campaigns

Now, if you think I'm going to get into all kinds of dark sinister corruption theories, let me disappoint you. I fully believe that every politician is a good person at heart that wants to do good for his society. But before they can do any good, they have to get elected, and that means they both have to take into account those who voted for them and those who make their campaigns possible.

That's just the way the system works, and even the most honest politician in the world has to play by those rules.

Still, it has become obvious that the TM movement, as a small non-profit educational organisation, is no match for the lobbying of the trillion dollar pharmaceutical industry, so we can forget about option two. But option number one is still feasible, and it only takes one thing: enough people have to know that transcending exists and understand how it works, and demand their governments use it.

If the will of the people is strong enough, the governments will do what their voters ask.

All we need to do is let our governments know what we want. One way you can help with this is by simply *ask your government leaders to read this book*, investigate all the scientific research, and implement the recommendations (TM reimbursed, TM in schools, etc.).

Just find the contact information of whomever you feel should read this book (your congressman or senator, minister, prime minister, president, etc. – you can find the contact details for politicians in your country on www.fieldparadigm.com/politics) and email/Tweet/Facebook share them the link (www.fieldparadigm.com) where they can download the book for free.

It really only takes a few seconds to send them a quick email or a tweet. If one person sends them this link, probably not much will happen, but if dozens or hundreds of people send it, then rest assured it will get their attention.

This is the main reason why I decided to give this book away for free, so that everyone, with just a few mouse clicks, can send it on to those who really need to read it.

Of course, if you *really* want to make a difference and can afford it, then it's much better to send them a physical copy of the book by mail. (you can order copies on www.fieldparadigm.com or, if you're reading a physical copy, simply send them this one. Though please finish reading first, the best part is yet to come). This will get their attention much more quickly, even if only a few people send such copies. Plus, they'll be much more likely to read it if they already have it on paper than if they have to download it and read it from a computer screen.

So don't think your single email/mail won't make a difference. It will. Do what you can do.

Unless of course you prefer to keep paying sky-high taxes to keep the bank accounts of the pharmaceutical companies fat and happy.

In that case, don't do anything.

I'm sure they'll all be *very* grateful if this thing could be ignored for another 45 years.

Am I implying here that the big pharma guys are bad people? Another dark sinister corruption theory? No. I believe from the bottom of my heart that everyone ultimately wants to do good for the world. A lot of pharmaceutical drugs are saving thousands of lives every day, and we can only be grateful for that.

But everybody does have their own paradigm. Try to convince a medical expert who is thoroughly trained in the Machine Paradigm way of thinking that a *meditation* technique is going to solve a wide range of problems that their drugs really can't solve (especially the chronic stress related ones, like anxiety, depression, insomnia, hypertension, ADHD, etc, those that create lifelong clients…and the biggest profits) and you'll get exactly the same reaction as the PSI or reincarnation researchers found. *Impossible.*

They are the experts, with billion dollar research budgets, and if they can't find the answers, nobody can. If there is any research that would show the contrary, there must be something wrong with the research.

> What I have seen, over and over again, is that the medical industry has been actively trying to discredit the TM research, and when they focus on just a few studies here and there, it's relatively easy to do so.
>
> Take the research as a whole, however, and there's *nobody* who can still discredit 350 published studies.
>
> The only reason why we haven't had a breakthrough yet, in spite of all the impressive research, is because people (or politicians) didn't know the full story.
>
> And this is just our health we're talking about, wait until we also start discussing creating world peace. The results of transcending are about to get a lot more spectacular still.

Spiritual Growth

While all the effects of TM that we can measure are rather amazing, the most impressive effects are the ones that are far more difficult to objectively measure, because they are subjective experiences.

This is where the real magic happens.

What is the subjective experience when the experience of separation gradually starts to be replaced by the experience of unity?

This was researched through a survey with 500 TM meditators in Italy.

The survey asked two simple questions:

1. How would you rank TM as an investment in your life? The options were the following:
    a. Money thrown away
    b. Very bad investment
    c. Bad investment
    d. Don't know yet – too soon to answer
    e. Good investment
    f. Very good investment
    g. Best investment ever

2. Which were the five most visible benefits in your life? [Out of a list of potential benefits]

The answers to the first question were largely in line with the surveys of the departments of education in San Francisco and Oaxaca, Mexico. Of the 461 people that answered the question*, 7% felt it was a good investment, 55% felt it was a very good investment, and 35% felt it was the best investment they ever made. Added together, this means that 97% felt it was a good investment or better.

Both the positive and the negative experiences (the 3% who did *not* feel it was a good investment) have been published online. You can read all the testimonies at http://meditazionetrascendentale.it/testimonianze/ (in Italian, obviously, but even if you run it through automatic translation software you'll get a pretty good idea).

Disappointing results

Whenever I discuss the 97% satisfaction ratio, I mention that I find this result disappointing because in my experience this technique works for *everyone*, and we should get a 100% satisfaction rate, rather than 97%.

So what happened with the 3% who did not think it was a good investment? In almost each and every case, it's the same story: they didn't take the follow-up part of the course as it was designed.

They learned TM during the first four days, but didn't come back for the follow-up program as much as needed. This means that they didn't get their TM practice checked. If something then went wrong, they felt that TM didn't work for them and gave up, rather than allowing their TM teacher to rectify it (which a TM teacher is trained to do).

TM is easy to learn, and it only takes a few sessions to learn, but that doesn't mean the course is done. Often, people forget some part of the instruction, their experiences change, which leads to doubts about their practice (which then automatically leads to the intellect trying to control it, and then they no longer practice correctly) or they need to have a little more patience before the effects become clear.

All these things are easy to rectify. This is why the course has been designed to include a 6-month follow-up program. If people do hold on and take the full 6-month program, in my experience the eventual satisfaction rate is between 99 and 100%.

---

* 41 people felt it was too soon to answer

However, what is more interesting for our discussion here is the answer to the second question, the individual experiences.

Here is a list of 42 benefits of TM practice that were reported by the 500 people who answered the survey, ranked based on the number of people who confirmed them. This gives an interesting insight into which benefits are most often noticed*.

Of specific interest are the more spiritual experiences, which we'll highlight here and discuss in more detail below.

	Benefit experienced from TM practice	Number of testimonies
1	Calmer	199
2	More emotional stability	158
3	More energy	125
4	Clearer thinking	122
5	Less impulsivity	107
6	Being yourself	99
7	More in touch with deepest desires	98
8	More connection to nature	97
9	Increased spontaneous happiness	93
10	Better sleep	91
11	Self-acceptance	91
12	Better concentration	90
13	More self-confidence	90
14	More creativity	78
15	Reduced anxiety	73
16	Better general health	71

---

* More specific improvements (like reduced ADHD) have fewer testimonies than general improvements (calmer) because fewer people who learned TM had the problem in the first place, it doesn't mean that TM would be less effective for ADHD than for being calmer.

17	Feeling better in my own skin	71
18	More connected to others	68
19	More spiritual experiences	65
20	Better intuition	63
21	More vitality	62
22	More love	60
23	Better personal relationships	56
24	Less conflict	49
25	More efficiency in tasks	42
26	Improved memory	37
27	Spontaneous fulfillment of desires	37
28	Standing up for oneself	31
29	Better work relationships	30
30	Reduced migraines	29
31	More luck (good fortune)	23
31	Reduced depression	22
32	Reduced obesity	22
33	Reduced muscle pains	20
34	Reduced hypertension	17
35	Reduced smoking	17
36	Reduced fibromyalgia/chronic fatigue	8
37	Reduced alcoholism	5
38	Reduced PTSD	5
39	Reduced heart problems	3
40	Reduced cholesterol	2
41	Reduced ADHD	1
42	Reduced cancer	1

You can read all of the more than 2600 testimonies (what people wrote about each subject): http://meditazionetrascendentale.it/testimonianze/

Here we'll focus on the more spiritual ones.

1. More in touch with one's deepest desires

A lot of people learn TM because they feel they're not on the path in their lives that is in tune with their deepest desires. They feel they have a particular purpose in life, and that is part of the reason they're unsatisfied with their lives is because they're not living that true purpose. This sense of purpose is often referred to as the *desire of the soul*.

What people refer to as the soul is that level of the mind where we are our true Selves. As we have seen, being yourself is exactly what transcending is.

Of the 500 people who replied to the survey, 98 noticed that one of the five most obvious changes was that they got more in touch with their deepest desires as a result of their TM practice. It's as if their soul started talking to them more clearly, now that they re-established the connection with themselves.

Here are some testimonies relating to this experience:

> *"The 'silence' of meditation allowed me to listen more carefully to the desires and goals that the 'noise' of life kept me from grasping."*
>
> *"When I meditate I realized that there were many things that I did not want to do but I did in automatism, or fear, or because 'it had to be done.' I stopped doing those things and feel much happier. Now I wonder how it was even possible for me to spend my time doing things I did not want."*
>
> *"I have a feeling of greater clarity on what I want, but most of all on what I DO NOT want."*
>
> *"The awareness of my deepest desires allows me to say NO more easily to those things that I think are dysfunctional and not in line with my values."*
>
> *"This [being more in touch with my deepest desires] was the simplest and most important change. Now I perceive distinctly a kind of direction or drive that is independent of my rational thoughts."*

2. More connection to nature and to others; more love, better relationships

This is related to the omnipresent quality of the Field, the fact that everything is connected to everything else. When this quality is enlivened, people will spontaneously feel a closer connection, both to nature and to other people, a connection they experience as love.

Out of 500 people that replied to the survey, 97 reported that one of the five most noticeable effects was a closer connection to nature; 68 reported a closer connection to others; and 60 reported more love.

Testimonies on a closer connection to nature

"This was the first wonderful feeling of a oneness with nature...I felt lighter, not belonging to material things but to nature, the breeze from the trees to the sky...impossible to explain...wonderful."

"Sometimes I get the feeling of being connected with a 'whole' and with a 'one' – I honestly do not know how to express myself better."

"While you meditate you feel in harmony with the world. It's a special feeling, difficult to explain, that everyone should try in life. Before learning the meditation I could never imagine what it is like to feel part of nature, as light as a cloud and harmonious as the universe..."

"It clearly improved my perception of the vibrations that constitute us and constitute the universe. I feel the flow of life, where death is nothing but a prerequisite for transformation and renewal."

"I was already living a deep contact with nature and continue to live it. Before, however, I reached a state of bliss only in the high mountains or in the woods, now I feel blessed even in a small room of the city, meditating on a chair."

Testimonies on a closer connection to others

"Sometimes I almost feel a state of empathy towards others, and I feel happy when I am with others, I can understand their feelings and sometimes their thoughts."

"I feel more connected...the pains and joys of others involve me more."

"I feel part of a whole that we are all a part of. I lowered the judgment against myself and others. I feel much closer to others, and I almost never feel alone anymore. It's a little as if outsiders are no longer strangers."

"After each meditation, I perceive a greater empathy with other people, less dependence."

Testimonies on more love

"It is easy to love when you feel good."

"I started to attract the right people. People who can give me love."

"Judge not others. Rather I feel a sense of compassion and solidarity with them, it's like I myself have lived and taken note of inner experiences of others."

"The love that comes over me every time I see my wife is indescribable ...I seem to be a little boy again."

"My worldview has expanded, everything has taken a new direction, and a new meaning. I discovered more insight, more sensitivity, less hostile, less fear, and more love and compassion for others, family members and other people, other beings, animals, plants, insects, our Mother Earth..."

3. Spiritual Experiences

These are usually the kind of experiences that are more of a direct experience of the unity of everything.

Out of the 500 people that filled out the survey, 65 reported such experiences.

"Sometimes it is as if I touched my spirit."

"During the TM I feel a sense of connection with the infinite...And a sense of peace and tranquility of 'being inside myself'."

"I feel in touch with God. A sense of love and gratitude towards the deity."

"Meditation connects me with God."

"Better concentration in Catholic prayer."

"In moments of meditation in which I experience the absence of thought, I feel in harmony with the healthy forces of the universe, and good, and this feeling extends to moments of ordinary life."

"No other technique has enabled me the kind of spiritual life that I can live today thanks to TM..."

4. Improved intuition

Intuition is related to the omniscient quality of the Field. We could say that at the source of thought, every thought we get will be perfect. It's like a supercomputer calculating the outcome of every possible thought one can have, and then picking the best one.

As we mentioned in the golf analogy before, the problem is that even if the putt is perfect, bumps on the green (accumulated stresses) will cause the ball to deviate and not reach the hole. Like that, even the most perfect thought can become distorted by the time it reaches our conscious minds.

> Improved intuition simply means:
>
> - the goal has moved closer because we can pick up thoughts at deeper levels before they deviate
>
> - there are fewer bumps on the playing field
>
> - or both.
>
> It means that our thoughts become more reliable; we seem to know certain things, even if we can't intellectually explain how we know them.

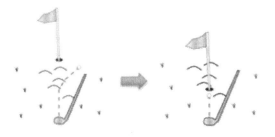

We could say that the Maharishi School students repeatedly winning the world championships in creative problem-solving is due to their brain coherence, but there's more going on. Creative problem-solving competitions present the participants with a problem and allow just a few minutes to find a creative solution. They're all about having the right thought at the right time – having that "universal supercomputer" at one's disposal. Basically, the Maharishi School students have an unfair advantage compared to other schools (though they'd be more than willing to share it).

Here are some testimonies on improved intuition:

> "Sometimes, I feel I have a sixth sense, allowing me to immediately avoid negative situations."
>
> "I follow my intuition more and discover that it is almost always right!"

> "Instant awareness in knowing that this choice is the right one."
>
> "I have more 'coincidences' and feel more people. Improves empathy."
>
> "I can understand if a road will take me to a goal or not."

5. Spontaneous fulfillment of desires, more luck (good fortune), more success

This has to do with the omnipotent quality of the Field. We have a desire and see that the entire universe starts to coordinate events just to fulfill our little desire. In the past, this was called "God answering our prayers."

The spontaneous fulfillment of desires is among the most spectacular effects of TM, something that seems so incredible (especially from a Machine Paradigm point of view) that even when it happens, people hardly even notice it, or don't even make the connection with their TM practice because it seems so implausible. They rather think it's a coincidence.

Still, out of the 500 people that filled out the survey, 37 felt that one of the most noticeable changes was an increased spontaneous fulfillment of desires, 23 noticed more luck, and 21 more success in their lives.

Testimonies regarding the spontaneous fulfillment of desires

> "I imagine something beautiful and...it happens. But I do not dwell too much on this, it's like an inner smile that winks at me and never ceases to make me smile."
>
> "Sometimes it happens that problems will resolve themselves without my intervention."
>
> "Some of my wishes come true in a natural way, unexpected."
>
> "I realized that if you stop trying to frantically get something, paradoxically you get what you want without effort."
>
> "At times I feel omnipotent."
>
> "Everything flows, everything fits together according to my needs that I had not even realized."
>
> "Facts and situations harmoniously converge to a solution favorable to you."
>
> "In reality, I am lucky, although it's still hard for my logical side to believe in spontaneous luck."

So How Does it Feel to Transcend?

In short: most of the times it will feel *spectacularly unspectacular*.

If you understand what transcending is according to the Field Paradigm (an experience of unity with the divine consciousness that is at the source of all of creation) and see all the wonderful effects it creates, you'll probably start to imagine that transcending must be a very special experience.

It is and it isn't. It has very special effects, but the experience itself is an experience of no experience at all.

Remember, the mind transcending is like a wave having settled down into the ocean. This means, however, that for a time, the individual wave is gone. There is no individual entity that can have an experience anymore.

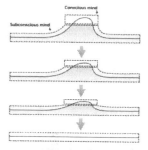

Very often people transcend multiple times during their TM session and don't even notice it. If they would hook up their brains to an EEG machine they'd be able to see the moments they transcended very clearly but in terms of a subjective experience, it won't feel spectacular at all most of the time. Sometimes people do feel something very enjoyable right before they transcend, like an expanded awareness, or a state of deep inner peace and happiness, but the experience of transcending itself is an experience of no experience.

What people do usually experience is a state of deep relaxation during their TM practice, but even this experience usually becomes less and less over time.

This all has to do with the integration of more and more silence in activity.

At first, when people learn TM, most people have quite a lot of tension, making it hard for them to relax. When they then have their first TM practice and dive into that deep silence, it feels like a deep dive, because the contrast between their rather tense state before their TM practice is so large.

Over time, however, the continued experience of transcending will remove more and more tension, so that people start to feel a lot more relaxed outside of meditation as well. As a result, say after two months, they may feel like the dive is not as deep.

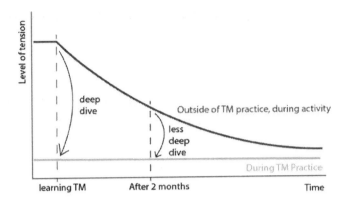

This is indeed the case. The dive is less deep and the contrast between before and during TM becomes less, because they are already diving from a far more relaxed state.

> **Do some people stop practicing TM?**
>
> This is a question people often ask me.
>
> When you read all the benefits that have been prescribed earlier, you'd have a hard time imagining that anyone would ever stop their TM practice.
>
> The attrition rate is certainly lower with TM than with any other meditation practice that's ever been researched. Most people who start will continue the practice for the rest of their lives.
>
> Still, the attrition rate is not zero. Some people do stop, and it usually has to do with a feeling that their meditations don't go as deep anymore, so they are wondering if they are still practicing the technique correctly, or just stop altogether because it doesn't seem to work anymore.
>
> This is another reason why the six-month follow-up program after the TM course is so important, people can have ever-deepening experiences over time, but it's equally important they understand their experiences as they change over time.

So, yes, the very fact that transcending is successful will result in more relaxation during activity, which means that the contrast between activity and rest will be less over time (less deep dive during TM) but it does create another situation as well. *Once we learn to integrate rest and activity, we can also learn to integrate activity into rest...*We can learn to *do stuff* during the experience of transcending.

This is where the fun really starts.

Transcending is just the start: The TM-Sidhi program

There is a great tragedy with the millions of people who have learned to transcend: most people are very happy with their TM practice and the effects it brings them, (as we've seen, a large percentage considers it the best investment they've ever done) but they never realized that learning to transcend *is just the beginning of the journey* – a first taste of the true magic of life. While this taste alone has already has incredible healing effects, the TM technique is in a way just the first preparation to learn even more advanced techniques.

If with TM we learn to "feel the Force", to use our Star Wars analogy, then with these advanced techniques we can learn to "use the Force". These techniques are designed to enliven the qualities of the Field that we mentioned earlier (omnipresence, omniscience and omnipotence) far more strongly than TM practice. This results both in a far faster growth towards higher states of consciousness and far more experiences of magic in their lives.

Here's the best way to illustrate this idea:

We're all on our path to develop our full human potential. We'll all get there in the end (there is nowhere else to go), the only question is, "How fast do we want to go?"

It's as if most people are walking, evolving slowly while going through their cycles of action and reaction.

Learning to transcend is then like getting a driver's license. Suddenly you're in a car. You're going so much faster, and you feel it. Things improve much quicker in your life.

You enjoy the ride. It's fast, and you might think this is as fast as it gets.

But what if the real benefit of being able to drive is that now you can drive to the airport and take the training to become a pilot – so that soon you can *fly* to your destination?

Sounds exciting?

The TM-Sidhi program is an advanced technique of TM, and it's like taking a flight. I referred to this earlier as the closest thing in real life to taking a Jedi Knight training or attending Hogwarts: it is a training that is purposely designed to bring far more magic into your life.

In the prologue we broadly defined "magic" as a collection of experiences like:

- feeling connected to others, or to nature
- an intuitive hunch that turns out to be right
- thinking of somebody you haven't spoken with in years, only to have him/her call you shortly after
- or desiring something, and watching the whole universe coordinate events to fulfill your desires.

All these things start to grow spontaneously when the experience of separation starts to be replaced by the experience of unity, which happens as soon as people learn TM.

For example, the Italy survey showed that of all the people who learned TM (of which the vast majority had been meditating less than one year), about 10% noticed that one of the most noticeable changes was that they felt "luckier" (spontaneous fulfillment of desires, more success), while roughly 20% felt a stronger connection with other people or nature. About 20% also felt that they could more be their authentic selves.

With the TM-Sidhi program, these qualities simply grow much more quickly. In his book *Supermind* Dr. Norman Rosenthal describes how a US/South Africa survey of 600 advanced meditators, of which most had taken the TM-Sidhi training, found that 73% felt luckier, 85% felt a greater connection with the universe, and 90% felt more empowered to be their authentic selves.

For our discussion here we'll focus on the spontaneous fulfillment of desires, feeling lucky. This is probably the clearest experience of magic one can have.

We've seen in the PSI research that every thought (and every desire) we have will create a ripple on the ocean that will ultimately influence the entire ocean. However, when we can only think our thoughts from the surface level of the mind, the effect will be very small and the results are usually negligible. Yes, you can measure it with sophisticated equipment and statistics, but it usually doesn't make much of a difference in daily life.

We've also seen that if influences are created from deeper levels of the mind, they appear to be much stronger. We tried to make sense of this by using an analogy of throwing a rock in the ocean. The closer you can come to the ocean, the bigger the rock you will be able to throw, and the stronger the influence you can create.

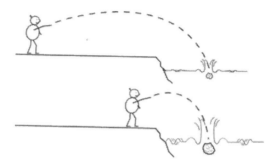

So now what happens when we transcend?

In this case, it would be like jumping in the ocean ourselves. *So any thought or desire we'd have from that level would be extremely powerful.*

There's a small problem, however: transcending is by definition a state of *no thought*. So any desire we'd have would be extremely powerful, but we can't have any desires in that state.

The mind is either active as a wave or quiet, merging with the silent ocean. You can't have both at the same time, right?

Well, what if we could train the mind to actually *have* both at the same time? What if we could expand our conscious awareness to such a degree that our minds can actively have a desire, without losing the awareness of the silence of the ocean?

This already spontaneously happens with TM practice over time. We learn to integrate silence into activity, resulting in a state of more relaxation also outside of TM practice, as we have just seen (the dive becoming shallower).

However, this means *we can also learn to integrate activity into silence*. This is what the TM-Sidhi program is all about.

> If TM is like learning to dive into the ocean, the TM-Sidhi program is like learning to swim at the bottom and create specific desires from the level where we are closest to the full omnipotent power of the field.

So in other words, this is more than just creating a bigger effect by throwing a bigger rock in the ocean, this is *jumping in the ocean ourselves*, and creating the influence from there, or at least very close to there.

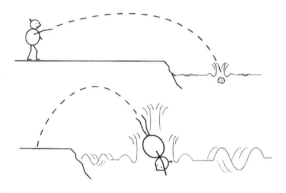

As we said, to some degree, this already happens when people learn TM. The more we alternate between waking state and transcending, the more we integrate both experiences at the same time, until we eventually have the active wave of the waking state without losing awareness of the ocean.

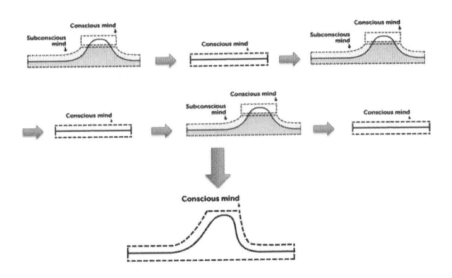

With TM practice this happens gradually, over time. All the effects that we've seen are really just side effects of the conscious experience of unity growing in our awareness.

166

We can clearly measure this by looking at EEG coherence. The degree to which the brain can remain fully coherent even outside of TM practice is the degree to which this integration of unity (awareness of the ocean) gets stabilized 24/7. The longer we practice TM, the more this high coherence gets integrated.

But it still takes time.

With the TM-Sidhi program, people learn to go to this state immediately. They can learn to have their attention on the level of transcending while projecting specific thoughts from there, where the thoughts are far more powerful. This has specific effects on the development of one's full mental potential.

As a result, any desires they have outside of meditation also become much more powerful, and they tend to get fulfilled more quickly.

Once more, the question then arises: *"Can this be measured objectively?"*

Yes, there are quite a few things about this phenomenon that can be measured. We'll discuss how the much stronger effect on the environment from the level of transcending can be measured in the next chapter (TM Field Effect). Here we'll focus on something that is clearly measurable during the TM-Sidhi program, for which we'll again use EEG coherence.

There is one part of the TM-Sidhi technique that we'll focus on, as this is a technique where *even the body will come into a state of activity, while the mind remains in transcendental consciousness.* This creates by far the fastest integration of transcending into activity.

This technique is called Yogic Flying.

To describe what exactly we do here, let's go back to our analogy of the Massively Multiplayer Online Games. Thousands of players have a connection to a central server, and with every action they do the virtual world is recalculated for every other player. These players are free to go where they want but are limited in their action by the laws that are programmed on the server. If the programmed laws say that the characters in the game can't fly, they won't fly.

But now imagine you have special access to the server, where you can actually *change these programmed laws:* instead of the law of gravity being programmed to pull you down to Earth, you make a small change, so that the law will now push you up instead.

As incredible as it may sound, this is what the Yogic Flying thing is all about: it's essentially a technique to levitate. Even gravity is just a waveform of the Unified Field, and if we can bring our minds to that level of the ocean, we can change this waveform.

Hey, didn't I tell you that you were going to learn to fly?

Now, it probably wouldn't surprise you if I told you that Maharishi was subjecting himself, and the TM movement as a whole, to quite a bit of ridicule from the scientific community by making claims of *levitation*.

Those who were laughing were missing the point, however. People who are practicing this aren't really levitating (yet). The body does come up in the air but immediately comes down again. To an outsider, it just looks they are making little hops. It doesn't look that different from people making these hops just with their muscles.

Yet it is *very* different.

First of all, tests were conducted where professional athletes were asked to mimic the actions of the Yogic Flyers. After 15 minutes the athletes were completely exhausted, while the Yogic Flyers could go on for an hour or longer *and have more energy at the end than before they started.* To do this with muscle power alone is virtually impossible.

Subjectively it also feels very different than just jumping with muscle power. Yogic Flying usually coincides with an incredible wave of inner bliss. People simply feel the qualities of unity being enlivened in their awareness, and a feeling of intense inner bliss is usually the first way to subjectively experience this.

But far more important is *what is happening in the brain* during the practice of Yogic Flying.

During TM practice we normally see an inverse correlation between EEG coherence and heart rate. This makes sense. During transcending the body will come into a deep state of relaxation, where one's heart rate goes down while the brain will become completely coherent. When we come out of the experience, heart rate will go back up and EEG coherence goes down. This is how we can visualize alternating between normal waking state and transcendental consciousness during TM practice.

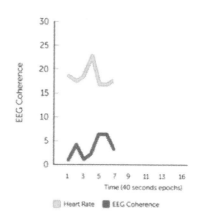

During Yogic Flying, at the moment a Yogic Flyer is about to lift off, we see that the heart rate goes up (body comes into activity) while at the same time broadband EEG coherence goes far higher than even during TM practice.

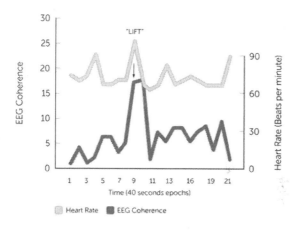

The long term effect of integrating transcending with activity now happens far more quickly. The body becomes active (increased heart rate) while the mind stays in the state of transcendental consciousness (increased EEG coherence).

This means the benefits of TM start to grow far more quickly as well, especially when it comes to more magic.

To learn the TM-Sidhi program requires a far more elaborate training than to learn TM, just like learning to fly takes more time than learning to drive a car.

First of all, the TM practitioner has to refine their experiences of transcending, and gradually learn to integrate activity during the process of transcending. This usually happens through four advanced techniques. These techniques generally make the TM practice itself a lot livelier (and a lot more fun as well), because we start to experience much more during our practice. It's advised to take a minimum of 3-4 months between each advanced technique to ensure enough practice.

After learning these advanced techniques, people can then learn the TM-Sidhi program itself. This usually requires a training of 3-4 in-residence weekend courses, plus a two-week in-residence course for the final part, where one learns the Yogic Flying technique.

It's a significant investment of time, but once people are done with this training they have usually experienced a personal transformation beyond their wildest dreams. Almost everyone I know who took this training considers it the best investment they've made in their lives.

Yet so far, out of six million people that have learned TM, only about 250,000 have taken this advanced TM-Sidhi course. I hope that more people will soon discover the joy of flying.

To find out more about how/where/when to learn the advanced techniques, the TM-sidhi program and Yogic Flying, fill out the form on www.fieldparadigm.com/advanced

So do all desires really just magically get fulfilled?
Can I promise that as soon as people take this TM-Sidhi course, all of their desires will be spontaneously fulfilled?

No, of course not. As we said before, it's just like no tennis coach will promise that you'll be ready for Wimbledon or the US Open as soon as you start playing tennis. Like everything, practice makes perfect.

What most people do notice is that when they start practicing the effects gradually start to appear and then become more and more obvious over time.

The other crucial factor to understand here is that in our new magical Field Paradigm universe we are all connected to each other, but that means we also influence each other. So the degree to which you'll see magic in your life does not only depend on your own level of consciousness, but also upon the collective consciousness.

This is a key concept to understand the TM Field Effect in next chapter (which is the most important section of the book), so let's try to explain it.

Imagine you are a glass of water, as are each of your family members.

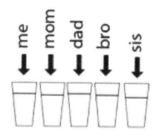

The temperature of the water in each of the glasses is your level of consciousness. If it's warmer you'll be happier, more self-confident, more peaceful, loving and positive, your brain will be more coherent, your intuition will be stronger, etc.

According to the Machine Paradigm, each glass stands alone. Consciousness is limited to the confines of your body. So whatever happens in your glass, stays in your glass.

According to the Field Paradigm, consciousness is everywhere. We could compare this to putting the glasses in a pot. There is water in the glasses, but also water between the glasses.

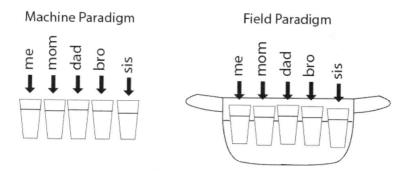

In this analogy, transcending is then like increasing the temperature in your glass. But as soon as you come out and spend some time with your family members, what will happen? The increased temperature of your water will warm up the water in the pot. This will also increase the temperature of the water in the other glasses. Your TM practice is improving the *collective consciousness* of your whole family. They somehow become less stressed and grumpy and a bit more positive.

At the same time the colder temperature of the other glasses of your family members will cool your water back down.

This balancing process will continue until all the temperatures in all the glasses reach an equilibrium: a little higher than before, but not as high as during your TM practice.

Likewise, every unit of society has their own collective consciousness. You can think of many family pots in a larger "city" pot, then many city pots into a national pot, and so on.

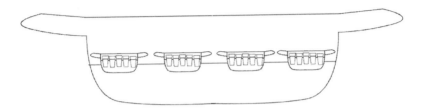

The temperatures of all these pots will interact with each other and influence each other.

This is the "collective consciousness", as simply as I can explain it. Carl Jung described this as the "collective unconscious", the part of our subconscious minds that we share collectively (the ocean) but it's essentially the same thing.

This means that if you learn to transcend, you'll probably take two steps forward; but if you then go out into a stressed environment you'll take one step back. Your temperature will always remain higher than before because you keep increasing it every day, but it may not go as fast as you'd like.

But what if you could be in an environment where the collective consciousness could lift you up, rather than drag you down? What if your glass could be in a pot where the water is even warmer than your own glass, so you take two steps forward during your TM practice, and then another step forward during the day?

Wouldn't that be something?

That's the situation we want to create for the whole world. And it's remarkably easy to do so. It could be done in a few weeks if enough people desired it. We'll discuss this in the next chapter of this book.

> Magical places
>
> Throughout my life, after more than 20 years of practicing the TM-Sidhi program, I've seen one magical event happen after another, starting with the first one (the radio song incident) a few weeks after I finished my training.
>
> I just desire something and one way or another it starts to happen.
>
> Sometimes it happens almost instantly. For example, you have a thought about an old friend you haven't seen in years and feel a desire to see them

again. Half an hour later you run into someone who, it turns out, has this friend as a roommate, and he invites you over for dinner that same evening.

At other times it happens more gradually, in small steps, like pieces of the puzzle that gradually come together. I just keep the desire in mind and gradually watch everything fall into place. I've built several successful businesses that way.

Obviously, the shorter the timeframe, the more magical it feels, because you experience a clearer connection between the desire and its fulfillment.

One thing I quickly learned in this regard is that in surroundings where the collective consciousness is high, the magic happens *far* more quickly and *far* more often. The time between having your desire and its fulfillment becomes so short that it sometimes almost seems instantaneous.

There have been three places in the world where I had this experience.

The first one was a kind of monastery in East Germany where I spent almost two years, participating in the most advanced TM program there is. This is called the "Purusha" program where you essentially live a monk's life, meditating all day long. I was spending almost the whole day to boost my "spiritual power", together with a group of around 30-40 others who had been doing this for most of their lives. Both the temperature in my own glass and the collective pot were very high, and, not surprisingly, I had magic happen almost every day. You just desire something (whether it is for a friend to call you or that they'll serve pizza at lunch) and it happens, almost instantly.

The other truly magical place for me was the little town of Fairfield, Iowa, where both the Maharishi School and the Maharishi University of Management are located, and where out of a population of around 10,000 more than 3000 practice TM, and most of them the TM-Sidhi program as well.

We'll see in the next chapter that when people practice the TM-Sidhi program together in a group, the positive effect on the collective consciousness becomes even stronger, with the power of the wave they create increasing with the square of the number of participants.

So now imagine a small town where anywhere between 500 and 2000 people do their TM-Sidhi and Yogic Flying practice together in big meditation halls *every single day for the past 35 years*. We'll see in next chapter that the wave that they can create is often strong enough to positively influence the entire US population. So you can imagine it must be quite a special place.

Whenever I visit Fairfield, usually driving from Chicago, I have the most amazing experience of an inner bliss that becomes stronger as I get closer

173

and closer. As soon as I arrive in Fairfield, it starts. Whatever I desire tends to happens so quickly (usually within 24 hours) that it really starts to feel magical.

If, somehow, my desires aren't fulfilled right away, it's usually only to discover that there was something even better around the corner. Sometimes we can desire something from our intellect, because we think this is what we want, but on a deeper level, the level of the soul, there might be a very different plan. In places where the collective consciousness is high, it's that desire of the soul that becomes much stronger, and that is the desire that will manifest.

This is true magic, that we will be on a path our soul desires, whether we like it or not ;o).

So it may sound a bit strange to call a small town in the middle of a lot of Iowa cornfields the most magical place on Earth, but in my experience that's exactly what it is. (How magical it feels greatly depends on how big the group of Yogic Flyers in Fairfield is. The numbers have been fluctuating wildly over the past 30 years, from 500 to 2000. The bigger the group is, the more obvious the magic).

It's quite obvious that I'm not the only one to whom this happens. Fairfield has been half-jokingly called "*Silicorn* Valley" due to the many highly successful tech companies that were started in this little town, in the middle of the Iowa corn fields. As a result, In 2009 the US National Center for Small Communities gave it their Grassroots Rural Entrepreneurship Award, recognizing Fairfield as the most entrepreneurial small town in the US.

I'm sure you can imagine that if you can start to develop all of your employees' full creative potential and on top of that, you can enliven that omnipotent power of the Field and have all your desires spontaneously fulfilled... it seems almost impossible *not* to be successful.

The most amazing thing about Fairfield is that people just got completely used to it. They just take the whole spontaneous wish fulfillment thing so much for granted that they hardly even notice it anymore.

The third magical place for me has always been the global headquarters of the TM organisation in Vlodrop, Holland. This is where Maharishi lived for the last 20 years of his life, and where a lot of people with a very high level of consciousness are living and working together. Just being there in that environment around Maharishi (before he passed away in 2008) and the other leaders of the TM organisation seemed to be enough to start the sparks of magic, usually also on a daily basis.

> While I'm trying to spend as much time as possible in these places (my wife and I recently decided to build a house in Fairfield, so we can spend a lot more time there), I would like to experience the true magic of our universe not just in these few places, but *everywhere* I go.
>
> That's the main, somewhat selfish reason I've spent the last 15 years writing this book. I hope that someday we can lift the entire world consciousness to such a level that everyone will simply be dragged along to experience the higher magical levels of life, and everyone can have the reality of unity consciousness present in their awareness.
>
> ...and I can have my fun everywhere I go. ;o)
>
> The ending of all wars, corruption, and crime will just be a small side effect.
>
> So now let's see how easy it actually is to raise the entire world consciousness. All it takes is a few relatively small groups of people practicing TM, and especially the TM-Sidhi program together.
>
> P.S. My current desire? That I can appear with this book on Ellen or Oprah, or both is okay as well. ;o) I realize this is a slightly bigger one than "I'd like to see this or that person again", but I am living in Fairfield now (even if the group of Yogic Flyers here is currently the smallest it has been in almost 40 years) so we'll see how long this one takes...it might be a bit more than 24 hours. Meanwhile I figured I better do a bit more fitness training and loose some weight, so I look good on television ;o).

Twenty Experiments that Will Change the World

This is the point where the book really starts, where we come to the heart of the Field Paradigm. Everything up until now has been an introduction of the concepts required to make sense of what is to come in this chapter: the TM Field Effect.

Let's recap what we've discussed so far:

1. We perceive ourselves as separate beings. In reality, we are all connected by an invisible Field at the source of our thoughts, a field of universal consciousness of which we are all part. The body functions like a radio, giving a local expression of the vibrations of this omnipresent Field.
2. Through this Field, we influence each other with every thought we have. Most people can only create this influence from the

most superficial level of the mind, where the influence is weak. Even though it can be statistically measured, it usually doesn't make much of a difference in daily life. Thoughts from deeper levels of the mind appear to create a much stronger influence.

3. Transcending is a direct experience of this Field, which enlivens the qualities of this Field (which we called Primal Love) in one's awareness. This has positive effects on all aspects of life: health, happiness, brain development, self-confidence, relationships, etc.
4. Any influence created from the level of the Field itself will have a far stronger effect on the environment than thoughts from the superficial level of the mind.

This last point is what we'll mainly investigate in this chapter.

Through a series of increasingly well-designed experiments, we'll see that:

1. The influence from transcending on the environment *is measurable.*
2. It *is* much stronger than ordinary thought.
3. It provides the most solid evidence to date that there is indeed a Field of consciousness. (We can't have field effects unless there is a field).
4. Changing people's behavior by enlivening the qualities of the Field in their awareness is far more effective than our current methods of dealing with negative behavior, at a far lower cost to society.

In short, Over the next few pages you'll discover the most powerful technology to change the world (in a positive way) that has ever been objectively researched.

In fact, it has *already* changed the world.

Do you want to know what really caused the fall of the Berlin Wall?

Read on.

Research on the TM Field Effect (the 1% effect)

In the 1960s, Maharishi made his most spectacular prediction on the power of transcending yet: if only 1% of the population would learn to transcend, the level of stress in the collective consciousness would reduce, resulting in a measurable change in the behavior of the entire population.

Here's how it works.

As we have seen, whenever we have stressful negative thoughts, we don't just damage ourselves but create an influence for our environment as well. We create stress in the collective consciousness. According to our earlier collective consciousness analogy this means we decrease the temperature of the water in the pot, and thereby in all the other glasses in the pot as well.

This individual influence is not very strong but if millions of people in a city create a similar effect it *will* start to influence our behavior, resulting in increased crime, corruption, traffic accidents, addictions, etc.

This doesn't mean that everybody in the city will automatically become a criminal. If a man with a peaceful mind (glass of warm water in our earlier analogy) arrives in a stressful city (pot with cold water) he will not start committing crimes right away. But if he's already stressed himself, the additional stress in the collective consciousness is certainly not going to help.

Transcending is like jumping into the lake yourself, which creates a much stronger influence than the power from ordinary thoughts, and it is purely positive (enlivening the connection that we call love between us). This is why only a small group of people transcending can positively influence a much larger group around them.

To light up a whole city you don't need to have light bulbs everywhere; just a few streetlights will do.

So let's see what happens when we turn on the light.

Experiment 1: Decrease in Crime in 11 Cities – the first study on the TM Field Effect

Title: Improved quality of life through the Transcendental Meditation program – decreased crime rate
Authors: Candace Borland., and Garland Landrith III
Reference: Collected Papers on the Transcendental Meditation technique, Volume 1; (98), 1975.

In the early 1970s, when the first scientific research came out showing the remarkable individual benefits of TM, Maharishi and the TM technique became household names. At that time TM and the word "meditation" were almost synonymous, and hundreds of thousands were learning to transcend every year.

By 1973, several cities in the US had 1% of their population practicing TM, so two brave scientists, Candace Borland and Garland Landrith III decided to take up the challenge to put Maharishi's prediction to the test. Would 1% of the population transcending indeed have a measurable effect on the behavior of the entire population?

Being well aware that this would be a highly controversial study, they realized they had to do their study as thoroughly as possible.

They identified 11 cities with a population between 25,000 and 50,000 where 1% of the population had learned TM. They then matched these 11 cities with 11 control cities in the same regions and with similar demographics, and examined the FBI crime statistics in each.

Using publicly available FBI statistics already gave them one significant advantage compared to a lot of other social science experiments: *objective data*. Often social science researchers collect their own data, through questionnaires for example, to try and prove their hypothesis, but that can often leave questions about the reliability of the data. Was it properly collected, was contradictory data suppressed, etc.?

In this case, the researchers felt pretty confident that nobody in their right mind would assume that the FBI would start to falsify their data to help the TM movement prove their point. So if there were an effect, at least nobody would question the data.

And there was indeed a remarkable effect. The result looked like this:

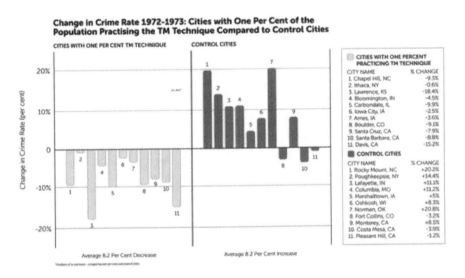

> Whereas the control cities had an average increase in crime levels of 8.3 per cent, the 1% cities had a decrease in crime of 8.2 per cent. The relative decrease was therefore 16.5%.

Could this be a coincidence? Yes it could, but the chance was not very high: the study had a p<.001, one in a thousand – 50 times smaller than the norm for which a social study is considered viable (p<.05). Such a large change, consistent over 11 cities, would be unexpected by chance alone.

The results looked promising, but there were still *a lot* of questions that were going to be raised:

- <u>What if the effect appeared because the researchers picked control cities that happened to have an increase in crime?</u>

    To answer this question the researchers looked at the average crime increase in all cities in the same population range in the US, 460 cities in total, and found that the average increase was 9.6% – even bigger than in the control cities.

- <u>What if the 1% cities had a trend of decreasing crime that began before people learned TM?</u>

    The researchers looked at the trends of the growth of crime rate of both control cities and 1% cities. The result looked like this:

Until 1973 both control and 1% cities had a trend of increasing crime. The increase was even stronger in the 1% cities than in the control cities.

In 1973, however, the trend of the 1% cities reversed, while the trend in control cities continued. So whatever was happening in the 1% cities, was unlikely due to trends.

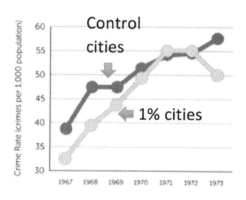

Or was it? One interesting thing was that the increasing trend of crime in the 1% cities already seemed to stop before 1973. How can this be explained?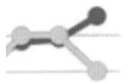

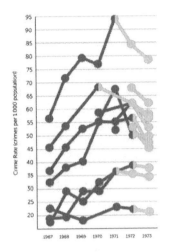

The researchers had to choose a starting point of their research period so they picked changes in crime rate from 1972 to 1973, but this was far from a perfect study. They had to choose the cities with 1% of the population meditating, but not all cities reached that threshold at the same time. This graph shows the 1% cities, with the line turning light from the moment the 1% threshold is reached.

What this graph shows is that out of the 11 cities, three already had 1% by the end of 1971. The crime in those cities already decreased in 1972, averaging out with the other cities to stop the trend of increasing crime from 1972 to 1973. This shows that the study underestimated the true effect of TM. If citizens in all cities had learned TM at the same time, the effect would have been stronger.

So a lot of questions seemed to be answered already, and there seemed to be a clear correlation between 1% of the population of these cities learning to transcend and a decrease in crime rate.

But correlation does not mean causation. There are many factors that will influence crime rate, and before anyone can be sure that TM was really the cause, the researchers needed to eliminate (or "control for") other possible causes.

This was done in a more elaborate follow-up study.

Experiment 2: Expanding the Sample to 24 Cities over Five Years

Title: The Transcendental Meditation program and crime rate change in a sample of 48 cities
Authors: Garland S. Landrith III, Michael C. Dillbeck, and David W. Orme-Johnson
Reference: Journal of Crime and Justice vol. 4, 1981, pp 25-45.

After the first study, Dr. Michael Dillbeck joined the team of researchers and used his expertise in statistics to significantly increase the quality of the TM Field Effect research.

First of all, they expanded the scope of the original study to 24 cities with 1% of their population practicing TM, and matched them with 24 control cities. This time, the researchers requested an independent investigator to make sure that there was an objective selection of 24 control cities.

Next, they looked into every factor that was known to influence crime and controlled for it, including population density, level of education, median income, percent unemployment, percent below the poverty line, and percent in ages 15-29.

Next, they looked at a longer period, over five years, rather than just one year.

If it was really the TM Field Effect that caused the drop in crime, rather than some other unknown factor, then the effect should be consistent with all these extra variables taken into account.

In the end, it turned out that with the more detailed study the results *improved*, the drop in crime rate was even bigger.

> With a larger number of cities and a more stringent control for other variables, the crime rate in the 1% cities decreased 22% in comparison with controls and trends (p<.001).

After the initial drop the crime rate also remained stable for the next five years, while in the control cities the growth in crime rate increased.

Dillbeck was so detailed in his statistical analysis that the research was accepted for publication in the *Journal of Crime and Justice*, offering the first breakthrough for the scientists involved. As unorthodox as the study was, the data was solid and the research methodology passed the peer-review test of the journal.

They later expanded the study to also include car accidents and suicides, and found similar highly significant decreases (p<.001 for both).

This makes sense. If the decrease in crime was really due to the TM Field Effect, then this effect shouldn't just manifest in terms of decreased crime, but in several other variables also related to social stress. We'll see an elaboration of the research where far more variables are included in future experiments.

Experiment 3: Causal Analysis in 240 Cities

Title: The Transcendental Meditation program and crime rate: a causal analysis
Authors: Michael C. Dillbeck, Garland S. Landrith III, Craig Polanzi, and Sheldon R. Baker
Reference: Journal of Mind and Behavior, vol. 8, 1987, pp. 67-104.

By 1982, hundreds of US cities had 1% of their population practicing the TM technique, so the researchers expanded the study to a random sample of 160 cities. With such a large sample they were able to do a more elaborate analysis to identify whether it was really the TM Field Effect that was *causing* the decrease in crime rate. The analysis involved a statistical method called cross-lagged panel correlation (CLPC) over a random sample of 160 cities, which measures the correlation between cause and effect. If the cause is there (1% TM meditators) does the effect (reduced crime) also show? If there is no cause, is there also no effect?

If a high correlation is found it strengthens the hypothesis, but if they find that the effect exists without the cause, the hypothesis is weakened.

> The research found that the statistical correlations between cause and effect were significant. It could then be said with a high statistical reliability that the TM Field Effect was indeed the cause of the decrease in crime rate.

This study was replicated with another random sample of 80 larger metropolitan areas, with similar results.

Research 4: The First Prospective Research – Cessation of Warfare in Lebanon

Title: The Maharishi technology of the Unified Field and reduction of armed conflict: a comparative, longitudinal study of Lebanese villages
Authors: Tanios M. Abou Nader, Charles .N. Alexander, and John L. Davies
Reference: Collective Papers vol. 4, No. 331 pp. 2623-2633.

The individual TM studies show a very clear trend: the bigger the problem (the more somebody is out of balance) the greater the balancing effect of transcending. For example people with severe PTSD, or a severe alcohol addiction usually see a much stronger improvement then those with only a moderate problem. The darker it is in the room, the greater the difference when we turn on the light.

Dr. Tony Nader wanted to test if the same held true for the TM Field Effect. It's certainly nice to see crime decrease by 20% in moderately stressed US cities, but what would happen in an area where stress is so high that people are at war with each other?

Dr. Nader was trained as a Lebanese medical doctor who went on to study neuroscience at MIT and Harvard, and eventually worked with Maharishi on the discovery of Veda in the Human physiology. Before embarking on his postgraduate studies, however, he decided to take the training to become a TM teacher and go back to Lebanon to try an audacious experiment: to stop the war in his hometown.

This study would be unique not only because it was done in a far more stressed environment, but also because it would be a truly prospective experiment.

As impressive as the earlier experiments were, they still had one major flaw from a scientific point of view: they were all *retrospective* studies. The effects could only be measured in those cities which happened to have 1% of their population already meditating. In this case, the researchers could only *look back* in the past and see if something happened (hence the name retrospective).

From a scientific perspective a *prospective* study is much more reliable. In this case scientists predict in advance that they will create a particular effect in a particular place and time. However, these studies were much more difficult to execute as one can't predict that 1% in a particular city will learn TM.

Still, Dr. Nader decided to try it, and his hometown of Baskinta was the perfect location. He would risk his life to teach people to experience peace in the middle of a war zone. He then wanted to see if the influence of radiating this peace to everybody else would be sufficient to stop the war in his hometown.

Fortunately, Baskinta only had a population of about 10,000. This meant that he only had to teach about 100 people in order to create the 1% effect.

Baskinta was in a strategic location for the fighting parties, and fighting had been continuously going on for four years before the experiment started. There were four other villages in the region with a similar population and in similar circumstances. Dr. Nader reasoned that these would be ideal control cities.

In May 1981, predictions were made to the media that the hostilities would reduce significantly in Baskinta and that the quality of life would significantly improve, both compared to its own previous trends and compared to the four neighbouring villages.

Dr. Nader started giving lectures on the TM technique and offered to teach anyone who wanted to learn for free. He purposefully didn't announce the goal of their experiment to the local population so that there wouldn't be any expectation effect.

By June 1982 he achieved his goal: 1% of the village population had learned TM and five individuals had also learned the advanced TM-Sidhi course. From this moment the experimental period began.

For the purpose of the study, three variables were measured: the number of incoming shells, the number of casualties, and the amount of property damaged. The primary source of data was *An-Nahar*, the most widely distributed newspaper in Lebanon, which was also considered the most objective.

When the researchers compiled their data, the results were astonishing. Whereas the level of hostilities was worse in Baskinta than in the neighbouring villages in the years before the 1% threshold was reached, the hostilities completely stopped from the moment 1% of the village had learned TM.

> Throughout the entire experimental period, from June 1982 till March 1984, there were *zero* incoming shells, *zero* casualties (even zero wounded), and *zero* property damage. War violence decreased by essentially 100% for a continuous period of over three years.

The hostilities in the neighbouring towns, on the other hand, had shown a strong *increase*, much more incoming shells, casualties and property damage then before the experimental period. The chance that the difference between Baskinta and the surrounding villages was due to coincidence was smaller than 1 in 100,000 (p<.00001).

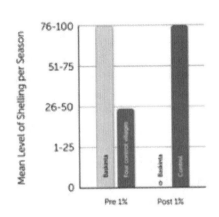

The other predictions also came true. While in the surrounding villages a few miles away people were still at war, in Baskinta people were getting adjusted to normal life again. They were forming a new soccer team, installing a tennis court, and built a new football field. The Lebanese government decided to start fixing some roads in Baskinta (the first time in 15 years) and to install an automatic telephone system, something that they had been requesting for four years before the experiment. None of these improvements happened in the neighbouring villages.

To somebody who doesn't know the science behind this experiment, this would do pretty good justice to the word "miracle". But this is a true story, with all events objectively verified and open to being checked.

With this study the 1% research had come full circle; from the first promising but imperfect study, to a complete causal analysis in 240 randomly selected cities, to eventually a real prospective study with mind-blowing results.

Maharishi later appointed Dr. Nader as the head of the Global Country of World Peace, (the global nonprofit organisation that is responsible for teaching TM and some other Vedic technologies) and gave him the title of Maharaja Adhiraj Raja Raam.

Did the TM Organisation Gain Anything from This Research?

It's natural to be suspicious whenever research is done by scientists who are connected to institutions that would gain from the research.

When it comes to the individual effects of transcending, the experiments done by scientists connected to the TM organisation were usually confirmed by independent scientists fairly quickly. They found the same or even better results and could conclude that the TM scientists were honest in their research. The results were really due to the effects of transcending, not researcher bias.

When it comes to the TM Field Effect, on the other hand, almost all the experiments were done by scientists from the TM organisation itself. (It wasn't until the mid-1990s before independent scientists dared to link their name to these experiments.)

So then the question becomes: Did the TM organisation have anything to gain by proving that the TM Field Effect works?

Well, no...quite the opposite, in fact.

> Imagine you have a "product" that could improve all aspects of life (health, happiness, IQ, brain development, self-confidence, etc.), would your marketing strategy be to try to convince people that they *don't have to buy your product*, because they'll get the benefits anyway?

This was essentially what Maharishi started claiming, that it's not even necessary for everyone to learn TM. One percent of the population is sufficient for the benefits to trickle down to everyone.

It doesn't sound like a very good sales strategy, if you ask me.

There was a far bigger issue, however. The research on the individual effect of TM was impressive and inspiring, but it didn't challenge people's belief system too much. Perhaps TM just created some profound relaxation which created all the changes? Perhaps something else happens on a physical level? It all still seems possible within the Machine Paradigm.

The TM Field Effect was different. This effect is only possible if the Machine Paradigm is just...wrong. They would indicate that there would be some kind of influence on a field of consciousness at the source of everybody's thoughts, which is impossible in the Machine Paradigm point of view that consciousness is created by the body, just like all the PSI, near death experiences, and reincarnation research is impossible.

And, as we have already seen with the PSI researchers, people don't like to be told their whole belief system is wrong.

In the case of the PSI studies, the effects were usually so small that it was actually rather easy to ignore them (even if they were highly statistically significant). They just labeled the researchers pseudo-scientists and that was it.

But in this case, the change was much bigger and much more difficult to ignore. It's not quite as easy to discredit FBI data showing a 20% drop in crime, or data from Lebanon showing a 100% drop in warfare for a continuous period of three years while only a few miles away the war intensity increased during that same period.

Normally, we'd think that when the scientific evidence grows stronger, people change their old beliefs and accept the new reality.

In practice, usually the opposite happens. Psychologists have researched this rather strange behavior and formulated a name for it: cognitive dissonance. When old beliefs are confronted with new evidence, then the stronger the evidence, the more people cling to their old beliefs. They just find more and more creative ways to dismiss the credibility of the evidence, rather than change their minds.

Max Planck, whose discoveries ultimately led to quantum physics, was already familiar with this phenomenon more than 100 years ago. He had a famous quote to describe his opinion on paradigm shifts (old beliefs confronted with new facts):

> *A new scientific truth does not triumph by convincing its opponents and making them see the light, but rather because its opponents eventually die, and a new generation grows up that is familiar with it...*
>
> *Science progresses...one funeral at a time.*

The TM organisation would also find out soon enough how unscientific people really were in our scientific age.

Almost as soon as Maharishi announced the results of the first 1% studies, and his intention to the use the TM Field Effect to create world peace, some people started using labels far worse than pseudo-scientist.

PSI researchers were mostly branded as just naïve people who were trying to prove something that was impossible. But this was different. In the case of the TM Field Effect, it was so obvious that it was so utterly impossible that whomever would make such a claim *would be deliberately misleading people*.

Suddenly Maharishi was portrayed as somebody who was preying on the weak-minded with promises of a better world based on claims that were just utter nonsense according to all (Machine Paradigm) scientific standards. This is the kind of thing that cults do.

So suddenly there were only two options. Either
1. the TM Field Effects were true, which means we'd have to dismantle our entire belief system that we've gotten so comfortable with over 300 years of scientific progress

    or

2. the TM organisation was a dangerous cult that was deliberately trying to deceive people.

For most people the choice was obvious. (This was 1975 we were talking about, after all, long before the Unified Field theories appeared and before most of the other experiments that were mentioned earlier were done).

As a result, the number of people who wanted to learn TM started dropping dramatically.

Around that time a lot of other meditation techniques appeared to fill the void. They all claimed that you could get all the same benefits as you'd get from TM (all meditation techniques were the same anyway) but without having to be associated with all the weird *world peace* stuff.

So, from all perspectives, the smart thing to do for the TM organisation would be just to stop talking about the TM Field Effect and just focus on the impressive individual effects.

> Why on earth would anybody want to expose themselves to the kind of ridicule or open hostility that the TM organisation was suddenly faced with?

Because Maharishi and the scientists who were involved in the research knew that *this could change the destiny of mankind*, that's why.

This was the technology that was going to change the world, and they were *going* to talk about it. If people weren't ready to understand it at that time, someday they would be.

Maharishi wouldn't even for a second consider toning down his claims about the TM Field Effect.

In fact, he was just getting warmed up.

Research on the Square Root of 1% Effect

When Maharishi started teaching the advanced TM-Sidhi program and Yogic Flying techniques in 1976, it quickly turned out these techniques didn't just have a far more powerful effect on individual growth. It was also discovered that it created a far more powerful influence on society as well (as predicted by the ancient texts*) especially when people were practicing it together in a group.

To explain this let's use our jumping-in-the-lake analogy again.

---

* One of the Vedic texts, the *Shiva Samhita* mentions:

"When the Yogi, though remaining in Padmasana (sitting position) can rise in the air and leave the ground, then know that he has gained Vayu-Siddhi (mastery over air), which destroys the darkness of the world."

Imagine three people jumping in a lake one after another. They will create three waves, each with a particular height and power. This power will determine how far the waves will travel before they die out, and how much of the surface of the lake they will influence.

Now imagine that instead of jumping separately, they hold hands and jump in the lake together. The wave they create together will become much bigger, and will travel much farther. There's a law in physics which says that the power of a wave increases with the square of its amplitude*. To illustrate this very simply we could say that if a wave is three times bigger, and will travel three times further, this means that *the area of the circle of influence* would theoretically increase with *the square of the radius*, or nine times.

With transcending, it worked according to the same principles. During the TM-Sidhi practice, and specifically Yogic Flying, people could stay in the transcendent for much longer, making it far easier to coordinate the transcending among a group of people. It was as if they were holding hands and jumping in the lake together.

This means that in terms of the amount of people positively influenced, the effect radius will grow with the square of the number of Yogic Flyers. Three Yogic Flyers creating the influence together in one group could theoretically create the same effect as nine individual TM practitioners meditating in their own homes at their own time, which according to the 1% formula is an effect for 900 people.

From here the curve grows very quickly:

- 20 Yogic Flyers together in one place will have the same effect as 400 individual (20^2) TM meditators, for 40,000 people.
- 200 Yogic Flyers will have the same effect as 40,000 TM meditators, for 4,000,000 people.

---

*LASER technologies, for example, make use of this law. LASER stands for Light Amplification by Stimulated Emission of Radiation. This means that, rather than a light source sending out light waves at random, in the case of LASER light the individual light waves (*emission of radiation*) are *stimulated* so that they are emitted coherently, and their individual amplitudes will add up. This way the resulting light wave has a much higher amplitude resulting in *light amplification*. The power of this light wave will be the square of the amplitude.

- 2,000 Yogic Flyers will have the same effect as 4,000,000 TM meditators, for 400,000,000 people.
- 9,000 Yogic Flyers together in one place will have the same effect as 81,000,000 individual TM meditators, for 8.1 billion people: the entire world population.

Sounds wonderful, doesn't it?

If people were already skeptical before, imagine how they'd react now.

A group of a few hundred people hopping around on a few mattresses can decrease crime, accidents, or even warfare in an entire country?

I think it's fairly safe to assume most people thought that now Maharishi and the TM organisation had completely lost their minds.

Maharishi didn't care one bit. Rather, as a scientist, he was excited that the far more powerful effect from Yogic Flying allowed them to create far more spectacular experiments.

Previously, other than in the Lebanon Experiment, studies could only be done if 1% of a city had learned TM, something the TM organisation had very little control over. Now, creating the effect, even for an entire country, only required a few hundred Yogic Flyers. This was relatively easy to organize. So now all the experiments could become prospective; they could predict the effect in advance, bring in a group of Yogic Flyers, see if the effect takes place, then remove the group and see if the effect goes away.

Extraordinary claims require extraordinary evidence.

The claims just got a whole lot more extraordinary…

…the evidence will be as well.

Experiment 5: The First Yogic Flying Study: Creating an Ideal Society in Rhode Island

Title: Maharishi's global ideal society campaign: improved quality of life in Rhode Island through the Transcendental Meditation and TM-Sidhi program
Authors: Michael C. Dillbeck, Andrew Foss, and Walter J. Zimmerman
Reference: Journal of Mind and Behavior, vol. 8, 1987, pp. 67-104.

This was the very first experiment to test the Yogic Flying Field Effect – or the "Maharishi Effect" as scientists started to call it. (It's common in science for an effect to be named after the person who first predicted it, like the Doppler effect.)

The idea behind this new experiment was simple: teach 1% of the population of a particular state to transcend and turn the state into *an ideal society* as an example to inspire governments in other states or countries to support similar projects.

As a first project, they selected the state of Rhode Island in the US.

In the summer of 1978, for a period of three months, 450 TM teachers went to Rhode Island to teach as many people as possible. They planned to teach anyone that wanted to learn, almost for free, until the 1% threshold would be reached.

At the same time these TM teachers, who had all taken the TM-Sidhi and Yogic Flying course, decided to do their meditations together in groups around the state, so that they could already create the effect themselves, just from their group meditations, during the three months they were there.

Rhode Island had a population of around one million at the time of the experiment. One percent of one million is 10,000, and the square root of 10,000 is 100. So only 100 Yogic Flyers were needed to create a measurable effect if they'd be in one group. In this case, the Yogic Flyers were in smaller groups, but still big enough to create the effect for the whole state.

As an "ideal society" involved much more than just a reduction in crime rate, the scientists chose a much wider range of variables. They selected everything that would be a good indication of increased collective consciousness. As usual, they would only use completely objective, publicly available sources, rather than gather their own data.

To make the study even more comprehensive, they would measure any changes both against previous trends in Rhode Island itself and against the situation in a nearby state (Delaware) with comparable demographics during the same period.

Here's a list of the variables measured and the official sources of data:

- Crime (FBI)
- Deaths (*Vital statistics of the United States,* US Bureau of Census, National Center for Health Statistics)
- Vehicle fatalities (Department of Transportation, Rhode Island and Delaware)
- Auto accidents (Department of Transportation, Rhode Island and Delaware)

- Unemployment (Department of Employment Security, Rhode Island, Department of Labor, Delaware)
- Pollution (particulates) (Department of Environmental Management, Rhode Island, Department of Natural Resources and Environmental Control, Delaware)
- Beer sales (United States Brewers Association, Washington D.C.)
- Cigarette sales (Tobacco Tax Council, Richmond Virginia)

Next, the scientists decided to group the variables together in an *Ideal Society Index*.

Creating an index of different variables requires scientists to add apples to pears, so to speak. For example, how do you add a 10% decrease in car accidents to a 20% decrease in cigarettes purchased?

There is actually an easy way to do this: by working with *standard deviations* rather than absolute changes.

For example, if the number of car accidents consistently fluctuates between 80 and 90 per month, the average number of car accidents is 85, and one standard deviation would be around 5 (meaning that we can predict with a high degree of certainty that the number will be somewhere between 85-5 and 85+5)*. If now we found a 10% decrease in car accidents this would mean there were 8.5 fewer car accidents. To now calculate this in standard deviations we divide 8.5 by 5 and we get 1.7.

Similarly if the amount of packs of cigarettes purchased per month fluctuates between 90,000 and 110,000 we could say that that average number of packs of cigarettes purchased is 100,000 with a standard deviation of 10,000. A 20% decrease in cigarettes purchased would mean 20,000 fewer packs, or a standard deviation of 2.

If we'd now want to put these two in an index we just average the two standard deviations, 1.7 and 2, and we come to an index of 1.85.

Another word for standard deviations is "effect size", which we've already seen in some of the earlier TM studies. Any effect size above 0.8 is considered large. The 10% decrease in car accidents in our example might not be that impressive at first sight, but compared to the normal fluctuations it translated to an effect size of 1.7, which would be considered a very big change[†].

---

* This is a very simplistic explanation of standard deviation, and the numbers should be taken with a grain of salt. My main focus was to keep it simple.
† Effect size is inversely correlated to probability. The larger the effect size the smaller the chance that it could be a coincidence.

Like this, the scientists created an index for all eight variables, which made the research a whole lot more impressive than just measuring crime.

Normally, if you have this many variables you'd expect the random fluctuations of each of them to cancel each other out. Sometimes car accidents will go up due to chance, but the number of cigarettes purchased might go down at that same time.

Combine eight variables like this and you should get overall index fluctuations close to zero, unless something is influencing all eight at the same time.

> That was exactly what the scientists wanted to measure, and a composite index was much more reliable than a single variable. If this index still showed a significant change, it would be far more difficult to assume it was a coincidence or due to some other cause. The only factor that influences all eight variables at the same time is a fundamental, positive change in the way everyone thinks and behaves, which would indicate a change in collective consciousness.

The researchers first had to make sure that there actually *were* no other factors that could influence these variables. One obvious factor was *seasonal trends*. During summer, for example, there might be fewer cars on the road due to people being on holiday and there might also be fewer cigarettes smoked.

So before the scientists could compile their numbers, they first also had to filter out any seasonal changes through a *time series analysis*. They looked at seasonal trends over the previous five years, and then checked if changes in the seasons influence the numbers. If this is the case, the seasonal changes are filtered out before the effect changes of the study are calculated.

All in all, this was becoming a pretty advanced experiment. If after all this analysis some kind of effect still appeared, it would be impressive, especially because the effects were predicted in advance.

To make their analysis as thorough as possible the scientists calculated a three-month average of their Ideal Society Index for a period of six years – four-and-a-half years before the experiment, three months during the experiment, and for a little over two years after.

Here is how the plot looks like over the entire six year period.

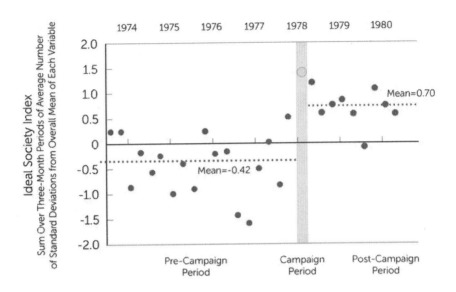

As we can see the experiment was *highly successful*.

Before the campaign period the standard deviations had a mean of −0.42. This meant that the quality of life, on average, was deteriorating over the 4.5 years.

> During the campaign period there was a standard deviation value of +1.5, indicating an exceptionally large effect size over all eight factors at the same time, which would be highly unlikely to happen by coincidence.

The highest positive deviation they saw in the 4.5 years before the experiment started was +0.25[*]. The chance that the index would now all of a sudden jump to +1.5 by coincidence was smaller than one in 1000 ($p<.001$).

But how do these effect sizes translate into changes in daily life?

Here the results become even more impressive. A separate study looked into some of the individual variables of the Index. The individual results of the three month period in 1978 were compared to the results in the five year period before:

---

[*] There was a +0.5 standard deviation during the three months before the experiment. This was due to the fact that the actual experimental period ranged from June 12 to September 12, while the three month average was calculated for July, August, and September. The fact that there was already a significant positive change in the standard deviation in the three month period before only confirms this effect.

- *Suicide*: dropped 42% compared to previous year, largest decrease of the five year period.
- *Divorce*: dropped 7.7%, the largest decrease of the five year period.
- *Marriages*: largest total number of marriages of any quarter on record.
- *Traffic fatalities*: increasing steadily at an average 18% per year, but decreased 54% during experimental period, first decrease on record.
- *Murder*: fell 49% compared to same period in the previous year, in spite of an overall general increase before the experiment.
- *Aggravated assault*: fell 22% compared to previous year; greatest decrease on record.
- *Auto thefts*: lowest number of thefts for any July-August period on record and largest decrease on record.
- *Beer and cigarette sales*: first decrease during experimental period, breaking the trend of increasing sales.
- *Total employment:* reached record-breaking levels during the period.
- *Environmental pollution (carbon monoxide and ozone violation days)*: largest decreases on record.

See how *in almost every case* we could use the words *largest decrease, lowest number, record-breaking*, etc.?

All this shows that the Yogic Flyers were not just having an effect, but that this effect was significantly stronger than what could be achieved with any of the current methods used to counter these issues…on many different variables at the same time.

It's like our analogy of warming up the pot of the collective consciousness. We put a fire underneath the pot on one location, and the water becomes warmer everywhere, in every single glass that is in the pot. When people's consciousness starts to change, they think differently. This manifests in all different kinds of behavior.

On top of this, a spontaneous change from inside is always far more effective than a forced change from outside.

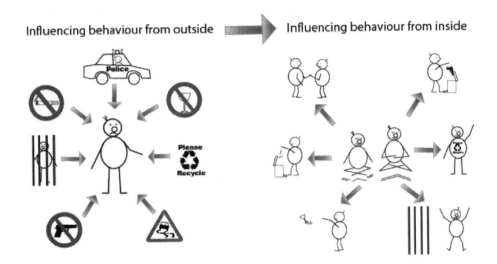

Can you already start to imagine what this could do for the world if this technology would be applied? Hang on. We're just getting started.

After the campaign, the group of Yogic Flyers left, but they did largely succeed in their goal of teaching 1% of the population, so even after they left there was a continuous improvement of the situation as shown by a +0.7 standard deviation per three-month period over the next two years.

Neither trends during or after the campaign were found in the control state of Delaware.

JMB This research was eventually accepted for publication in the *Journal of Mind and Behavior*, as part of a larger paper combining three later experiments where Yogic Flyers also significantly reduced crime in New Delhi, Puerto Rico, and in the Philippines (in each case the drop in crime rate was publicly predicted in advance).

The additional studies only made the paper more impressive, as now it was shown that the effect seemed to happen independently of culture, religion, or other regional variables. Also, the chance that it could still be a coincidence is obviously a lot less if an experiment can be successfully repeated several times. The overall chance of coincidence of these four experiments was less than one in a million ($p<.000001$).

The editor of the journal, Dr. Raymond Russ, professor of Psychology at the University of Maine, was intrigued by the paper. He said:

On one hand the paper was based on an extremely unconventional idea. On the other hand, this idea was backed up by rigorous statistical analysis, a level of mathematical sophistication rarely seen in psychological or sociological studies... I'm afraid that many times, new ideas don't lose out on their merits. They lose out because established people in the field don't want to see their power eroded by new ideas which threaten their expertise and authority. In any event, Michael Dillbeck had written a strong paper with solid evidence. I didn't see how I could deny that paper publication.

Less violence, fewer cigarettes, sure, but fewer traffic accidents???

Once you understand the concept of stress in the collective consciousness, and how this influences everybody's individual consciousness, it's starting to make sense that things like violence and cigarette sales can be influenced by a group of Yogic Flyers, but what about traffic accidents?

Are they also related to stress? Aren't they usually due to coincidence or just inattentiveness.?

Sure stress will play a direct role in car accidents, but there's something more going on. If we raise the collective consciousness (warm up the water in the pot of the entire state) we don't just decrease collective stress, but enliven *all* qualities of the Field in people's minds. So people don't just experience being more connected to each other in terms of "loving thy neighbour" (or at the very least not killing them, if at all possible), but also in terms of the omniscient qualities.

It's like our previous example with the starlet birds, where thousands of birds can fly criss-cross through each other in one big flock without ever having an "accident". They are part of the field that knows everything, and just intuitively, instinctively, feel each other's movements. Now, Can you imagine thousands of cars all randomly changing lanes on four five-lane highways that are all crossing each other from all sides. How long do you think it would take us, super-intelligent human beings that we are, before we'd have an accident. I'm sure the answer would be measured in milliseconds rather than seconds or minutes.

But what if the omniscient qualities of the Field would become a bit more lively in our minds as well, and we'd start to instinctively feel the other drivers and adjust our own driving to this, in real-time, just like the starlets do? Can you imagine how, if this would happen even to the smallest degree, accidents would go down?

> For me this is not a concept but a practical (quite possibly life-saving) experience. I've experienced many times that I'm about to turn on a crossing, not seeing any other cars, only to have that instinctive voice (the same one as the one with the radio contest, but a bit more urgent) say: "Look again !!!". So I look again and suddenly see a car coming at me from my blind side at high speed.
>
> So yes, from the Field Paradigm perspective, fewer traffic accidents are a consequence of increased collective consciousness that's as logical as fewer crimes.

Experiment 6: Using the Maharishi Effect to Stop Wars

Title: An experimental analysis of the application of the Maharishi technology of the Unified Field in major world trouble-spots: increased harmony in international affairs
Authors: David W. Orme-Johnson, Michael C. Dillbeck, Jean G. Bousquet, and Charles N. Alexander
Reference: Collected Papers on the Transcendental Meditation technique vol. 4 no. 322 pp. 2532-2548.

Around the time the Rhode Island experiment was coming to an end, the mayor of a small village in Nicaragua sent out a message through United Press International. *"Anyone who can help, please help."*

Nicaragua had been torn apart by a civil war that had killed 1200 people in the previous month alone. People were getting desperate.

When Maharishi heard this message he decided to answer. The Rhode Island experiment had proven that the Maharishi Effect worked; with only a relatively small group of Yogic Flyers they could create a real change. Now he wanted to use this powerful new technology to start creating peace around the world.

Nicaragua wasn't the only place where tensions were running high. There were several regions around the world in autumn 1978 where the fire of stress was burning so intensely that it was leading to civil and international wars. And like fires, social stress can spread to larger regions, or even the whole world if they are not contained.

In our personal lives we know that stress is like a vicious circle, often leading to more stress. When we are already stressed and somebody says something we don't like, we'll lose our balance much more quickly than when we are calm and relaxed. Likewise, tensions between groups of people can often escalate to more and more tensions until war breaks out.

Due to the vicious circle of stress, it rarely happens that fires like these go out by themselves. Peace treaties almost never last when there is no peace in the collective consciousness of the groups. If the underlying tensions remain, it's usually only a matter of time before the treaties collapse.

The late 1970s was a time when the world was at great risk of these fires spreading, and it was already happening. The Cold War tensions between the superpowers were running dangerously high, and social stress was spreading rapidly in Central America, the Middle East, Africa, and Southeast Asia.

> Maharishi reasoned that if some peace and harmony was brought to those hotspots of collective stress it might calm things down in the entire world. He predicted it would even ease tensions between the two Cold War superpowers.

As such it was decided to call this new endeavor the Global Peace Project. Yogic Flyers from around the world were asked to take a holiday from their jobs...to travel to the world's most violent places and stop the war (try explaining that one to your boss).

In total, 1400 Yogic Flyers responded to the call. The TM movement took a bank loan to finance their travel and staying expenses. They were either sent to the countries that were at war themselves, or to nearby countries if the situation was deemed too dangerous.

<u>Central America</u>: Other than the civil war in Nicaragua, tensions were also running high in the neighbouring countries of Honduras, Costa Rica, Guatemala, and El Salvador. One hundred forty Yogic Flyers were sent to Nicaragua and another 160 to the neighbouring countries.

<u>Southern Africa</u>: Like in Nicaragua, more than a 1000 people died during the war in Rhodesia (Zimbabwe) in September 1978 alone, and the war was already spreading to neighbouring Zambia and Mozambique. Fifty six Yogic Flyers traveled to Zimbabwe and 40 more to Zambia.

<u>Middle East</u>: The continuous war in Lebanon was creating tension in the whole region. A potentially explosive situation in Iran was developing. Two hundred Yogic Flyers were sent to Iran, 100 more to Cyprus and Syria, and 400 people took part in a TM-Sidhi course in Israel.

<u>Southeast Asia</u>: The tensions that led to the war in Cambodia were starting to engulf Thailand. Two hundred sixty Yogic Flyers traveled to Thailand.

One thing that encouraged all these Yogic Flyers to travel to remote places around the world was that they weren't *only* doing it for world peace. Many of them had already experienced that *doing Yogic Flying in a big group was far more powerful for themselves as well*. One could imagine that a wave of positivity strong enough to influence an entire country must be something quite special for the person who is involved in creating the wave.

While we said earlier that the experience of transcending during TM practice is usually spectacularly unspectacular, with Yogic Flying, and especially group Yogic Flying, it's different. This was a very blissful experience, and the bigger the group the stronger the waves of bliss in their own awareness. There was something strangely addictive about it.

So a lot of them were very happy to grab the opportunity to be part of a big group again. If that opportunity turned out to be the first large-scale demonstration of the Maharishi Effect to stop wars and change the destiny of mankind, all the better.

As with the previous experiment in Rhode Island, significant positive changes were predicted and publicly announced beforehand: effects that nobody in their right mind would have predicted based on the rapidly worsening situation in all four regions.

As before, the changes happened exactly as predicted and, as before, they were dramatic. You can read the detailed stories of what happened in the book Permanent Peace, by Robert Oates. Here's a quick summary.

Central America (Nicaragua)

Only a few days after the group's arrival the number of conflicts was reduced sharply, as objectively confirmed by the international press.

President Somoza suspended the state of military siege, began to eliminate radio and TV censorship, and granted unconditional amnesty to political prisoners and exiles. He said that: "...*due to the tranquility in the country after the events of September, we have been able to stop the censorship of the press, and this has produced a better climate of communication...*" (*None Dades*, Dec 8, 1978). The President also agreed to a public referendum on whether he should stay in office, saying: "*I am not afraid of a vote, what I really want is peace for Nicaraguans.*" (*International Herald Tribune*, Dec 2, 1978). This was a dramatic turnaround.

So the experiment was successful. Or was it? To determine a cause and effect relationship the cause has to precede the effect, which clearly happened, but also as soon as the cause stops, the effect should also stop.

Turn on the light in people's minds, and the darkness disappears. People start thinking differently and behaving differently. But turn the light back off and the darkness should return.

Did this happen also? Unfortunately, yes. Immediately after the group left at the end of December 1978, President Somoza rejected the proposed public referendum, negotiations broke down, and violence again broke out in the country. A few months later Somoza was violently deposed and rebel leaders took control of the country.

Southeast Asia (Thailand)

Maharishi felt it was crucial to reduce the tensions in Southeast Asia as this was an area where the superpowers were directly facing each other. After the Vietnam War, a new war broke out between Cambodia and Vietnam, with the US siding with Cambodia and the Soviet Union siding with Vietnam.

It looked more and more likely that this conflict would escalate to Thailand, where tensions between the government and insurgents had already led to warfare earlier in the 1970s. In the interest of keeping the Yogic Flyers safe they weren't sent to the actual war zone, but to nearby Thailand. One hundred fifty Yogic Flyers arrived in Thailand on November 11, with another 110 arriving thereafter.

The feared escalation into war did not take place; Thailand remained in peace.

While this experiment was the least scientific of the four, as it's impossible to say whether the war would have broken out or not, Maharishi felt it was an important one. This was the first time that a group of Yogic Flyers were reducing stress in the collective consciousness for the whole Southeast Asia region, and it did seem to have a calming effect on the relation between the Cold War superpowers (see section on improvements in worldwide relations later).

Middle East

Lebanon

The civil war that had been going on for many years was getting ever more intense. At the beginning of October 1978, the fight reached the highest levels in years and Lebanese leaders were predicting a total economic collapse. To give an objective idea of the situation, here are a few quotes from the Washington Post: *"a new crisis"* (June 15), *"war of vengeance"* (June 23), *"Beirut's hopes for a normal life fade"* (July 12), *"32-65 killed"* (Aug 8), *"hundreds of deaths"* (Aug 31), *"New fighting flares in Beirut"* (Sept 8), *"220 die in Lebanon before guns still"* (Oct 1).

It was considered too dangerous for the Yogic Flyers to go into Lebanon itself, so the effect was created from the surroundings. One hundred Yogic Flyers traveled to Syria and Cyprus on October 23, and a TM-Sidhi training course was organized in Israel near the Lebanese border where another 400 Yogic Flyers were in training.

As soon as they arrived and started doing their group TM and Yogic Flying sessions, something changed in the environment. A new cease-fire lasted for almost the entire time the project was going on, three months in total. This was longer than ever before. During this time refugees began to return to their homes in Beirut (*The New York Times*, Nov 14); the Lebanese army, the Arab League forces, and local security units formulated a security plan which was subsequently discussed by the Lebanese Government (*Lebanon News*, Dec); and the Lebanese began to rebuild (*The New York Times*, Dec 6). Something had changed, and positivity was returning to Lebanon.

When the Yogic flyers left in early January, however, the cease-fire came to an abrupt end. The number of casualties jumped back up to levels before they arrived in what the *Lebanon News* called the *"worst onslaught since October."*

Iran

Iran was on the brink of a revolution. Violent demonstrations took place around the country. The oil industry had been brought to a halt by continuous strikes, and the US supported Shah had declared martial law. The exiled Ayatollah Khomeini became increasingly critical of the Shah day by day.

On October 17, the first 50 TM-Sidhi practitioners arrived in Tehran. They were told for their own safety not to leave the hotel.

Immediately after they arrived, however, something changed in the environment. Four days later the BBC ran a story commenting on how the demonstrations were suddenly more peaceful, saying this was a *"remarkable illustration of changed conditions in Tehran."* The numbers were far from high enough to create a stable influence around the country, so two weeks later 150 more TM-Sidhi practitioners spread out over different cities in Iran. By December, *Time* magazine reported that Iran was relatively peaceful, oil strikers returned to work (bringing much needed funds to the country), and that 477 political prisoners were released.

<u>Personal experience of a Yogic Flyer in Iran</u>

A friend of mine, Dr. Stuart Rothenberg, was one of the group members who were in Iran during the project. He describes his experiences as follows:

My experience in Iran on the World Peace Project transformed my life. During the project I had the clear, recurring experience of my individual awareness being connected to the consciousness of our group, and of the powerful nourishing influence of our group on the collective consciousness of the society as a whole. These experiences were very concrete – similar to direct perception – so much that the subsequent changes in the quality of life in the city seemed merely to be ancillary confirmations of my direct experience.

Returning home, I felt much more powerful and effective. My family enjoyed immediate benefits. Within a month, a new business opportunity arose that transformed our financial and our overall living situation. Since then I have had many such dramatic experiences of support of nature.

The World Peace Project gave me direct insight into the power of my individual awareness to change the world.

Stuart Rothenberg, M.D. Boynton Beach, Florida[25]

Unfortunately, like in other places, the time soon came when the Yogic Flyers had to leave again. The change that happened in Iran when they left was perhaps the most dramatic of all, as Dr. Keith Wallace recounts:

> *In Iran the situation was potentially so explosive that removing the Yogic Flyers at the end of the project had to be orchestrated like a military withdrawal. Maharishi told us that the peacemaking effect would collapse almost immediately after our groups left the country. Therefore it was imperative to take them all home on the same day. Otherwise, an upsurge of violence would engulf any small group left behind. We had groups scattered around the country, in Tehran, Isfa-*

han, Tabriz, and Shiraz. To move them all out on the same day required that the groups in the south fly across the Persian Gulf at the same time that the northern and central groups flew to Tehran Airport. Then both contingents departed simultaneously for America on synchronized flights from Tehran and Saudi Arabia. Maharishi was emphatic about this maneuver, and we quickly understood why. Four days after our evacuation, mobs forced the Shah to flee Iran, and a few days later, amidst near chaos, the Ayatollah Khomeini returned from exile to assume power.

Africa (Rhodesia/Zimbabwe – Zambia)

The civil war in Rhodesia (now Zimbabwe) was even more intense than the one in Nicaragua. More than 1000 had been killed in September 1978, and the military was bracing itself for even more intense fighting. Terrorists were getting ready for a major offensive from both Zambia and Mozambique. They were expected to come to the border at any time.

The 56 Yogic Flyers that were on their way to Rhodesia on Nov 4, 1978 immediately realized how serious the situation was when their plane was landing, as Robert Oates reported in his book *Permanent Peace*. Rather than going down gradually, the plane stayed up high in the air for a long while and then descended sharply to the runway. This maneuver, as it was later explained, was necessary to stay out of the range of shoulder-launched missiles as long as possible.

The moment they arrived, however, something changed.

> Before the Yogic Flyers arrived, an average 16 Rhodesians were losing their lives every day. From the first day the Yogic Flyers started creating the influence, the average dropped to 3.1 deaths per day, as reported by the *Rhodesian Chronicle*.

A BBC correspondent reported that after months of extreme chaos there was an unexplainable calm in the atmosphere. Towards the end of November, Bishop Abel Muzorewa, who would later become Zimbabwe's prime minister, said *"Peace has at last taken hold of our war-torn society."* (*International Herald Tribune*, Nov 27). Rural people returned to normal life and the schools, which had almost all closed as a result of the conflict, were re-opened.

The experiment in Rhodesia took an interesting twist when on November 15 it was decided to split the big group into two smaller groups, with one in the north and one in the south, to ease tensions in both regions. It had a reverse effect, with violence going back up. This actually fits the theory of the power of the wave increasing with the square of the number of participants. One big group will have a stronger effect than two smaller groups. Unfortunately, the results were showing in Rhodesia. The number of deaths increased from three to an average six per day.

Similar to what happened in Nicaragua, *the day* after the Yogic Flyers left on November 27, the violence shot back up to the same levels as before they arrived, back to an average 16 deaths per day.

Forty more Yogic Flyers were sent to Lusaka, the capital of neighbouring Zambia. Rhodesia had started bombing Zambia to deter the terrorists trained there from entering the war in Rhodesia. The day the flyers arrived the *Lusaka Times* reported: "*Lusaka bombed again.*" It was an almost daily report.

However, from the day they arrived and for the next six weeks not a single bomb was dropped and no serious events of violence, either domestic or from neighbouring countries, took place.

The government officials from Zambia, whom the Yogic Flyers had contacted upon their arrival to declare their intention of creating peace, noticed that something strange was going on. They came to ask the group to stay for two more weeks. The two government officials that came to visit them – the governor of Lusaka province and a senator – told them that the month before the Yogic Flyers arrived was the worst since Zambia's independence and the change they had brought to the environment was obvious and much needed. The election was two weeks away and a lot of violence was expected in Zambia. Could they stay until the elections were over? The Yogic Flyers stayed, and the elections took place in an atmosphere of calm throughout the country.

After the elections they really had to leave, however. They were all volunteers who had to go back to their day jobs. So on December 22 the group took the morning flight to London.

That same afternoon Lusaka was bombed.

Convincing government leaders

The intention of the Global Peace Project was to give a demonstration of what could be done, hoping that governments around the world would take it up and start training Yogic Flyers in their own countries.

Several government officials did notice the difference, and not just in Zambia. But their enthusiasm usually didn't last very long. As one of the scientists who met several leaders explains:

> It often happened, when we presented our program, that government officials showed tremendous enthusiasm while we were physically with them. We expected to hear from them afterwards, but there would be only silence. The gap between their situation and the solution we were presenting was too great for them to bridge alone.

In other words, the gap between their Machine Paradigm way of thinking and the new Field Paradigm understanding that is required for these effects to make sense was just too big.

Objective scientific analysis of events

Based on the reports above we could say that the World Peace Project was a big success, but reports and newspaper articles are subjective. Who's to say that articles noting the positive changes weren't selected to fit a narrative?

So the question that the researchers asked themselves was, "How do you make a study like this objective and scientific?"

Fortunately, it turned out that there was a source of purely objective data they could use.

The Conflict and Peace Data Bank (COPDAB) was at that time the largest news database in the world, keeping a daily record of all newsworthy conflict events around the world and objectively scoring them in three major categories: hostile acts, verbal hostilities, and cooperative events. The purpose of the database is to give a balanced, objective view on state of events in every country around the world every single day.

From 1968 to 1977 the COPDAP file contained 172,938 recorded events. In 1978, the year of the World Peace Project, there were 14,567 events. More than enough to create a thorough statistical time series analysis for the purpose of this research.

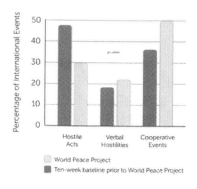

The study suddenly became an objective statistics numbers game. In order to make the numbers more statistically reliable, the scientists grouped all the data from the four regions together to get one overall number.

The results spoke for themselves. Even though the changes were more dramatic in some regions than in others, on average the hostile acts in the four trouble spots decreased by approximately 30%, while cooperative events increased by 30%.

Statistical analysis revealed that this was a very big change compared to the normal fluctuations, which would have occurred by chance only once in 10,000 times (p<.0001).

Improvement in worldwide relations

Maharishi predicted that if the Yogic Flyers could reduce stress in the collective consciousness in these four most stressful regions the situation would also improve in the world as a whole.

The number of Yogic Flyers was insufficient to create an effect for the whole world, but Maharishi said, *"When milk is about to boil even a few drops of cold water can prevent it from boiling over."*

Warming up the Cold War between US and Russia

There was indeed a real improvement in relations between the two superpowers during the time of the Global Peace Project, even if neither could explain why.

For example, on November 18, 1978 the *International Herald Tribune* quoted President Carter as saying: *"I think that in recent weeks there has been an alleviation of tension between us [U.S.S.R and USA], and I would like to see it continue. I can't say why there has been an improvement in US-Soviet relations."*

A week later *Newsweek* reported that Soviet leader Leonid Brezhnev also observed the reduction in tension. *Newsweek* reported Leonid Brezhnev saying to US senators that, *"US-Soviet relations have improved substantially since last summer,"* while quoting President Carter, *"The remaining differences are minor compared to what they were a year ago."* (Dec 18). Meanwhile, *Time* reported, "*At the same time that Washington and Moscow are maneuvering against each other at a number of the world's hot spots, they are also sitting amiably around negotiation tables discussing myriad projects and possibilities.*" (Jan 22, 1979).

Other improvements around the world

- In November, China and Japan ended the technical state of war they were in since 1931, and signed the Treaty of Peace and Friendship (an event *Time* magazine called "stupendous").
- China re-opened its doors to trade with the West (Nov 20).
- The US and China restored full diplomatic relationships after 30 years of estrangement, as announced by President Carter (*Newsweek, Time* Dec 25).
- The Soviet Union and Vietnam signed a Treaty of Friendship (Nov 13).

The mood in the world at the height of the World Peace Project was accurately portrayed by a US newspaper, saying: "*No nations are actively engaged in open warfare at the moment, a history rarity.*" (*Des Moines Register*, Nov 30, 1978).

To again make sure that their data was objective, the scientists looked at the COPDAP database for all events around the world before and during the experiment.

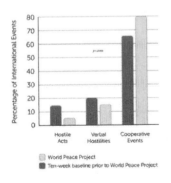

The percentage of hostile acts decreased by 60%. As a result, of all news stories around the world during the time of the World Peace Project 80% were stories of increased cooperation (p<.0001).

Comparison of worldwide events during the same period over the last 10 years showed that the decreases had nothing to do with seasonal effects, the improvements in 1978 compared to the same period over the past 10 years were again significant to the p<.0001 level.

Experiment 7: Increased Brain Coherence 1200 Miles Away
Ref: International Journal of Neuroscience (16, 203-209)

The Maharishi Effect researchers reasoned that if group Yogic Flying creates a measurable effect on people's thoughts and behavior, then there must also be an effect in the brain. Could this effect be measured?

So when a group of 2000+ Yogic Flyers gathered in Massachusetts during the first major experiment in the US, (a group that was big enough to theoretically create an effect for the entire US) a few scientists from Maharishi University of Management investigated if this could have a measurable effect on brainwave coherence in subjects more than 1200 miles away, at their university in Fairfield, Iowa.

Earlier studies in Mexico had already found that subjects could influence each other's brainwaves, and that the influence always came from the one with the more coherent brainwaves. If somebody with highly coherent brainwaves has their attention on another person with lower coherence, the coherence in the second person will start to increase.

These studies were confirmed by research published in the *International Journal of Neuroscience*[26] showing how people practicing TM were found to influence non-meditating subjects in the next room who were doing a computer test. When the TM meditator started TM, both the EEG coherence and test results of the person in the next room improved significantly.

But would there also be an increase in coherence at the moment when the Yogic Flyers were doing their thing halfway around the country? Scientists have found a strong correlation between brainwave coherence and improved moral reasoning, impulse control, emotional stability and reflex times, all of which clearly influence things like criminal behavior, car accidents, substance abuse, etc. So if the coherence could be influenced through field properties, this would provide a neurological explanation for the changes in behavior, and the improvements on a wide range of variables.

For their tests the researchers introduced a new element. Rather than trying to find an increase in coherence in one subject they decided to measure coherence among three different subjects. If brainwaves from three different brains would show more phase coherence (meaning electrical impulses fire at the same time), then this would imply a Field Effect; it would imply that all three brains were being influenced by a single source.

To do their test as thoroughly as possible the researchers took continuous coherence measurements before and during the period when Yogic Flying was going on. They also repeated these measurements at the same time one week later after the Massachusetts course had ended. If this effect was only measurable while the Yogic Flyers were flying in Massachusetts 1200 miles away, but not when the course had ended, it would provide a stronger indication that the Massachusetts course was the cause.

There was indeed a fundamental improvement, especially in alpha coherence, at the moment when the Yogic Flyers started flying ($p<.001$ to $p<.02$). During the control period (when the course ended) there was no difference between the time periods.

The research may have been unorthodox, but was considered solid enough for publication in the *International Journal of Neuroscience*[27].

The Massachusetts experiment itself was also very successful. As predicted in advance there were highly significant decreases in crime, car accidents, air traffic fatalities, and 14 other categories of fatal accidents across the entire United States, with p values from $p<.02$ for crime rate (3.4% decrease) to $p<.0001$ for automobile fatalities (6.5% decrease). It even appeared to have a positive effect on the stock market.

In Massachusetts itself, the changes were far bigger than in the US as a whole, which would be expected (the effect is always the strongest near the source), with p values ranging from $p<.05$ for automobile fatalities (18.9% decrease) to $p<.00001$ for crime rate (10.1% decrease).

Experiment 8: A Permanent Group of Yogic Flyers in the US, Ensuring an Ongoing, Positive Effect...and 1,300,000 Fewer Crimes

Title: The long-term effects of the Maharishi technology of the Unified Field on the quality of life in the United States (1960 to 1983)
Authors: David W. Orme-Johnson and Paul Gelderloos
Reference: Social Science Perspectives Journal, (2 (4), 127-146).

Even before the scientific data from the Massachusetts experiment were compiled, Maharishi felt that a big improvement had taken place in the collective consciousness of the US*. But he also warned that there would be a sharp decline in national coherence if the group now simply disappeared, similar to what happened during the World Peace Project.

As we have already seen, when people are in the dark, they are used to it, but when the light is turned on and then turned off again, the darkness can feel even darker than before.

---

* Although Maharishi never said as much, and it's not something that can be scientifically proven, it was widely believed that he could feel how a nation was doing, how coherent the collective consciousness was. He simply was in that state of consciousness where he could experience a connection to everything around him, the whole world consciousness.

At such a precarious time for the world, during the height of the Cold War, Maharishi felt this should be avoided at all cost. So a permanent group with a minimum of 1500 Yogic Flyers – enough to create a continuous effect for the US as a whole according to the square root of 1% formula– should be created as quickly as possible.

The most suitable location for this was also the most unlikely at first sight: a small farming town in the American Midwest – Fairfield, Iowa – where the Maharishi University of Management* was located. There was already a permanent group of 300 Yogic Flyers, composed of students and faculty from the university, and they had a lot of room for expansion. They had bought a campus from another university that had gone bankrupt and had room for more than 1500 people.

So Maharishi casually asked everyone: "hey, why don't you move to this small town in the middle of a lot of cornfields (which basically meant in the middle of nowhere) in Iowa, so that a permanent group of 1500 Yogic Flyers can be created".

That was a *big* request. To travel somewhere for a few weeks is one thing, but to move your entire household and family to a small, Midwestern town with only 10,000 population, with the nearest decent city 50 miles away? Where would people find jobs?

Nevertheless, more than 800 incredibly brave people took the plunge. Some came as students or as staff for the university, others relocated their businesses to Fairfield. Others still just came, not having a clue how they would support themselves.

They knew they were doing something extremely important for the whole world, but also for themselves. Yogic Flying in a big group was so enjoyable, and causes such a rapid growth towards higher states of consciousness for themselves that the idea of being able to do this every day was just too appealing.

Within two weeks more than 800 people from the Massachusetts course had moved to Fairfield, and the numbers jumped up from 300 to 1,100. A lot of those who couldn't relocate offered financial support to those who could.

The Maharishi University of Management board decided to build two massive meditation halls (they called them "the Golden Domes"), so people could meditate together.

---

* At the time it was called Maharishi International University.

Architects and builders estimated that it would take two years before such a project could be finished. Maharishi wanted it done in three months. They started on Oct 1, 1979 and finished in January of 1980. It was a beautiful example of the power of the TM-Sidhi program. A large group of Sidhas collectively desired something, and all circumstances simply fell into place for the desire to be fulfilled.

For the next 30 years, the hundreds of Yogic Flyers in these two domes would become the unsung heroes of the United States.

They changed the town of Fairfield, for sure. As we already mentioned, in the next few decades this small farming town would grow to become the most successful small business town in the entire United States, and home to the most successful school in the world*.

But the housewives, businessmen, workers, students, and artists who were gathering in the domes twice a day would also fundamentally change the USA as a whole...and eventually would play a major role in changing the destiny of the whole world, as we'll examine in the next few experiments.

But let's start with some changes in the US itself.

To measure the effect that the group in Fairfield had on the US, the researchers again looked at a wide number of variables that are influenced by social stress. Similar to the Rhode Island experiment they were compiled into a single US Quality of Life index, which was then calculated for a period from 1960 till 1983.

In this case, 12 variables were chosen, again with all data collected from publicly available publications from governmental institutions:

- *Crime and justice:* crime rate, percentage of civil cases reaching trial.

---

* As measured by the amount of local, national, and international competitions won per student capita.

- *Health:* infectious diseases rate, infant mortality rate, suicide rate.
- *Health habits:* cigarette and alcohol consumption per capita.
- *Economic welfare:* GNP per capita.
- *Creativity:* patent application rate.
- *Education:* degrees conferred per capita.
- *Marital stability:* divorce rate.
- *Safety:* traffic fatality rate.

In a way, this research is a collection of 12 individual experiments, and again it provides a control for itself. If this index went up it would mean that on average *all* 12 variables would improve, which could not be due to random behavior (different random fluctuations normally cancel each other out). It would also be very hard to come up with a plausible alternative hypothesis that could explain improvements in all these variables at the same time. The only explanation that makes sense is that the level of the collective consciousness – and as such in every US citizen's individual consciousness – would go up.

In essence, they were measuring whether the group in Fairfield could be strong enough to warm up the water in the entire pot of the USA, and all the 300 million individual glasses that are in it.

This is how the evolution of the index looks from 1960 (baseline) to 1983:

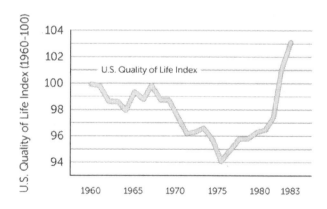

It shows a continuous downward trend that bottoms out in 1975. Then there is a reversal until 1980 and a strong increase from 1980 to 1983.

What caused this reversal and the big increase from 1980?

Here is the graph of the index again, but this time with another index plotted for the same period, the Maharishi Effect index: the predicted influence of the TM Field Effect based on the sum of the effect created by the number of people practicing TM individually *and* the effect created by the group practicing the TM-Sidhi program in Fairfield:

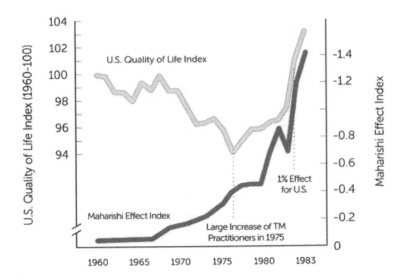

TM was first introduced in the US in 1959. By 1970, 200,000 people had learned, but during the 1970s, this number increased rapidly. In 1975 alone, almost a quarter of a million people learned TM. As such the 1% threshold was reached for several cities, causing a reversal in the index.

But the biggest boost to the Maharishi Effect index came from the group of Yogic Flyers in Fairfield. In 1982, the required number of Yogic Flyers to create the effect for the whole US was reached for 30% of the time, and in 1983 it was reached continuously.

The US Quality of Life index followed very closely. The chance that such a sudden rise in 1982 and 1983 could have been a coincidence was less than one in ten thousand (p<.0001).

So what does that mean in terms of the individual variables, especially in 1982 and 1983, where the biggest change took place? As with the earlier Rhode Island experiment the results were fascinating, to say the least. Almost all the variables showing improvements in this period, with 5 out of 12 variables even setting records:

1. <u>Crime:</u> In 1976 and 1977, after the large increase in TM meditators in 1975, crime rates fell for two consecutive years, which had *never happened before*. But then from 1981 to 1983, crime fell for *three* consecutive years (0.78% in '81, 4.3% in '82, and 7.6% in '83).
2. <u>Percentage of civil cases reaching trial:</u> This is a good measure of harmony in collective consciousness resulting in fewer conflicts. It dropped 7.6 % in '82 and another 11.5 % in '83, to reach an all-time low.
3. <u>Infectious disease rate:</u> Dropped 4.23% in '82 and 7.02 % in '83 (largest drop in 16 years).
4. <u>Infant mortality rate:</u> Continued its long-term decreasing trend (-1.08 % in '82 and -2.3% in '83).
5. <u>Suicide rate:</u> Increased 1.08% in '82 and 2.3% in '83, the only negative variable that increased in both years.
6. <u>Cigarette consumption:</u> Decreased 1.90% in '82 and 6.26% in '83 (largest decline in the 23 years under consideration).
7. <u>Alcohol consumption:</u> Decreased 3.52% in '82 and 2.64% in '83 (second and third largest decreases in 23 years).
8. <u>GNP per capita:</u> Decreased 2.81% in 1982, as part of a three-year-long recession (even though the second half of the year showed one of the strongest economic recoveries on record). Increased 2.25% in 1983.
9. <u>Patent application rate:</u> Increased 2.51% in 1982, but dropped 11.26% in 1983 as a result of an increase of the application fee. This was somewhat compensated in 1984 with an increase of 12% (largest increase in 23 years).
10. <u>Degrees conferred:</u> Rose slightly (0.31% and 0.98%) after declining for the previous five years.
11. <u>Divorce rate</u>: Decreased 4.46 % in 1982 (a decrease three times larger than the previous record set 21 years earlier) and again 0.18 % in 1983 (the only time divorce rate decreased in two consecutive years).
12. <u>Traffic fatality rate:</u> Decreased 10.95 % in 1982 (largest drop ever, apart from 1975, when the 55 mph speed limit went into effect) and again 4.60 % in 1983.

So here we have it again. Doesn't it blow your mind that a small group of around 1600 people practicing Yogic Flying together could cause such a dramatic change all over the US on so many variables at the same time?

Of course, the question remains whether the change in the Maharishi Effect index really *caused* the changes in the Quality of Life index.

To determine this, the researchers used the best-known statistical method to determine causality: cross-correlation analysis. The results (described in more detail in the paper itself) show that the changes in the Maharishi Effect (ME) index predicted the changes in Quality of Life (QL) index, while the reverse was never the case. The correlation between changes in the ME index and changes in the QL index was significant to the $p<.0001$ level.

So yes, the changes were indeed due to the Maharishi Effect. Another statistical analysis showed that in 1982 and 1983 the Maharishi Effect index accounted for 86% of the variance of the Quality of Life index.

Like with the Massachusetts experiment, if the changes were indeed due to the Maharishi Effect, then the changes should be greater in Iowa in comparison to the rest of the US for 1982 and 1983. The effect may spread over the entire US, but we'd still predict it would be the strongest near the source, just like light is brightest near the light bulb. This was the case for all of the variables that were investigated ($p=.0065$).

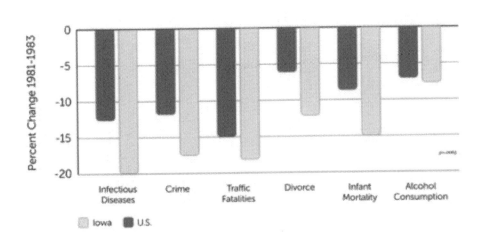

So the Maharishi Effect works, and it seems to be especially powerful on a large scale. For example, the changes in national crime rate in 1982 and 1983 resulted in 1,300,000 fewer crimes.

Can you even imagine that 1600 people, simply doing their TM meditation and Yogic Flying sessions for about one hour every morning and evening resulted in 1,300,000 fewer crimes over 1982 and 1983?

Maharishi was not interested in *fewer* crimes, however. He wanted to see *all* crime, and all negativity – of which crime is just a dramatic expression – eradicated. But for that he predicted we would need bigger groups.

In fact, the researchers were able to calculate that a group of 3000 Yogic Flyers would improve the quality of life by 13% every year. With 5,000 Yogic Flyers, an annual improvement of 36.4% would be expected, and with 7,000 Yogic Flyers, quality of life would improve by 71.6% every year.

We have seen that transcending has a wide range of benefits on the individual level, from less stress to spontaneously reduced smoking and alcoholism to more creativity. Now we see that all these benefits start to happen for the population as a whole. It's not even necessary for everyone to learn to transcend. Just a few hundred to a few thousand Yogic Flyers appears to be enough to create the effect for the whole nation.

...and we're just getting started.

Experiment 9: Increased Serotonin with Randomly Selected People During Yogic Flying

We have seen that the TM Field Effect was creating increased EEG coherence, not just with those practicing the Yogic Flying, but even with ordinary people 1200 miles away. As EEG coherence is related to a wide range of benefits, from improved moral reasoning to more creativity to faster reflexes, it offered one explanation how the TM Field effect can create changes in people's behavior.

In this study, researchers tested another hypothesis: that Yogic Flyers in the Fairfield domes would also influence serotonin levels in non-meditating Fairfield inhabitants. This would give another level of insight into how the Maharishi Effect works, as low serotonin levels correlate with negative emotional moods and even increased aggressiveness and violence.

The researchers found that when the numbers of Yogic Flyers flying in the Golden Domes were high, the serotonin levels measured in 40 locals in Fairfield were up to 400% higher than on the days of the lowest group attendance.

The study was published in the *Journal of Social Behavior and Personality*.

Increased happiness: my personal experience of being near groups of Yogic Flyers

To read about the power of Yogic Flying regarding increased serotonin or improved behavior is one thing, but to experience it for yourself is something else entirely.

The analogy of jumping in the lake and creating waves is a very real experience for me. Whenever I practice Yogic Flying and create this stir, I feel it very clearly as waves of light and bliss arising in my own awareness. It is such an enjoyable thing to do! After Yogic Flying I usually feel that my whole body is filled with light and feel full of energy and happiness.

But the most powerful experience for me was to experience that same stir in my own awareness when *others* were flying.

This experience was most obvious during the time when I was on the Purusha program: the program Maharishi had developed for those who wanted to be solely focused on the development of higher states of consciousness, living a monk's life in deep meditation.

Often I would do my TM meditation in my room but would go to the big meditation hall to do the Yogic Flying as part of the group.

Sometimes I'd lose track of time, however, and I was still meditating while the Yogic Flying started, say, at 6 p.m. Every single time this happened I'd suddenly notice waves of light and bliss becoming enlivened in my awareness during my meditation, and I already knew, "It's 6 p.m." All I had to do was open my eyes and look at the clock and, sure enough, 6 p.m. sharp. Basically, I could feel how the Yogic Flying at the other side of the building was creating a stir on the Field, and how this was influencing my own awareness.

For me, this experience of the TM field effect was more convincing than 100 scientific studies combined.

Experiment 10 (the most spectacular one to date): Quality Of Life Index Following Numbers of Yogic Flyers on a Daily Basis

Title: International peace project in the Middle East: the effects of the Maharishi technology of the Unified Field
Authors: David W. Orme-Johnson, Charles N. Alexander, John L. Davies, Howard M. Chandler, and Wallace E. Larimore
Reference: Journal of Conflict Resolution, vol. 32, no.4, Dec 1988, pp. 776-812.

On August 1, 1983, Yogic Flyers from around Israel were gathering in a hotel in Jerusalem to participate in what would become the most impressive experiment to date, although the reason why it became so impressive was, ironically enough, because it didn't go as planned.

The idea was simple: do another demonstration, with predictions in advance on how a small group of Yogic Flyers in Jerusalem can both change the quality of life in Israel as a whole *and* stop the war in neighbouring Lebanon.

To measure these changes the researchers again chose to investigate a number of variables on a daily basis from publicly available data for the city of Jerusalem, Israel as a whole, and Lebanon, and combine them together in a single index.

Jerusalem
    1. Crime: total crimes per day (Israeli Police Department).
    2. Auto accidents involving personal injury (Municipal Government of Jerusalem).
    3. Fires (Fire Extinguishing Service).

Israel
    4. Crime (Israeli Police Department).
    5. Stock market changes (Tel Aviv Stock Exchange).
    6. National mood (the affective tone of the most prominent story of the *Jerusalem Post**).

Lebanon
    7. War deaths (daily Israeli newspapers, *International Herald Tribune,* BBC World service reports).
    8. War intensity scale (a content analysis scaling of the intensity of the hostilities in Lebanon each day as reported in news stories in the *Jerusalem Post* †).

---

* Stories scored from 1 (very negative, unpleasant) to 7 (very positive, uplifting). Scoring was blind and used the average scores of two raters independent to the project.

† The 5-point scale ranged from 0 (no reported fighting) to 4 (full-scale land battles, etc.) Again the rating was blind with regard to dates and events and the analysis used the mean of three independent raters.

Similar to the Rhode Island experiment, a Quality of Life index was composed of the standard deviations for each of the eight variables. As with previous experiments, it would be expected that this index would swing very little (unless there was a single cause influencing all of them at the same time), as the random fluctuations from each of the variables would normally cancel each other out.

With the 40,000 individuals who learned TM in Israel already contributing to the Maharishi Effect, the researchers calculated only 122 Yogic Flyers were needed in one location to create an effect for Israel as a whole, and that 197 Yogic Flyers were needed for Israel and Lebanon combined.

With all the variables fixed the experiment should be simple: come with 200 people, stay for two months (August and September 1983), and see if the individual variables and the composite index improve with any statistical significance. Then leave and see if the situation deteriorates again. A simple before-during-after experiment, that was the plan.

Things didn't go as planned, however. The researchers had to rely on volunteers for the experiment but that made it hard to keep the group at a stable size. Students in the group had to go back to school, others had return to work, others still could only come for the weekend, etc. In the end, the size of the group had a huge variation over the two months, ranging from 65 to 241. When plotted day by day over the course of two months, the numbers looked like this:

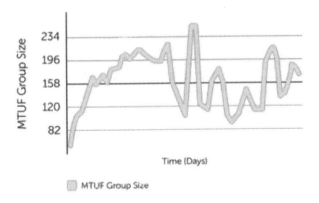

These wide fluctuations made the research far more impressive than originally planned, however. Rather than just having one single before-during-after experiment, the researchers could instead plot the changes in the Quality of Life index *on a daily basis*. If there was a correlation with the size of the group of Yogic Flyers, that would make the results far more impressive.

And there definitely was a clear correlation. Here are three graphs of how the stock market, the Israeli national mood, and the Lebanon indexes clearly fluctuate with the group size.

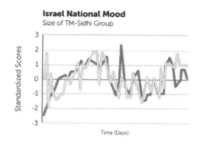

These graphs showed that the general trend was definitely following the numbers of Yogic Flyers, but imprecisely due to the inherent random fluctuations of each of the variables (the stock market, for example, will be influenced by several factors). Theoretically, if we add up all the variables together in one index, the individual random fluctuations should be filtered out. In that case the influence of the group of Yogic Flyers, if any, should show much more clearly.

And that's *exactly* what happened.

Dr. Howard Chandler, one of the researchers, described how personal computers were just becoming available when this study was being conducted. Their computer didn't even have a graphics card yet, and the monitors could only display numbers, not the graph. The only way they could see the actual graph was by printing it, with an old matrix line-by-line printer that took a few minutes per page.

Chandler described how the researchers' mouths dropped open as the graph slowly appeared from the printer. They could not believe what they saw.

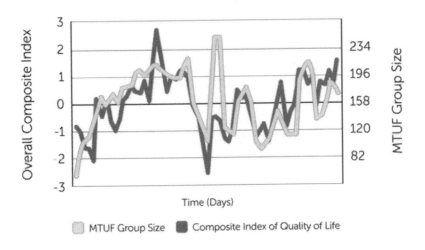

Dr. Orme-Johnson also recalls his feelings when he first saw this graph:

> *At first I felt like jumping and laughing with joy. The effect was so much stronger than I ever had hoped. What we were seeing was the otherwise invisible collective consciousness of society made visible – and moving society to a new and better destiny. But a few minutes later I just wanted to sit down and weep. We had demonstrated the existence of a technology to create world peace – and nobody knew about it*[28].

The fact that this index swings at all, sometimes as much as three standard deviations, was a miracle in itself. *All eight variables under consideration would have to change in a positive or negative direction at the same time*, and significantly more than their usual random fluctuations. The fact that they followed the size of the group so closely made it all the more impressive. As you'd expect the chance that this could be a coincidence was almost nonexistent (p<.0001, 500 times better than the norm in science).

This wasn't just another experiment where they turned on a light in people's minds and saw what happened when they were no longer in darkness. Instead, it was as if somebody was using a dimmer, gradually turning the light up and down, and then looking if things got darker or more light in people's minds. That's what made it so impressive.

> Before the experiment, an average of 24.5 people died in the Lebanon War every day. During the last two weeks of August, when attendance was at its peak and the numbers were high enough to theoretically influence Lebanon, only 1.5 people died on average per day, a 94% drop.

This meant that during those two weeks the 200 Yogic Flyers in Jerusalem saved more than 300 lives.

With such a dramatic result Drs. Alexander and Orme-Johnson felt they should aim high. They tried to get their study published in the top journal in the field of peace studies in the world, the *Journal of Conflict Resolution*, edited at Yale University. The struggle to get it published is an epic story on its own – a story of old paradigms being confronted with new facts.

The study was so unorthodox that the editor decided to send it out to four referees instead of the usual two.

- One referee replied that the study was *"logically and methodologically coherent"* but advised against its publication anyway, since the idea seemed absurd.
- The second referee said that the paper had a great deal of merit and was done in a professional fashion even though it was outside currently accepted scientific knowledge.
- A third referee said that he would only advise publication if it was done by an independent body, such as the National Academy of Sciences.
- The fourth referee said that before he'd advise in favor of publication, he first wanted to see a statistical analysis to determine whether the change in Yogic Flyer numbers was really the cause of the changes.

Dr. Russett – the journal's editor – was faced with different recommendations. He didn't feel it was correct to simply reject the study only because it didn't fit the current paradigm. He also didn't agree that such a study would only be valid if it were done by an independent agency. After all, only the people who believed in the central hypothesis would ever go through the trouble of organizing such a study, and somebody has to do the first studies before an independent body will want to replicate them. He felt the fact that the study was done by those who were connected to the TM movement didn't diminish its impressive results, especially since the numbers all came from objective sources.

In the end, Russett decided to follow the advice of the last referee, Dr. Duval – professor of political science at West Virginia University – who wanted to see a stringent statistical procedure performed to make sure the change in numbers in Yogic Flyers really preceded the change in other variables. Maybe the news of decreased deaths in Lebanon had caused several Yogic Flyers to come to the group so that it appeared as if the Yogic Flyers caused it but, in reality, it was the other way around.

Orme-Johnson and Alexander spent more than two months conducting the requested analysis. The results showed that the increase in Yogic Flyers always came first and the changes in the index followed, never the other way around. They often happened at the same time.

In the end, Duval recommended in favor of publication and Russett decided to publish. He did include an 'editor's comment':

> *The following article presents and tests a hypothesis that will strike most readers (myself included) as, to say the least, unorthodox...Yet the hypothesis seems logically derived from the initial premises, and its empirical testing seems competently executed. These are the standards to which manuscripts submitted for publication in this journal are normally submitted.*

Duval also offered to write a commentary, which was also published with the research:

> *The fundamental assumptions of a 'Unified Field' and a 'collective consciousness' are not within the paradigm under which most of us operate. Yet if one will, for the sake of argument, accept these premises as plausible, then the research conforms quite well to scientific standards.*

The Maharishi Effect researchers had landed their most impressive publication to date, even if it took them three years before the research was published.*

---

* This was probably the moment when many in the scientific world turned from ignoring and ridiculing to openly attacking. It was not possible to simply ignore such a high profile publication anymore, so several other scientists went into attack mode, claiming that the effects were due to the choice of statistics, or due to national holidays or whatever other thing they could come up with. The communication between the Maharishi Effect researchers and the critics went on for several more years, and was all published in the *Journal of Conflict Resolution* as well. Each time the critics thought they had found an alternative way to explain the effects, the Maharishi Effect researchers were able to discredit the alternative explanation. Ultimately, this only made the Jerusalem study a lot stronger.

Experiment 11: The Global Demonstration of 7000 TM-Sidhi Practitioners Creating a Measurable Effect for the Whole World

Title: The influence of the Maharishi technology of the Unified Field on world events and global social indicators: the effects of the taste of utopia assembly
Authors: David W. Orme-Johnson, Kenneth L. Cavanaugh, Charles N.. Alexander, Paul Gelderloos, Michael C. Dillbeck, Audri G. Lanford, and Tanios M. Abou Nader
Reference: Collected Papers on the Transcendental Meditation technique, vol. 4, no.337, pp 2730-2762.

After the spectacular success of the Jerusalem study, Maharishi announced that he wanted to do a global demonstration of the Maharishi Effect. He called it the "Taste of Utopia" course – something that sounded way too good to be true...and now the world was going to get a taste of it.

According to the square root of 1% formula this course would require about 7000 Yogic Flyers to come together in one place. (The world population in 1983 was 4.8 billion, of which 1% is 48 million, of which the square root is 6928.)

Coordinating 7000 Yogic Flyers from all over the world together in one location would be challenging enough, but Maharishi added another little challenge: *he wanted the whole thing organized in three weeks.*

How on Earth do you organize for 7000 Yogic Flyers to come together with three weeks' notice? Nobody understood why there was such a hurry, but people had learned that when Maharishi wanted something done with such great urgency, there was usually a good reason for it.

It was decided to hold the course in Fairfield, Iowa, as the town already had 1600 Yogic Flyers gathered together, so *only* 5400 more were needed. Enough Yogic Flyers had been trained to reach this goal, but they would have to come from all around the world. Then there were the logistical issues: where to house them? A town with a population of only 10,000 didn't have the capacity for 5,500 more on a moment's notice.

The university campus had 1,700 rooms. Even if three people stayed in one room, they could only house 5,000 people. The solution? Buy 200 mobile homes large enough to house six people each, have them shipped across two states, and install the water, electricity, and plumbing... all in three weeks. As by some miracle, they did it.

The next question was where they could do their Yogic Flying? The two meditation domes already had a capacity for 3,000 people, but they needed a place for 4,000 more. They calculated that an additional 60,000 square feet of building space was needed.

The previous industry record for a hall of that size this was three months – and that record was probably not set during a cold, snowy Iowa winter – now they had to build one in three weeks? The manager of a company known for fast construction of halls decided he liked a good challenge (and felt competitive, as the previous record was set by their main competitor) so he decided to go for it. He did it in a little over three weeks.

Meanwhile, the student kitchen prepared to cater food for 7,000 people – six times more than usual – and the purchasing department ordered a couple thousand mattresses.

While the Maharishi University campus organizers were tripping over themselves to get everything organized, a team of researchers was selected that included all the most experienced Maharishi Effect researchers to date. They were David Orme-Johnson, Kenneth Cavanaugh, Charles Alexander, Paul Gelderloos, Michael Dillbeck, Audri Lanford, and Tony Nader. They worked day and night to determine the proper scientific variables. They lodged their predictions in advance, both with a body of independent scientists across the US and with the press, giving one press conference after another announcing their intention to give the world their "Taste of Utopia". They announced the course to 105 leading newspapers and magazines in 30 countries around the world.

> Maharishi's predictions about what would happen during the assembly were simple:
>
> *"Anything that is good will rise. Anything that is not good will vanish, as darkness disappears with the first ray of light."*

The researchers' jobs were to find ways to formulate this in objectively measurable changes. The experiment would take place from Dec 17, 1983 to Jan 6, 1984. During that time, the variables for which they predicted a significant positive change were:

1. Increased progress by heads of state in solving problems.
2. Increased calming influence in the world's trouble spots.
3. Increased progress towards a peaceful resolution of the Lebanese conflict.

4. Significant rise in the World Index (an international stock index representing 19 countries), and a simultaneous rise in stock indices in all countries.
5. Decreased highway traffic fatalities worldwide.
6. Decreased air traffic fatalities worldwide.
7. Increased patent applications worldwide (as a measure of increased creativity).
8. Decreased indices of infectious diseases worldwide.

As with previous studies, this study was actually a collection of eight separate experiments.

Around mid December, The Yogic Flyers started arriving from around the world; 100 from Germany, 200 from Japan, 150 from Australia, etc. The numbers grew from the regular 1600 to over 4000. More and more continued to join and by December 28th the goal of 6900 was reached. When this was announced, people in the grand assembly hall stood and cheered for five minutes. Over the next few days, even more arrived, peaking at almost 8000.

Creating a wave that was strong enough to influence the whole world just sounded like too much fun. Everybody wanted to be there for the party, even if that meant traveling halfway across the world.

Here's a picture of all the 8,000 Yogic Flyers in front of the meditation dome:

And here is a graph of the numbers in the three weeks before, during, and after the assembly:

As the graph shows, the threshold to create an influence for the entire world was only reached for about half of the experimental time. This was unfortunate. The predictions were made for the entire three-week period, so this was what the researchers had to stick to. It meant that whatever results they would find would be an underestimation of the real global effect.

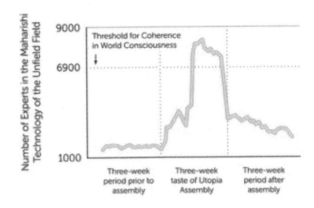

But even then the results spoke for themselves.

The first variables the researchers kept an eye on were the stock markets. The earlier Jerusalem experiment had already shown this appears to be an objective measure of the collective mood. The effect of Yogic Flyers on the stock market seemed to be instant, so this was the quickest way to measure the effect for the whole world, as the numbers were available in real time.

The world index is a weighted average of the world's 19 most important stock markets published every day by the *Wall Street Journal*. The numbers were projected on big screens for all the participants every day, and they followed the figures as though they were following scores of a football game. Based on previous experiments everybody expected a positive change to take place, but nobody expected what would happen over the course of the next three weeks.

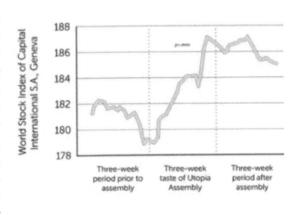

Out of the 19 markets that were considered, 18 increased simultaneously. Of the 11 largest markets around the world, eight all-time records. Japan set seven new records in a row during the three weeks of the course, West Germany broke a 23-year-old record, while the Netherlands, Great Britain,

228

France, Switzerland, Australia, and Singapore all set new records. The US Dow Jones came within one point of its all-time record.

This was all the more remarkable because before the course the entire world was engulfed in a deep economic recession.

The Times in London reported:

"*Everything suddenly seemed to come together...It was as though investors everywhere had made a new year's resolution that the recession was over.*"

The *London Sunday Times* agreed: "*The world's stock markets are buoyant and governments are once again talking about economic growth... After four years of gloomy prognostications, there is, at last, something to cheer about.*"

As soon as the course was over, the cheering stopped. The Dow Jones plummeted again to its old levels and world index started falling again. The individual markets went back to their seemingly random patterns, with some increasing and some decreasing. Nobody could find any alternate explanation for the positive change during the assembly, or why it suddenly stopped once the assembly was over. The chance that 18 markets going up at the same time continuously over a three-week period could be a coincidence was one in 25,000 (p=.00004).

The other variables under consideration changed almost as dramatically.

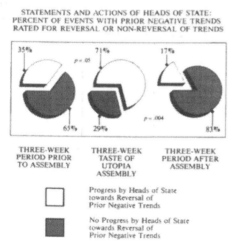

Media analysis revealed that wherever there were negative trend in relations between countries, those relations became much more constructive during the three weeks (from 35% of all statements and actions positive before the assembly to 71% during the assembly, p=.05). The positive mood ended immediately after the course ended, going down to 17% positive statements (p=.004).

A similar trend was visible in the international conflicts at the time. The sum of positive and strongly positive events increased from 19.8% before the course to 36% during the course (p=.015) and decreased to 14.6% after the course was over (p=.001).

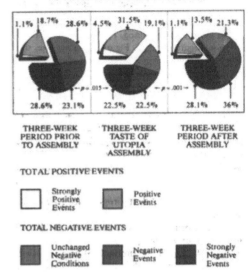

In Lebanon, the region where societal stress was probably still the highest in the world, the results were even more impressive, from 9.6% positive events before to 57.1% during the three weeks, (p=.001) to 9.5% after the Taste of Utopia assembly (p=.001). The chance that both changes occurred by coincidence was one in 5000 (p=.0002).

During the assembly, rival fractions came closer to a peace agreement than ever before, but the day the assembly ended everything collapsed.

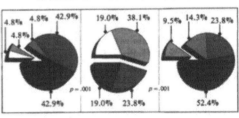

This data showed something very interesting for which Maharishi had already warned in the past. When darkness has taken over human minds, they are capable of some pretty inhumane behavior, but as soon as we turn on the light, this behavior largely stops. However, if we then turn it off again, the darkness feels even darker. The negative events, even though significantly less during the assembly, actually appeared to increase immediately after the assembly compared to before. It's kind of like pressing a spring and then releasing it.

This was the reason why Maharishi eventually stopped giving demonstrations of the TM Field Effect once there was enough scientific evidence. Eventually his only focus was on creating permanent groups of Yogic Flyers.

The other variables under consideration also improved exactly as predicted, and they were no less impressive. In general, we see a stronger effect in the US than in the rest of the world, confirming the radiation effect. An effect is always strongest near its source.

Variable	US change	International change	P value
Traffic accidents	-31.5%	-10% to -20%	p<.0001
Air traffic fatalities	only international data	-49%	p<.0001
Patent applications	+15.3%	+6% to +33%	p<.0001
Infectious diseases	-32%	-17%	p<.0001
Crime	-4%	-13%	p<.000002

This meant each of the eight experiments was successful, and each had a chance of coincidence that, on average, was smaller than about one in ten thousand. (p<.0001). The chance that this could have happened by coincidence eight times was...well, really small.

A few remarks about these numbers:

- As with the stock market and the increased positivity in international relations, most of the other variables returned to their previous levels immediately after the assembly was done.
- Crime data was the only variable where the change in the US was less than in the rest of the world, but that discrepancy was mostly due to the selection of the city. For the US, Washington, DC was measured, but this city had its own permanent group of 300-400

Yogic Flyers before the Taste of Utopia course started. Most of the flyers from the DC group left to go to Fairfield during the global demonstration. So while the global influence was created, the local influence stopped. As such it's expected that the improvement would be smaller than in other cities.
- Seasonal effects have been investigated as a possible cause for all the variables under consideration. Maybe heads of state were getting friendlier during Christmas and New Year. Data analysis from previous years did not show any trend in this direction. Seasonal effects, weather patterns, and other factors were excluded as possible causes by the statistical evaluations of the research.

So the world had had its Taste of Utopia, a taste of what Maharishi's technologies could accomplish on a global scale. To make sure that the world would notice what had caused the changes, Maharishi took out full-page advertisements in all of the leading newspapers around the world to explain his technology and invite governments to create a permanent group of Yogic Flyers.

In spite of the impressive research, it would take another 10 years before governments would take up his invitation.

So why the hurry? A fascinating background story

As exciting as the Taste of Utopia experiment was, the background story about why Maharishi wanted it to happen so quickly is even more interesting.

In the months before the experiment tensions between the US and the USSR were running dangerously high. On Sept 1, 1983, Soviet fighter planes had shot down a South Korean Boeing plane with 269 passengers, including a US congressman, which had strayed into Soviet airspace. A month later, on Oct 23, the US Embassy in Lebanon was bombed. Two hundred and forty two US servicemen and 62 French soldiers were killed. The US blamed Syria and the USSR. On Oct 25, US troops invaded Grenada to oust Cuban soldiers, trained and equipped by the USSR.

Everyone knew tensions were high but few knew the situation was far more dangerous than anyone could have imagined. This was only revealed 14 years later, in 1997 when secret KGB files were found in the East German military archives. These files confirmed an earlier story from Oleg Gordievsky, a senior Soviet intelligence officer who fled the USSR, bringing information about top secret KGB files to the West.

Time magazine wrote a major story based on Gordievsky's book on Oct 22, 1990, which revealed that during the time of the Taste of Utopia experiment the world was on the edge of nuclear annihilation, without anyone even being aware of it.

President Reagan had spoken publicly about fighting and winning a nuclear exchange, which fueled fears in the USSR that the US was actually planning such an attack. In 1981, KGB chairman Yuri Andropov held a secret meeting where he convinced the Russian government that the Americans were actively preparing for nuclear war. He put his intelligence officers on the highest state of alertness and launched the largest peacetime intelligence operation in Soviet history, code-named RYAN (*Raketno-Yadernoye Napadenie*, or *nuclear missile attack*). The US had begun their "Star Wars" program and deployed cruise missiles in Europe, which the Russians interpreted as a sign of aggression, fueling fears even more. Then the Soviets accidentally shot down the South Korean airliner, believing it was a spy plane. The Russians were so certain that the US would retaliate that they decided they should be first; they would strike before the Americans had the chance.

The Russians started creating scenarios of how the Americans might attack, and concluded it was most likely the US would disguise an attack as a military exercise. This way the Americans could prepare everything without raising suspicion, and then launch the missiles when the enemy was unprepared. The Russians reasoned that's what *they* would do if they were to launch an attack.

Then, in a weird twist of fate, NATO actually began a military exercise, code named Able-Archer 83, designed to practice nuclear-release procedures. The Russians were almost certain the time had come. *The Sunday Times* reported:

> The East German papers reveal how in November 1983... the Soviet military was planning a possible strike. Barely 800 miles from London, aircraft capable of delivering nuclear strikes were placed on standby at East German air bases.

Then, on Nov 9, telegrams were sent to the KGB that US bases had been put on alert, implying that the countdown to a nuclear first strike had already begun. The Russians had thousands of intelligence officers working day and night. They were observing every move by the West, looking for any confirmation for the nuclear war they were sure was imminent.

The Russians practically had their fingers on the nuclear launch button. If it was going to happen, they were going to be the first to launch. The US was unaware of this dangerous paranoia on the Soviets' side. But the situation was so explosive that any small action the Americans did, if understood the wrong way, could have caused nuclear annihilation for the whole world.

It will always remain a mystery whether Maharishi intuitively knew something that even the US and British intelligence officers didn't know. Was this why he felt such an urgency to create the effect for the whole world immediately, making everybody do the impossible to organize an assembly of 7000 people in a matter of a few weeks?

Whatever the reason, tensions between the US and Russia did decrease dramatically during the three weeks of the Taste of Utopia assembly.

On Jan 2, President Reagan declared a *"cease-fire in the war of words"* with the USSR and softened his approach and outlook. On Jan 4, London's *Financial Times* reported *"The new year is coming with signals from both East and West suggesting that the chill... between the two power blocs may be moderating."*

Top level communication started again, and Moscow began to understand that maybe, just maybe, the US didn't have the intention to bomb them to oblivion anyway. Operation RYAN began to wind down and, in the spring of 1984, Margaret Thatcher convinced President Reagan to begin talks on arms reduction.

> So here we have it, the most impressive demonstration of the Maharishi Effect to date. For the first time it was demonstrated that it's possible to create the effect on a global scale. And, coincidence or not, it now seems all this happened at a time when the world may have needed it more than at any other point in the history of mankind.

Experiment 12: An Approach to Reduce Terrorism that Works

Title: Time series impact assessment analysis of reduced international conflict and terrorism: effects of large assemblies of participants in the Transcendental Meditation and TM-Sidhi program.
Authors: David W. Orme-Johnson, Michael C. Dillbeck, Charles, N. Alexander, Howard M. Chandler, and Robert W. Cranson
Reference: Journal of Offender Rehabilitation 36: 283–302, 2003.

After the Taste of Utopia assembly, Maharishi organized three more large assemblies to continue to calm international tensions. These next gatherings were meant more to simply create the effect than for thorough scientific demonstrations, as there were only so many studies the five or six researchers that were always involved could take on. Nevertheless, the researchers still decided to use the opportunity to study one more variable that they hadn't researched yet: the effect of a worldwide Maharishi Effect demonstration on terrorism.

To have enough data points to reach a statistically significant conclusion, the scientists did their study across the four major world assemblies that had been organized (the Taste of Utopia assembly and three new ones).

Location	Date	Number of participants
Fairfield, Iowa (Taste of Utopia)	Dec 17, 1983 to Jan 6 1984	6,900
Fairfield, Iowa	July 1-13, 1984	5,100
The Hague, Netherlands	December, 28 1984 – January 6, 1985	6,100
Washington, DC	July 8-17, 1985	5,500

Even though three out of four assemblies didn't have the required number to influence the whole world, the researchers still hoped the effect would be strong enough to create a significant change in the number of terrorist events.

It certainly looked like that.

With normal seasonal changes controlled for, the researchers found that on average terrorism casualties and injuries decreased by 72% ($p<.025$) during the four assemblies.

Of course 72% is not 100%, so could this technology be used to make us all 100% safe from terrorism?

The indications certainly look good. These decreases came from assemblies that only lasted 2-3 weeks, while the positive effects usually accumulate over time. Moreover, three out of the four assemblies didn't even reach the required number to influence the whole world. This should give us a renewed hope there is finally a practical solution for the biggest threat to our national security today. With larger groups coming together for a longer time, much larger decreases should be possible.

The reason why terrorism is so terrifying is simple: as long as there is *a single person* with a desire to kill, *nobody on the planet is safe*. All it takes is a

235

suitcase and an internet connection to find the recipe to make a bomb, or access to a machine gun, or even just the ability to rent a truck and drive through a busy street.

Keeping an eye on every single person 24/7 would require three or four full time jobs for every single person in this world. We know that this is impossible...and that is what makes it so terrifying.

But what if there is another way? What if we could create an influence from a single source that is guaranteed to reach every single person on the planet, and where we would enliven the source of humanity in their consciousness (love, connectedness, etc.) to the point where the thought of behaving inhumanely to each other simply wouldn't even come up anymore?

What if all we had to do was maintain one big fire that is warm enough to warm up the entire global collective consciousness pot, which would be guaranteed to influence the warmth of every single glass in it?

Would this change our world?

You bet...overnight.

Maharishi always said that to guarantee the effect 24/7 we should have not just one group that is big enough to influence the whole world, but ideally one on every continent. This way the effect can be created around the clock: when Yogic Flyers in the East go to sleep, those in the West wake up.

This time it's personal

For someone who used to live close to Brussels, the terrorist attack on our airport in March 2016 was a big shock for me. The Belgian authorities *knew* that an attack on our airport was planned. When I was flying in and out of the airport during the weeks before the attack in 2016, I was impressed by how many soldiers with heavy machine guns were guarding the airport – and still, they were powerless to prevent what was coming. Terrorists can easily achieve their objective of creating constant fear because they know that nobody can stop them.

After 15 years of writing and rewriting this book, the attack on the Brussels airport was a strong reminder to finally finish it as quickly as possible. If there is a proven solution, it's time for this nonsense to end. Our government spent a fortune of our tax money trying to fight the darkness, while it's not only much more effective, but also 1000 times cheaper (we'll come to that) to turn on the light.

Have you shared the link to download this book (www.fieldparadigm.com) and sent it your government leaders yet?

Experiment 13: Winning the Lottery

Title: Alleviating political violence through enhancing coherence in collective consciousness: impact assessment analysis of the Lebanon War
Author: John L. Davies and Charles N. Alexander
Reference: Journal of Social Behavior and Personality 17(1): 285–338, 2005.

As we have already seen, in human sciences it's never possible to say with 100% certainty that a particular cause creates a particular effect. However, it *is* possible to come really, really, *really* close.

We've seen that, the larger the effect size and the more consistent it is successful over a larger number of data points, the smaller the chance is that the effect could be due to coincidence.

Each of the individual Maharishi Effect experiments shows such extraordinary effects that even with one single study, the probability is often smaller than one in 10,000, ($p<.0001$), which is already 500 times better than the accepted norm in the social sciences ($p<.05$).

But what would the chance of coincidence be that these experiments could be successfully repeated multiple times?

That's what Charles Alexander and John Davies decided to put to the test, by going back to Lebanon once more. Unfortunate as it was, the continuous warfare that had been raging for many years made Lebanon an ideal location for such repeated experiments.

Other than the Jerusalem experiment and the four big global assemblies, there were two more assemblies that were large enough to theoretically influence the Lebanon War, one assembly in Lebanon itself and one in Yugoslavia. In most of the cases the effects on the Lebanon War were predicted beforehand.

The seven assemblies that were predicted to have an effect on Lebanon were:

Location	Dates	Number of Yogic Flyers
Jerusalem, Israel	Aug 1 – Sep 30, 1983	200
Fairfield, Iowa (Taste of Utopia)	Dec 17, 1983 to Jan 6 1984	6,900
Beirut, Lebanon	March 1-17, 1984	70
Yugoslavia	April 16-23, 1984	2,000
Fairfield, Iowa	July 1-13, 1984	5,100
The Hague, Netherlands	Dec 28, 1984 – Jan 6, 1985	6,100
Washington, DC	July 8-17, 1985	5,500

A first study was done from Nov, 1983 till May, 1984, during which three assemblies took place: Taste of Utopia, Beirut, and Yugoslavia. As usual, the researchers used newspaper content analysis from some of the world's top newspapers to get an objective source for the state of affairs in Lebanon. A daily index was plotted on a graph. When the line goes up it indicates more peace, when it goes down it means more war. When you look at the chart, try to make your best guess when the assemblies took place (where the line was going up for a longer time):

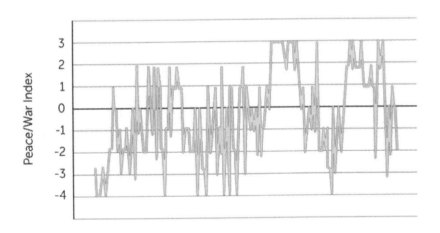

Here's the same chart with dates and indications when the assemblies were organized. Let's see if you guessed correctly.

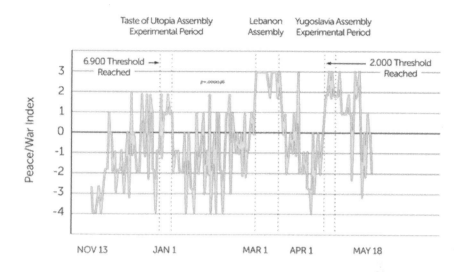

Pretty impressive, isn't it? The correlation is imperfect – the positive events outlasted the Yugoslavia assembly, for example – but I'm sure people in Lebanon didn't mind that somehow the mood stayed positive a bit longer.

In spite of its imperfection, the correlation between the group of TM-Sidhi practitioners and the peace/war index was still significant to the p=.000046 level, meaning that only once in roughly 50,000 would such a result occur by chance. The Lebanon assembly itself was perhaps the most impressive one, especially since there were only 70 participants in the assembly. The probability at this single assembly by itself was already one in 30,000 (p=.000036)[29].

Later on this research was expanded into a much larger study. Researchers took daily data of the peace/war index over a period of *2.5 years* and compared the periods during which the seven assemblies were going on (a total of 93 days) to all the other days during the 2.5 year period when no influence of coherence was generated*(close to 700 days). The results were spectacular.

---

* To conduct their study as thoroughly as possible the researchers contacted the leading institute on peace studies in the US, the Center for International Development and Conflict Management at the University of Maryland, and asked for their recommendations. The recommendation was to have a person with no knowledge of the experiment analyze daily data over the 2.5 year period about Lebanon from 10 different media sources and make an average point for that day in terms of a war and peace index.

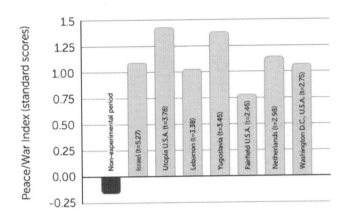

During the control period the index was negative, indicating Lebanon was at war, but during all seven assemblies it shot up in the positive direction, meaning the war had mostly stopped and peace efforts started taking place.

What was the chance of this happening by coincidence *seven times in a row*? A statistical time series analysis will start to work with as few as 40 data points. For this study the researchers had more than 800 data points for the 2.5 year period. If the effects were big and they were consistent over such a large amount of data points, then this was going to yield some truly impressive results.

And impressive they were.

It was found that during the 93 days of the assembly there was an average:

1. 66% mean increase in the level of cooperation among conflicting parties (p=.0000004)
2. 48% reduction in level of conflict (p=.000000003)
3. 68% reduction in war injuries (p=.0000005)
4. 71% reduction in war fatalities (p=.0000000001)

And what is the overall chance that all these positive changes were happening at the same time? Brace yourself for a lot of zeros...
p=.00000000000000000009, the chance was smaller than one in *ten million trillion*.

So what does this number mean? Let's put it in perspective.

The chance of winning a national lottery this week typically ranges from about one in 5 mil-

240

lion for a small country like Belgium to almost one in 300 million for the US Powerball lottery.

> In other words, **the chance you'll win the lottery this week is anywhere between 30 billion and two trillion times higher** than the chance that the Maharishi Effect could be due to coincidence.

If I were you, I'd go buy that lottery ticket *right now...*your chances *never* looked so good.

As far as I know, there is no other study *in the entire history of social sciences* that can demonstrate a correlation between cause and effect with this kind of statistical certainty. Basically, this is as statistically certain as it gets.

The study resulted in another major publication for the TM researchers in the *Journal of Social Behavior and Personality*. The people at Maryland University who were consulted for the study design were so impressed with the study that they offered one of the researchers, John Davies, a job at their prestigious center for peace studies.

Experiment 14: What our governments really should be doing

This is a combination of several publications
Authors: Michael C. Dillbeck, Kenneth L. Cavanaugh, and Paul Gelderloos
References: Social Indicators Research, 1990, no. 22, pp. 399-418 (crime), *Proceedings of the American Statistical Association, Business and Economics Statistics Section*, 1988, pp. 491-496 *Proceedings of the Midwest Management Society*, 1989, pp 183-190 (economy), *Social Science Perspectives Journal 2(4), 127–146,* Proceedings of the American Statistical Association, Social Statistics Section, 1990, pp. 297–302. *(International relationships)*

> What if it turns out that the size of the group of Yogic Flyers had more influence on how a country was doing than anything the government decided to do?
>
> What if it turns out that government decisions themselves appeared to be influenced by the size of the group of Yogic Flyers.

There are a few things we'd expect our governments to do for us, in return for all those taxes we're paying them:

1. Keep our country safe from invaders (military) and manage international relationships (diplomats)

2. Manage the economy (make sure everybody can earn enough)
3. Keep our streets safe (police)
4. Make sure everybody has sufficient access to healthcare
5. Provide education

In order to achieve these goals, governments continuously try new technologies and programs, some with more success than others. But what if there was solid scientific proof that there's *one* program that is far more successful than anything else, because it takes care of most of the above goals at the same time at a far lower cost?

Since the end of the 1970s, the numbers of Yogic Flyers in the meditation domes in Fairfield were recorded on a daily basis*, going up and down for a period of more than 10 years. That's a massive amount of data points for the researchers to have fun with... and it seems like they were having a lot of fun.

They demonstrated that there was a close correlation between the daily fluctuations in the number of Yogic Flyers and:

1. crime rate and car accidents
2. the economy, and
3. relations between the US and other countries.

One more time, brace yourself for some pretty impressive numbers...and a lot of zeros.

1. Keeping our streets safe: Crime rate and car accidents

Dr. Michael Dillbeck took weekly Yogic flyer attendances in Fairfield for a period of six years, from 1979 to 1985, and found a strong correlation with weekly fluctuations of the three strongest indicators of social disorder: deaths through homicides, suicides, and traffic accidents. *Each* of the three correlations were significant to the $p<.0001$ level, a far better result than most social studies with other programs can show.

The study showed that just from these three variables the 1500 Yogic Flyers in the meditation domes in Fairfield Iowa *saved on average 5,528 lives per year*. The statistics showed that each additional Yogic Flyer saved 3.6 additional lives every year. The study was so impressive that it got accepted for publication in one of the most prestigious social science journals in the world, *Social Indicators Research*.

---

* The meditation halls had doormen counting and logging the number of people going in.

2. Making sure people can earn enough: Economy

Dr. Kenneth Cavanaugh also had some fun with the numbers. Rather than measuring the state of the collective consciousness in terms of violent deaths, he started looking at it in terms of economic variables. Specifically he mapped the Yogic Flyer numbers against the US *Misery Index*, a well-known social indicator that takes both unemployment and inflation into account. If the index is high, the situation is...well...bad, indicating low employment and high inflation. It means that a lot of people are not making money and that the value of whatever money is being made is decreasing rapidly.

If we look at an annual overview of the Misery Index we see a similar trend to the earlier US quality of life chart. We see a first decrease in 1975, when a large number of people learned TM. Next, there is a much stronger continuous decrease (the longest continuous decrease since recording of misery index numbers began) from 1980 till 1988, a period when the Maharishi Effect was continuously created from Fairfield.

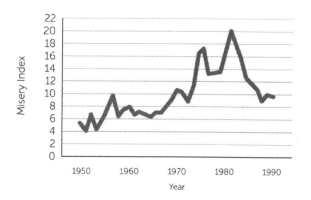

When monthly data of Yogic Flyers were mapped against monthly data of the misery index over a 10-year period, from 1979 till 1988, the results were even more impressive. The results were so obvious that no statistical analysis was even needed to see the correlation. You could simply visually see the trends on a chart. As the size of the group of Yogic Flyers increased, the Misery Index decreased.

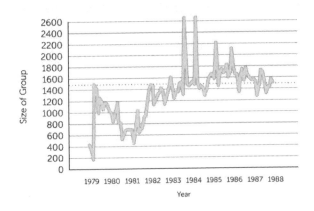

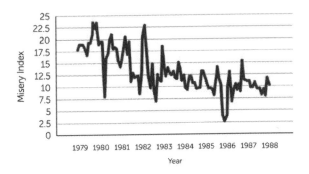

The researchers did their statistical analysis and found that the chance that the correlation between the group size and the misery index could be due to coincidence was a staggering 1.6 in one trillion, p=.0000000000016.

The Yogic Flyers appeared to be having a bigger influence on the US economy than anything other program the government was implementing.

One interesting note was that when the group size was above 1700 and was theoretically big enough to also influence Canada, the economy improved in Canada as well (p=.0000043). (Another research had also found that crime and traffic accidents also decreased in Canada every time the group was big enough to include Canada in its radius of influence.)

The papers impressed a lot of statisticians and the authors were invited to present them at the Annual Meeting of the American Statistical Association in three subsequent years, while the papers themselves were published in their proceedings.

3. Keeping our borders safe: International relationships

As incredible as those studies were, the most impressive, and probably most controversial study showed that the number of Yogic Flyers in Fairfield were also closely correlated to how the US was managing its international relationships, specifically with Russia, as this was the time at the height of the Cold War.

> This research essentially demonstrated the unthinkable: according to the data, a group of people hopping around on foams in the middle of a bunch of cornfields in Midwest America *played a more important role in eventually ending the global Cold War* than anything else.

The media gave most of the credit for ending the cold war to Russian President Gorbachev, for which *Time Magazine* even named him "man of the decade". A more scientific picture, however, reveals another reality.

When timings of statements of both US sides and Russian sides were put side by side, it showed that *it was almost always the US who first softened their stance and took a more positive approach with Russia, and then Russia followed suit.*

The changes in approach from the US side at first glance seem completely random, sometimes being negative, at other times more positive. A more detailed look reveals that they were not just random changes but were actually closely related to the changing numbers of Yogic Flyers in Fairfield.

Before this can even remotely make sense, we have to introduce another new paradigm, this time in the area of politics. Maharishi always said that the decisions a government makes simply reflect the state of the collective consciousness. In our system of democracy, this is expressed in a rather superficial way already, where the politicians feel they have to stay in touch with the "will of the people" but it works at a much deeper level. This is how Maharishi explained it:

> *If the people in the country are disorderly, only the fruit of disorderly action will come to the nation. If the people create chaos in society, then this can only result in chaos in government. Every experienced member of a government knows this from his own experience. A new man in government may have a great desire for accomplishment. The same man, full of enthu-*

siasm and ambitions for his community, when he comes to the legislature and sits there – he finds his whole thinking changes.

So many legislators are beautiful people – when you have them to your home for dinner they are so intelligent and full of good will – but when they sit in the legislature, what they do is so different. This has always embarrassed the leaders of governments everywhere. They are not able to think in the halls of government what they are able to think at home. It's because their thinking gets tossed about by the effects produced by all the people in the nation, by the disorder in the collective consciousness of that nation.

In essence, Maharishi describes how the collective consciousness drives government decisions as well as the clarity of thinking of its leaders. If the nation's collective consciousness is gripped by a war fever, the government goes to war. If the collective consciousness of the nation becomes more harmonious, suddenly the government wants peace, as we have already seen in numerous studies. For example, every time the influence was created for Lebanon, the leaders of the fighting parties suddenly started to think differently and started looking for solutions that will bring peace.

This is also exactly what the researchers wanted to confirm in much more detail here. Could the presidential statements be linked to the numbers of Yogic Flyers in the Golden Domes? It took a rather brave researcher to tackle this one, as this would be a far more controversial study than anything else that had been done so far. Dr. Paul Gelderloos, a Dutch researcher who had already worked on several earlier studies, felt brave enough to give it a go.

In his first study on the subject, Dr. Gelderloos took the weekly numbers of Yogic Flyers from April, 1985 to Sept, 1987 – 129 weeks in total. He then compared the weekly fluctuations to all statements from the US president[*]. They found 347 statements, which two independent raters (who knew nothing about the purpose of the study) examined on a scale from -7 (war) to +7 (peace). To exclude personal bias the average of the two raters was taken. These 347 scores were then matched against the Yogic Flyer numbers in Fairfield.

He found that when the numbers were above 1500, the threshold to theoretically create the Maharishi Effect for the US, the statements from US side suddenly became remarkably more positive, which was then followed by more positive statements from the USSR. This correlation was highly signifi-

---

[*] As published by the Office of the Federal Register of the National Archives and Records Administration as the *Weekly Compilation of Presidential Documents.*

cant (p=.0066) and the study received another high-profile publication in *Social Science Perspectives Journal*[30]. As bizarre as it may have sounded, the data was impressive enough for another journal to link its reputation to it.

A second research study looked at weekly data over a much longer period (from 1979 till 1986), correlating the size of the group of Yogic Flyers to the statements between US and Russia.

As always, if the effect stays the same over a larger number of data points, the chance that the effect could be due to coincidence, rather than the Maharishi Effect, will become a lot smaller. In this study the chance of coincidence was one in 100,000, (p<.00001). As we mentioned earlier the standard in science to consider an effect significant is one in 20.

> Here we have a statistical near-certainty that the group of Yogic Flyers was influencing the Cold War. The chance that it was a coincidence was 5,000 times lower than the norm in science.

This study was published in the *Proceedings of the American Statistical Association*.

A third study looked at how the Yogic Flyer group influenced the relationships of the US with *all* other countries in the world. They took the Fairfield dome numbers from 1981 to 1988 and used data from another independent organisation that collected and rated events between the US and other countries, the World Event Interaction Survey coded at the US Naval Academy at Annapolis.

Again, *if* an effect is consistent, then the larger the amount of data the smaller the chance of coincidence. In this case, the researchers had a *huge* amount of data. Was the effect consistent?

Yes, it was.

The statistical analysis revealed a p value equaling 0.0000000000005, one in twenty trillion.

Have you bought that lottery ticket yet?

So basically, from the several researches over this 10 year period, all with probability values so low that we can call it just about a 100% certainty (okay, 99.999999999995% to be exact, but given that scientists are usually happy with 95% certainty, this is *one trillion times* better), we see that governments really need to do *very little* to improve society (something that will make US Republicans very happy).

All they have to do is maintain a big group of Yogic Flyers to create coherence and enliven positivity in the thinking of every single citizen so that the negativity disappears. Then suddenly we see that crime and accidents go down, the economy improves, and all international relationships become so much better that the animosity spontaneously disappears.

Maharishi always said: *"Don't destroy the enemy, destroy his enmity."*

This was Maharishi's definition of "Invincibility" for a country. A state where the collective consciousness is so high that nobody would even think about harming the country anymore.

Not only does this work a lot better than current methods but it's also far cheaper, allowing for more money to be made available for the other government programs, like education, healthcare, social security, etc., so that everybody can have a decent standard of living (something that will make US Democrats very happy as well), while at the same time taxes could be reduced (Republicans twice as happy).

In our next experiment we'll investigate just how much cheaper Yogic Flying actually is.

Experiment 15: A Thousand Times Cheaper…While Being Far More Effective

Title: The Maharishi Effect: a model for social improvement. Time series analysis of a phase transition to reduced crime in Merseyside metropolitan area
Authors: Guy D. Hatchard, Ashley J. Deans, Kenneth L. Cavanaugh, and David W. Orme-Johnson
Reference: Journal of Psychology, Crime & Law (1996, vol. 2, pp. 165-174).

Fairfield wasn't the only place where a permanent group of Yogic Flyers had gathered. The same happened in the small town of Skelmersdale in the UK, part of the Merseyside metropolitan area.

This created an ideal setting for another experiment, this time also allowing the researchers to calculate precisely how much the government would save.

In March 1988, when the threshold was reached to provide an influence for all of Merseyside (150 permanent Yogic Flyers for the population of a little over two million), the researchers predicted on television that crime would start to decrease.

Needless to say, not many people took the claim seriously. Nothing seemed to be able to stop the trends of increasing crime and Merseyside had the third highest crime rate of the eleven large metropolitan areas in England and Wales.

However, as it is evident on the chart below, the results happened exactly as predicted.

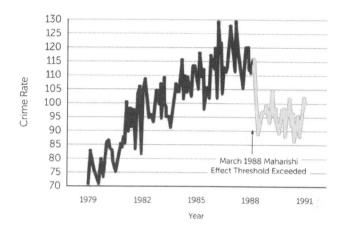

After an immediate drop of more than 20%, crime rate remained stable while it kept increasing in the rest of England. After five years the decrease in crime compared to previous trends in Merseyside was 45%. Compared to continuing trends of increasing crime for England as a whole, the crime rate in Merseyside dropped 60%.

By 1992, Merseyside had gone from having the third highest to the *lowest* crime rate of all the metropolitan areas in England.

This stable decrease in crime rate allowed the researchers to do a thorough cost-benefit calculation. It resulted in 225,000 fewer crimes for Merseyside and, at an average cost of $7500 per crime, the Yogic Flyers saved the administration of Merseyside close to $2 billion in those four years.

It was calculated that for every hour a Yogic Flyer was doing his thing, Merseyside saved $6000 in crime related expenses.

Imagine the government would pay them $20 per hour, then the cost to maintain such a group, and preventing crimes, would still be *300 times* cheaper than the cost of dealing with crimes after they happened. Three hundred times lower means a 99.7% reduction of cost.

Imagine what that would do to a government's budget.

And this is all still on a relatively small scale. If the group could be 10 times as big, due to the effect growing with the square of the participants, they'd be able to create an effect for 100 times as many people. This means that the cost per person affected would be 10 times less, so that means 3000 times cheaper. (We'll actually see far better numbers still in a later research)

Also, this is only taking into account the cost of crime related expenses, while many other factors improved in Merseyside as well, similar to what we've seen in all the other studies: decreased car accidents, improved employment, and economy, etc. Overall our claim that the cost can be 1000 times cheaper seems to be an understatement.

This paper turned into yet another high-profile publication for the TM researchers, in the Journal of *Psychology, Crime & Law*.

Experiment 16: Calculating the Economic Benefit of Groups of Yogic Flyers
Unpublished experiment

New Zealand economist Guy Hatchard who was involved in the Merseyside experiment also did a cost-effectiveness calculation for both New Zealand and the US.

For New Zealand, he found that for every dollar invested in creating the Maharishi Effect, the national government would save $320 per year in its budget; plus they'd see $700 in increased gross domestic product.

Hatchard compared it to installing a new piece of technology in your car. It would cost you only $10 but would save you $3200 in maintenance over the next 10 years, while significantly increasing the economic value of your car as well. Would you want that in your car?

In the US, due to the vastly increased economies of scale, the results were far more impressive still. Hatchard calculated that every dollar invested in supporting a group of Yogic Flyers could generate $17,500 in increased GDP, plus enormous cost savings through reduced crime and conflict, improved health, etc. The return of investment was calculated to be up to 14,000%.

Now imagine your government is asking you to pay sky-high taxes, but decides to not make use of an investment opportunity which would create such a high return that they'd easily be able to lower your taxes. Furthermore, this investment has a *far* lower risk of failure than anything else they're trying. Do you think any of their current programs can show statistical certainties that they work of 99.99999999%? For most of their programs there is actually little proof they work at all.

Basically, by deciding not to use this, the government prefers to keep asking you to pay your sky-high taxes.

Would you agree with this?

Should you agree with this?

So *why aren't we using this?*

That is really the million dollar question now, isn't it? Actually, by now it has probably become a trillion dollar question.

If all the research that we've seen is true, then compared to almost any other program that's ever been researched, the Maharishi Effect:

- has more solid scientific evidence that it works

- has a far lower chance that it could still be due to coincidence

- has far better results

- all at a far lower cost.

So it works better, it's cheaper, and the scientific evidence is a lot more solid.

And why aren't we using it?

Because research, no matter how impressive, doesn't convince anyone if they're not wearing the right glasses to see the research properly. So that's the first thing we had to do, which I hope we accomplished with this book.

The other problem with the Maharishi Effect research, which I hoped to rectify in this book, was that few people ever seemed to bother to bring all the different Maharishi Effect researches together in one document.

Each research that has been done is impressive on its own, but it's never perfect. If the materialists want to find the flaws, they will probably find them. If they don't want to be convinced, nothing will convince them.

What really makes the Maharishi Effect research impressive is *the collection of all the studies together*. It's going to be very hard to find an alternative explanation that will explain *all* the effects from *all* the experiments combined.

And the most impressive studies are actually still to come.

Experiment 17: Did 7000 Yogic Flyers in India Cause the Fall of the Berlin Wall?
Unpublished experiment

After the four global assemblies, and when the group of Yogic Flyers in Fairfield appeared to be big enough to create a permanent warming effect on the Cold War, the TM organization largely stopped giving Maharishi Effect demonstrations, and focused all their attention on creating permanent groups of Yogic Flyers.

They continuously invited the governments around the world to create such groups, pointing out how much money they'd be saving compared to their current methods of dealing with negative human behavior.

> At one point, in 1983, the TM organisation even placed a full-page announcement in most of the world's biggest newspapers, inviting governments to create groups of professional peacemakers. *They offered to pay for the full implementation of the groups of Yogic Flyers to prove that it works.* Only if the desired effect was achieved, the government would reimburse the TM organisation. It was a zero risk proposition for governments.

Even then, it would take ten more years before a government responded (as we'll discuss in our last experiment).

But meanwhile, they did get a response from one wealthy family who decided to do it on their own. They had studied the research that had already been done in detail and were convinced, so the family decided to offer their private funds to start creating a group that was large enough to create the effect for the whole world on a permanent basis.

It was decided to create this group in India, as the salary and living costs were much lower there than in the West, plus the permanent Yogic Flying professionals could also be trained in other additional Vedic procedures to create world peace.

Throughout the late 1980s, this group in India started to grow until it reached 7000 people in 1988, enough to create the effect for the whole world. As such on Jan 12, 1988 Maharishi announced 1988 as the *"Year of achieving World Peace."*

And that was exactly what appeared to be happening.

One year later, on January 2, 1989 *Newsweek* summarized 1988 as the *"year of miracles."* Here's why:

- The Soviet Union withdrew it's troops from Afghanistan after eight years of fighting (May 1988)
- The Cold War ended, with President Reagan declaring: *"Iron Curtain opening"* (*The New York Times*, June 4 1988)
- The Soviet Union started the process of ending communism (July 1988)
- The Iran-Iraq war that had been raging for eight years and claimed up to one million lives suddenly came to an end (Aug '88)
- The government of Estonia issued the first declaration of sovereignty from Moscow of any Soviet or Eastern Bloc entity (Nov 1988)

As an interesting side-note, 1988 was also the year when the connection between each and every one of us started to manifest in a physical form. In 1988, the first seeds of a global network called the World Wide Web, the internet, were sown by Tim Berners-Lee.

This "year of miracles" continued from 1989 to 1991, as long as the Yogic Flyers were creating the effect from India, and it was about to get a lot more miraculous still. Here are a few more examples of clear signs of improved collective consciousness in countries around the world:

- The fall of the Berlin Wall 28 years after it was built, resulting the reunification of east and west Berlin, and eventually the reunification of east and west Germany (Nov 9, 1989)
- The end of Apartheid in South Africa and the release of Nelson Mandela after 27 years in prison (starting in 1989, ending in 1991)
- Vietnam withdraws the last of its troops from Cambodia, ending an 11-year occupation (Sept 1989)
- Brazil holds its first free presidential election since 1960
- Romanian communist dictatorship of Nicolae Ceaușescu comes to an end after 22 years (Dec 1989)
- The collapse of communist Soviet Union, starting in 1989 and ending in Dec 1991, creating freedom for many former Soviet-bloc countries. The Soviet army, the largest in the world with 12 million soldiers, spontaneously dissolved.

The Fall of the Berlin wall

Yet after three years of miracles around the world, the 7000 Yogic Flyer project in India had to come to an end. The private donors were no longer able to support it and still nobody else, government or private, had come forward.

> All these remarkable events resulted in 1988 till 1991 becoming *by far* the most positive three-year period in all of last century, perhaps even in our entire history.
>
> Could it be a coincidence that this happened exactly at the time when, for the first time in history, a group was maintained that was predicted to create exactly these effects on a global scale?
>
> It's kind of the same as asking: *"Could it be a coincidence that the darkness disappears when the light goes on?"*

Somebody could probably try to calculate the chance that this was a coincidence, but the researchers already didn't bother anymore. They had already proven the correlation between the groups of Yogic Flyers and a positive change in events beyond any doubt.

So what would it take to maintain such a global group on a permanent basis?

Less than one day of US military expenses!

To engage Yogic Flyers as professional peacemakers in India (including salary and living expenses) costs about $250 per month.

The US military spends about $1 billion per day. If we put $1 billion in a bank account or an investment fund with a 5% interest rate, we'd get a return of $50 million per year, ($4 million per month), the *interest alone* would be enough to engage 16,000 professional peace makers. So with the US defense expenses of *one day*, we could permanently engage a group that is twice the size of what is needed to create the effect for the whole world, which was Maharishi's goal. (Maharishi always said he wanted a safety margin of twice the minimum amount to create the effect stronger and quicker.)

Currently, the TM organisation is trying to create such a new permanent group of Yogic Flyers in India. They purchased 2000 acres of land in central India where they hope to build a city for their 16,000 professional Yogic Flyers (called "Vedic pandits"). They already engage around 2,000 Yogic Flyers on a permanent basis, all funded by the TM organisation's own funds and private donations.

Permanent world peace, as you probably understood by now, *just depends on money*. We have a proven technology here that's so powerful, at such a low cost, that *any* government, or even any one of the more than 8000 billionaires in the world, can forever change the destiny of mankind.

Ideally every continent and every country would have their own group of permanent Yogic Flyers large enough to create an effect for their whole population. But with those smaller groups it's usually just a matter of one school, prison, or business, implementing this program. Or the government can turn the police force or military into Yogic Flyers.

There are many ways this group could be created, at almost no additional cost for our governments. We'll discuss a few more later.

Experiment 18: The Final Demonstration...and the Ultimate Scientific Study

Title: Effects of group practice of the TM program on preventing violent crime in Washington, DC: results of the national demonstration project, June-July 1993
Authors: John S. Hagelin, Maxwell V. Rainforth, David W. Orme-Johnson, Kenneth L. Cavanaugh, Charles N. Alexander, Susan F. Shatkin, John L. Davies, Anne O. Hughes, and Emanuel Ross
Reference: Social Indicators Research (1999, vol. 47, no. 2).

No matter how impressive the Maharishi Effect experiments had become, people still weren't convinced. The Maharishi Effect story turned out to become a classic case of cognitive dissonance: The more impressive the new research challenging old beliefs, the more people find creative reasons to dismiss the research rather than change their view.

For all those who held on to the Machine Paradigm, the Maharishi Effect research was a bit like a David Copperfield magic show: you know it can't be true, but they make it look so convincing. So people start searching for the trick. If they can't find it, it doesn't mean that they're convinced that magic suddenly works (or in this case, that the Field Paradigm is real). No, they just look even harder for the trick.

In 1993 the TM researchers, led by quantum physicist Dr. John Hagelin, decided to organize one more demonstration and turn it into the *ultimate scientific research*, something so thorough and foolproof that there would be no questions left. This way they were hoping that the focus could finally shift to actual implementation of the Maharishi Effect around the world rather than finding the "magic trick".

There was no magic trick.

They decided to hold their experiment in Washington, DC, which at the time was the national capital with the highest murder rate in the world.

The DC police spent $1 billion per year to fight crime, only to see crime rate increasing by 10% per year. Whatever they were doing, it wasn't working. Actually, a National Institute of Justice commissioned review of over 500 crime prevention programs (supported by $3 billion in federal funds) concluded that *"by scientific standards, there are very few programs of proven effectiveness."* (Sherman et al., 1997)

So when a public claim was made (and faxed to 1600 media organisations, scientists, and politicians) that in June and July of 1993 a group of Yogic Flyers would decrease violent crime in Washington by 20%, quite a few eyebrows were raised. In fact, as soon as the prediction was made, the Chief of the DC police department came on television to say that, *"The only thing that would decrease crime by 20% would be two feet of snow."* As snow is not very likely in the middle of summer, it was his way of saying: *"Impossible."*

As usual, the researchers also predicted that the quality of life would improve, measured from a mix of different variables. They also picked a new element. They predicted that as a result of improved collective consciousness, the government effectiveness and standing would improve, which they would objectively measure through the popularity ratings of President Bill Clinton. (I'm assuming the reasoning for including this one was that if they want to convince presidents or other government leaders to support the Maharishi Effect, it won't hurt if it turns out to be good for the leader himself, as well.)

To make sure every aspect of the study was flawless, the scientists gathered a review board of 27 independent scientists and leading citizens to monitor the entire experiment: sociologists, criminologists, members from the Washington DC government and police.

None of these scientists were connected to the TM organisation, and almost everyone was skeptical about the effects they were asked to investigate. Still, they all agreed to help with the research design, advising on every aspect of the study, from the use of statistical models to the gathering of data. The time series analysis model they built considered everything there was known to influence crime rate – seasonal trends and weather variables, historical crime trends and annual patterns in the District of Columbia – as well as trends in neighbouring cities.

Up until the moment the experiment started, the model predicted the actual levels of crime with an incredible accuracy, over a period of several years. As such they could conclude that, if a deviation from predictions from the model would indeed come during the experiment, they could be fairly certain it would be due to the influence of the Yogic Flyers.

As usual, that's exactly what happened.

As soon as the TM-Sidhi practitioners started to arrive (4000 coming from all over the world - my father was one of them), the crime rate started to deviate from what was predicted from the model.

Similar to the earlier study in Jerusalem, the group didn't arrive at the same time but increased gradually. This made the study even more interesting because they could again measure the drop in crime not just once, but on a weekly basis over the eight-week period. The following graph shows that as the size of the group increases (dark line), violent crime rates (homicide, rape, assault, or HRA crimes) drop more and more from their predicted levels, culminating in a 23.3% drop when the group reached 4000 people.

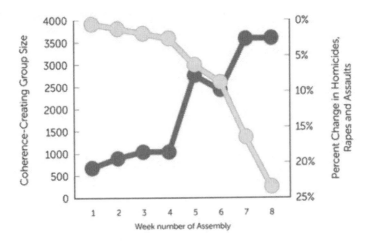

This was such a big drop in crime rate compared to predicted values, and there was such a close correlation between the size of the group of Yogic Flyers and crime rate decrease, that the chance that this could still be due to coincidence was one in 500 million (p=.000000002). This was the lowest probability of any single Yogic Flying study ever done.

Here's a picture of the 4000 Yogic Flyers in front of the White House.

All the other predictions also happened, as predicted, with the changes for President Clinton being especially impressive. In the months before the experiment, President Clinton's approval rating had been steadily dropping, to a record low 36% right before the experiment started. But as soon as it began there was a remarkable turnaround.

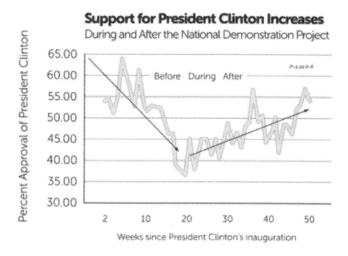

The chance that this sudden change in public approval was due to coincidence was one in 200 million (p<.000000005).

This study got the researchers yet another high-profile publication in a highly respected journal on social studies, *Social Indicators Research*. The Washington, DC police ultimately became a co-author of the study.

So did it change anything? Were the non-believers suddenly convinced?

After such a thorough experiment, and such impressive results you'd think that this would settle the discussion. In reality, surprisingly little happened.

The Washington, DC experiment is the most frequently mentioned of all the Maharishi Effect studies: Dr. Hagelin was even invited to discuss it in both *What the Bleep Do We Know* and *The Secret* movies, two films about the possibilities of consciousness as a field. However, it still didn't really move the needle in terms of mass adoption of the Maharishi Effect technologies.

It seems like people still weren't ready to shake off their Machine Paradigm glasses yet.

Fortunately, eventually another private donor came forward, allowing for yet another spectacular experiment to take place.

Experiment 19: The $100 Million One

Title: Societal violence and collective consciousness: reduction of U.S. homicide and urban violent crime rates
Authors: Michael C. Dillbeck and Kenneth L. Cavanaugh
Reference: SAGE Open. 2016; April-June: 1-16, *SAGE Open* March 14, 2017

In 2006, Howard and Alice Settle felt that the United States had waited long enough for the government to create a professional group of Yogic Flyers. Like the Zimmerman family before them, they simply decided to do it themselves.

While the group of Yogic Flyers in Fairfield was larger than the required number to create the effect for the entire USA during most of the 1980s, during the 1990s the numbers dropped again. People can only volunteer for so long and the most pressing reason to create coherence – to end the nuclear threat of the Cold War – was already gone.

Even though a core group of between 500 and 1000 Yogic Flyers kept coming to the Golden Domes to do their group meditations, more and more people started staying home and from the early 1990s till 2006 the numbers were continuously below the threshold to create the effect for the US as a whole.

The Settles decided to change this by simply paying a salary to anyone who wanted to do Yogic Flying as a profession. They announced they were ready to fund more than 1000 Yogic Flyers this way, partly through local Yogic Flyers who'd they pay a salary, partly by bringing a group of Vedic Pandits from India (for which they built a special village north of Fairfield).

They eventually kept this project going for more than eight years, spending close to $100 million on the project.

Especially during the first four years, (Jan 2007 till Jan 2011) this resulted in the numbers of Yogic Flyers consistently reaching, and often exceeding, the minimum threshold to create an effect for the entire US. According to the square-root-of-1% formula this was about 1700 people by that time. This was the first time since the late 1980s the group was consistently big enough to influence the entire US again.

This was a beautiful opportunity for yet another series of studies.

When the initiative was announced towards the end of 2006, the scientists once again organized press conferences and predicted that the crime rate would drop across the country once the required number of Yogic Flyers was reached.

As always that's exactly what happened. From 2007 onwards the crime rate started to decrease by 4-5% per year, similar to the changes seen in the early 1980s when the group size in Fairfield first reached the threshold.

But then, in 2008, something unexpected happened when Lehman Brothers collapsed and the financial crisis started.

Millions lost their jobs and *every* expert on criminal statistics in the US predicted that crime would see a strong increase again, as this *always* happens when unemployment rises.

This time it didn't happen.

The crime rate kept going down by about 5% per year, even during the height of the financial crisis when unemployment was twice as high as normal. By 2010 homicides and violent crime rate had decreased by 20% across the US, *in spite of all circumstances predicting a strong increase.*

Here are the monthly homicide and crime rates from 2003 till 2011 (per 100,000 population).

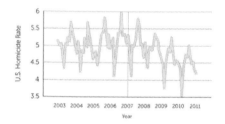 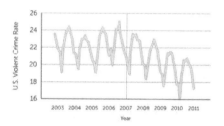

As you can see crime rate always has seasonal trends, going up in summer and down in winter, but you can still clearly see the long-term trends, an increase before 2007, and a decrease afterward, exactly as predicted[31].

Using the FBI statistics[32] it's relatively easy to calculate that close to 800,000 violent crimes and 10,000 homicides were prevented from 2007 to 2012 compared to trends the previous 5 years.

But that's just one variable. As we have seen numerous times before, a change in collective consciousness doesn't just cause a decrease in crime rate, but improves many different areas at the same time.

Far more convincing: doing your own research

Researchers don't always have time to investigate each area affected by the Maharishi Effect, so just for fun, I decided to see if I could find something myself.

Car accidents seemed to be a consistent variable that decreases as well, so I wanted to find an objective source for car accident data and see if there was a noticeable effect during the same four-year period. It actually turned out to be quite easy. The number of fatal accidents per hundred million miles driven was readily available on Wikipedia[33], with annual data from 1921 till 2015. The numbers showed a continuous decline, which is normal. As older cars get replaced by newer ones with better safety technology (airbags, etc.) you'd expect fewer fatalities.

Still, there was a clear sign that the group of Yogic Flyers were creating an influence. From 2001 to 2006, the number of traffic fatalities decreased by only 1.2% per year. Yet from 2007 until 2011, traffic fatalities decreased by an average 5.9% per year, resulting in a 20% additional drop over the 4 year period compared to previous trends. This was very similar to the crime rate drop, and similar to the changes that were seen in previous experiments. A quick calculation showed that 20,204 lives were saved between Jan 2007 and Dec 2010.

But as soon as the group of Yogic Flyers decreased, the effect was gone. From 2011 till 2015, car accidents *increased* by 2%. The last time car accidents increased over a 4-year period was in 1964.

For me, the fact that I could do my own analysis is even more convincing than reading about research from others.

Since then, right before the deadline of the manuscript for this book, the TM movement scientists also did the same analysis, with almost exactly the same results, finding a 20.6% decrease and 19,435 fewer traffic fatalities. They were also able to calculate the chance that such a dramatic change could have occurred by chance, and found it to be 3.7 in ten trillion. (p=.00000000000037)

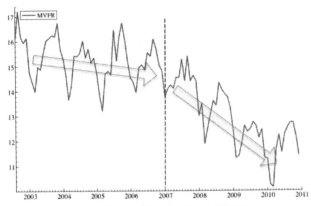

Figure 1. Motor vehicle fatality rate 2002-2010.

262

Additionally they also found that all other fatalities from other accidents decreased by 13.5% over the same period, saving an additional 16,795 lives. (p=.0000084).

And that's still not all. Just before this book went to press, Sage Open published two more studies, showing that infant mortality also went down by 12% during the same period compared to previous trends, saving another 992 lives, while drug-related deaths dropped by a whopping 30.4%, saving an additional 24,425 lives.

If we add all this together, this means that the group of Yogic Flyers saved no less than 71,500 lives (10,000 fewer homicides, 36,000 fewer fatal accidents, 1000 fewer infant deaths and 24,500 fewer drug-related deaths). The question is now how much "value" would this have created for the US government?

The US Office of Management and Budget estimates the economic value of a US human life in the range of $7 million to $9 million[34]. Even if we take the lower range of $7 million then the 71,500 lives that were saved resulted in *half a trillion dollars* of value. Yes, that's $500,000,000,000. And that's only counting deaths, we didn't discuss the other costs that were saved from reduced non-lethal crime (the psychological cost of assault or rape or any of the other 800,000 crimes that were prevented, for example), reduced addictions, material damage from car accidents, etc.

Yet, after spending $100 million on the project, of which $50 million over the four years when the research was going on (*10,000 times less* than the value that was created), the Settle family, like the Zimmerman family before them, had to face the reality that their funds were not unlimited and eventually they had to gradually reduce their support. From 2011 onwards the Yogic Flyer numbers dipped below the US threshold again and gradually started to go down more and more. By 2015 the group was consistently below the threshold. By 2016 it had almost completely dissolved again, and the Fairfield dome numbers were back to their old levels of around 500. It's probably no coincidence that now we see crime, accidents, and all the other variables rising again. 2015 saw an *increase* in car accidents of 10.5%, the highest increase since 1946.

So here we have yet another tale of heroism...and a complete lack of support from the institution that most benefits from this technology: the US government.

The US government would be able to support a group in Fairfield that is large enough to again create an influence for the US (even the whole world) at a cost that is peanuts for them, 10,000 times less than the money they'd save. All they'd have to do is the same as what the Settles did privately, pay a salary to a group of Yogic Flyers to again create the effect.

Make America Great Again? Anyone? It could be arranged in a few weeks.

The earlier researches have shown that with a group of 2000, variables like crime rate and car accidents improve at a rate of around 5% per year. However, the earlier long term studies (experiment 8) have shown if the group becomes twice as big, the effect becomes more than 4 times as big. With a group of 4000 the expected improvements would be closer to 30% per year (in Washington, they saw a 20% drop in crime rate in just a few weeks). This means that the effect would be noticeable almost immediately, while the long term effect would create an America that would be almost unrecognisable in just a few years time.

There are already more than enough Yogic Flyers in the US to create this group almost immediately, and there is an entire campus that was custom built to provide housing to more than 1000 professional Yogic Flyers from India (currently standing empty because the project was ended due to lack of funding). So a group of 3000 could really be arranged in a few weeks, just from the Yogic Flyers that are already living in Fairfield, and by bringing back the Indian professionals. A group of 4000 would take some extra planning, and more Yogic Flyers from accross the US moving to Fairfield, but even that could probably be arranged in a few months.

And while we're at it, why stop at creating the effect only for the US? Why not the whole world? That would only take 9000 Yogic Flyers, a large number for any private donor to support, but still peanuts for the US government. The biggest effect would still be for the US itself. According to the previous long-term study, such a large group would improve the US quality of life index by a whopping 70% per year.

This is why we ask everyone to send the link to download this book for free (or much better, a copy of the actual book) to anyone who has an influence in the government decision process, asking them to read it. Please find the contact data on www.fieldparadigm.com/politics for the politicians closest to you on.

Oh, and there might be one person whom we should really enourage to read it. Why don't you quickly tweet the link to download it to @IvankaTrump

Why Ivanka? Because Ivanka and her husband already practice TM. Nobody has to convince them about the benenfits of transcending anymore, they already know, and already publicly support it. She openly talks about how great TM is in her book, in interviews, etc. But before they'll bring this to their father, they have to know that the public supports this as well.

According to all the research we've seen, President Trump could *still* put America First, as he so much likes to do, by creating a massive positive transformation in the entire country, but in this case it would be in a way that makes both republicans and democrats happy, and both Americans and the rest of the world.

Whether you like the current US president or not (assuming he'll still be president by the time this book comes out), or agree with his decisions so far or not, if all the research that is presented in this book is true, he'd only have to make *one* decision and still could create the most progress any US president has ever created for his country. And one thing, at least, everyone would have to agree on: President Trump doesn't shy away from making controversial decisions if he feels it's right.

Of course, in case our governments are too slow to make the right decision in spite of the overwhelming evidence that is presented in this book, we also have quite a few multibillionaires who have pledged to donate a large portion of their wealth to make the world a better place. Given that there's nothing else that would even come close in terms of the impact it could make per dollar invested, they should all be very interested in this. And for them the cost of maintaining a group of 9000 Yogic Flyers in the US (or a group of 16,000 in India) would be peanuts as well.

All we have to do is make sure they know this solution exists and understand how it works.

So why not tweet the link to download the book, and ask them to read it, a few more gentlemen, such as:

@Jeffbezos
@Billgates
@warrenbuffet
@finkd (Mark Zuckerberg)
@elonmusk

And if you really want to go wild, on www.givingpledge.org you can find a list of 169 of the world's wealthiest people, all multi-billionaires, who all joined Bill Gates' pledge to give away the majority of their wealth to a good cause. All we have to do is let all of them them know that here's a really, really good cause.

Should we wait, or just do it ourselves? Here's a simple way to make a difference

The more people are aware that this possibility exists, and ask that governments or wealthy philantropists start using it, the more quickly it will happen. So the best thing you can do is share the link to download this book for free with as many people as possible, and ask them to read it.

But while we wait for them, there's something we can easily do ourselves as well that has an immediate effect.

There's a cool project that allows us to start to fund a permanent group of Yogic Flyers in Fairfield ourselves, without it costing us anything.

One Yogic Flyer who spent more than 6 years as part of the group in Fairfield wanted to do something to create more financial support for the project. So he started contacting a wide range of online retailers and created a referral program.

Basically every time somebody shops online through the links that are found in this website, the retailer will donate some percentage of the sales value (usually between 5 and 10%) to a non-profit organization that uses the funds exclusively to support professional Yogic Flyers in Fairfield.

Eventually he got more than 1000 online retailers on board, including most the big players like Amazon, Walmart, Target, itunes, Ebay, Best Buy, iherb, etc.

So whenever you want to buy something online, simply first go to www.fieldparadigm.com/shop-for-peace, select your retailer and then do your shopping as you'd regularly do. It doesn't cost you anything, (the price at which you buy will be the same) but you'll be literally shopping for peace.

Fortunately, there are a few governments around the world who *are* willing to take up the opportunity to change the destiny of their country, which brings us to our final experiment.

Are there cases where the Maharishi Effect *didn't* work?

No official study that was done on the Maharishi Effect has ever failed to produce the results as predicted/expected. Still, there one case where, if you take very limited data, it would *appear* that way. This one also involves Fairfield and has been cited by critics numerous times, but the numbers the critics use only tell a small part of the story. The moment the data is investigated more thoroughly, it only confirms the Maharishi Effect. I won't go into detail here - this book is already long enough - but if you ever hear the argument "but it didn't work in Fairfield" then be sure to read the full story: www.fieldparadigm.com/fairfield-crime.

Experiment 20: The First Government-Sponsored Implementations of the Maharishi Effect in Mozambique and Cambodia

Unpublished experiment

In July 1992, President Dr. Alberto Joaquin Chissano of Mozambique received an unusual visit. A group of representatives from the TM organisation who were claiming they could end all of the country's troubles.

Countless other heads of state had been visited by Maharishi's representatives, but the difference here was that President Chissano decided to act on it, becoming the first head of state in the world to actually use the Maharishi Effect for his country. As he says himself:

"First I started the practice of Transcendental Meditation myself, then introduced the practice to my close family, then to my extended family, then to my cabinet of ministers, then to my government officers, and then to my military. The result has been political peace and balance in nature in my country."

By February 1993, in less than six months, more than 16,000 soldiers in Mozambique had learned TM and 3000 went on to learn the TM-Sidhi program and Yogic Flying. As always when groups of Yogic Flyers started to do their thing, things started to change dramatically. The civil war, which had been going on for 17 years, came to a sudden end, and the economy started to rebuild.

In 1992 Mozambique was the world's poorest country. By 1997 the economy was growing at 12.4% per year, the highest in Africa. By 2000 Mozambique had the world's fastest growing economy.

In 1999 the *New York Times* wrote:

Seven years after the guns fell silent, jackhammers are ringing, new hotels are rising, new schools are opening, and newly paved roads are rolling across the land.

The war-torn, once ravaged countryside is now lush with corn, cashews, and mangoes. Inflation has dropped to 2%, from 70% in 1994. The economy has grown an average 10% a year since 1996. After years of relying on donated food, Mozambique now grows nearly enough to feed itself.

Once a symbol of Africa's calamitous wars, Mozambique is now a success story.

President Chissano was the first president to accept the simple truth that peace has to start within our own minds.

> *For what do we need this support of nature, this coherence, this Unified Field? We want it to keep peace in the world. We have been fighting for freedom and peace, and we want peace in order to develop our country and to develop the world...peace is the basis of development and this peace has to start in our own minds.*

However, even this project had to end eventually. When President Chissano's term as president ended in 2005, his successors didn't understand the Maharishi Effect, didn't see (or didn't want to see) the connection between the groups of Yogic Flyers and the sudden outbreak of peace, and didn't feel the need to continue the project. As such, the military project was gradually discontinued and tensions and civil conflicts in the country have recently been on the rise again.

Chissano is now trying to create a new group of Yogic Flyers by establishing a Maharishi School in his country.

Around the same time President Chissano was creating his group of Yogic Flyers in Mozambique, the government of Cambodia also started creating a group by opening a Maharishi University. Over the next few years their group of Yogic Flyers was also big enough to influence the whole country.

At that time, Cambodia was ranked alongside Mozambique as one of the poorest countries in the world, torn by civil war and the violent Khmer Rouge regime. As soon as the Yogic Flyer group started coming together inflation decreased dramatically, from over 100% per year to under 5%. Economic growth averaged more than 5% between 1992 and 2002 and Cambodia rose 24 places in the international rankings of economic prosperity.

So governments *have* been supporting the Maharishi Effect already...all we need is a few more to do so.

So What Did the Government of Guinea-Bissau Decide?

We still have to finish the story that we started with: Our meeting with the president of Guinea-Bissau.

With the impressive results we showed the president and his ministers, our delegation was convinced they'd take up our offer to change the destiny of their country.

After a few hours of deliberation, the ministers came back and told us that, as much as they liked our proposal, they wouldn't be able to make a decision until it was debated in parliament.

Everybody of our delegation knew what that meant...that very likely *nothing* would happen.

The difference with Mozambique was that President Chissano could decide himself. That meant they only had to educate one person in the Field Paradigm way of thinking where the research on the Maharishi Effect would make sense. But from the moment politics and public opinion get involved, it appears to be hopeless. Politicians do what their voters want, and voters won't support something they don't understand.

As we expected, in the end nothing happened in Guinea-Bissau.

> In 2007, one year after our visit to Guinea Bissau, Dr. Chissano received the African Leadership award – one of the highest awards an African leader can receive, coupled with a $5 million prize.
>
> Around the same time, the president of Guinea-Bissau was assassinated by his own military.

Let's hope more countries follow Mozambique's example, rather than Guinea-Bissau's.

> <u>A different time.</u>
>
> Since our visit to Guinea Bissau 10 years ago, a lot has changed in the world. Thanks to Social Media, something that is good can now spread far more quickly. What people know and the opinion they form no longer depends on the mass media (which could be controlled, either directly or through advertising money, by forces who may not want the world to know about transcending and the TM field effects). Instead, people can now decide themselves what their friends deserve to know.
>
> Perhaps it now no longer has to be hopeless once public opinion gets involved. If enough people understand what transcending can really do for the world and share it, public opinion could change *very* quickly these days, and governments would have no choice but to follow.
>
> Who knows, world peace could very well be just a few Tweets or Facebook shares away.

Five Ways to make it happen...At Virtually No Cost

Convincing governments to create groups of Yogic Flyers shouldn't be that difficult. We've already seen that the costs to train and maintain such groups are far lower than anything else they've ever tried to improve human behavior (even up to thousand times lower).

In this chapter, it gets even better. We'll see that creating and maintaining such groups actually barely has to cost *anything at all*.

The benefits that people who transcend experience for themselves are so substantial that they alone pay for the costs involved. We've already gone over some of the benefits, and they are explained in more detail in the Appendix. They include keeping ourselves healthy but also developing those skills that are considered most valuable today to improve our economy, yet for which there is no conventional training (like creative problem solving, IQ, EQ, self-confidence).

Developing these skills is among the most important investments our governments can make. World peace can simply be a free side effect.

Here are five ways how we could create groups of Yogic Flyers at virtually no cost.

1. Creating Groups of Yogic Flyers in Schools

We've already seen that the best thing we could do for our children is to incorporate TM in the curriculum of our schools, but why stop there? If we incorporate the advanced TM-sidhi program and Yogic Flying as well (for those who are old enough, minimum age is 16), it will also be the best thing we could do for our country. The only "cost" of creating groups of Yogic Flyers in schools, other than the cost of the initial training, is that students spend about 45 minutes twice per day (15 min TM practice plus another 30 minutes for their TM-sidhi and Yogic Flying practice), leaving fewer hours in the school day for the curriculum, unless the school day would be extended to accommodate the program.

The benefit is that:

> 1. The students are *far* more attentive during the rest of the day, learn far more quickly, and classes become efficient, so more learning is achieved in less time. Ultimately the time that is lost with the practice of the TM-Sidhi program and Yogic Flying is regained through improved student performance during the rest of the day.

2. In addition to the knowledge the students gain from books, students start learning skills that really matter in life. In an age where all information is just a few mouse-clicks away, people rarely stand out based on the amount of knowledge they have. Rather, they stand out based on skills that can't be learned from books, like learning ability, creative problem solving, IQ, EQ, and relationship skills. All these areas improve spontaneously with transcending, and they grow even far more quickly when children learn the TM-sidhi program and Yogic Flying.

This is why, even though hundreds of other schools are also incorporating the TM technique into their school curriculum, the Maharishi School children still keep winning the creative problem solving world championships, because they *still* have an unfair advantage. They're also learning Yogic Flying and are even able to practice it as part of the large group in Fairfield. Let's hope this unfair advantage will disappear soon, when we'll have such large groups everywhere.

Wouldn't we want every school in the world to first of all start teaching children to develop their full brain potential? Wouldn't this on its own be the best investment our governments could make? World peace will then simply be a free side effect.

2. Creating Groups of Yogic Flyers in Businesses

Let's imagine that a company paid for their employees to learn TM and Yogic Flying and practice it during work hours. This company would then invest in the most important capital it has: its employees.

The skills we mentioned before (creative problem solving, IQ, EQ, etc.) are normally considered talents – people are either good at it or they aren't. People who *are* good at it are considered highly valuable, and can command ever increasing salaries from their employers.

But what if we can train every factory worker, or every low-level employee, to develop more of their brain potential? The "cost" of this would be that they'd spend about 20% of their work time on their TM, TM-sidhi and Yogic Flying practice, which is a significant cost. But as long as the benefits outweigh the costs, the investment makes sense.

This was tested at a mid-size factory in the chemical sector in the US, where employees were able to learn TM and practice it as part of their work routine. The results were spectacular. As the percentage of employees practicing TM grew, sales income increased, productivity increased, the number of sick leave days was reduced, and overall profit grew.[35]

Productivity and Profit Increase
THROUGH THE TRANSCENDENTAL MEDITATION TECHNIQUE

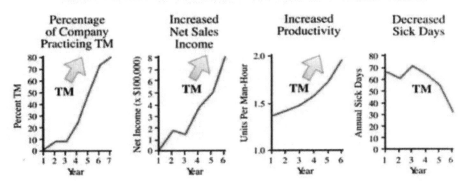

The correlation is obvious. The graphs above show that even though the amount of actual work hours decreased (as the employees now spend part of their work time practicing TM) the productivity (total amount of units produced divided by the total amount of hours worked, including TM time) actually increased from 1.4 to 2 – a 40% increase.

So the TM practice was more than paying for itself (if the productivity had remained the same, it would already have paid for itself, but it actually increased) and this company saw a significant increase in profits.

This is why more and more companies are now paying for their employees to practice TM (and Yogic Flying) during work hours: it's good for their bottom-line. Any benefit for society through the Maharishi Effect then comes as a free side effect.

Here's a nice video of how Oprah describes what happened when she paid for all of the 400 employees in her company to learn TM (3 min): www.fieldparadigm.com/oprah/

3. Creating Groups of Yogic Flyers in Prisons

Here's an obvious one. Prisoners tend to have a lot of time, and they need transcending more than anyone. The cost to create groups of Yogic Flyers in prisons is virtually nil. Transcending is the most effective prison-rehabilitation program ever researched, because it fixes the one fundamental problem in the brain that causes people to become criminals. (reactivating the prefrontal cortex, so that people are able to make a proper judgment before they act). This is a problem no other prison rehabilitation program addresses, which is why almost all other programs are largely ineffective.

Studies have shown significantly reduced recidivism when inmates learn TM, as well as better behavior inside of prison. As such any costs that is associated with learning TM and Yogic Flying pays for itself because we now finally have an effective prison rehabilitation program.

For more information (and some more inspiring videos) go to https://www.davidlynchfoundation.org/prisons.html

The only downside with this program is this: if it's effective the prison population will significantly decrease. This was found in a government-sponsored prison program in Senegal where 11,000 prisoners learned TM. The project was so successful that the government eventually closed three prisons due to lack of inmates. It's a good way to create groups of Yogic Flyers in the short term, but (hopefully) not in the long term. The better TM is for prisons, the less prisoners there will be to practice it in groups. Also if the groups of Yogic Flyers start creating their effect, there will be a lot less people going to prison, because the crime rate will drop in the whole country.

So, not a good long-term project, but I'm sure nobody would mind.

4. Creating Groups of Yogic Flyers in the Police Force and Military

The first job of the police and military is to maintain orderliness and peace. What better way to do this than by becoming professional peace makers? Research has shown that whatever time is invested in Yogic Flying typically has a 100 to 1000 fold return in terms of less time needed to fight crime, deal with car accidents, or fighting wars. On top the Police officers and soldiers would benefit so much themselves that the program would pay for itself.

What if the UN peacekeepers would all become Yogic Flyers and as such become real peacekeepers? What if every government around the world would train their soldiers and police officers to be real peacekeepers?

We'd have world peace in a matter of weeks.

5. Creating Groups of Yogic Flyers with the Unemployed

People who can't find a job (about 5% of the population, if times are good) are a huge burden on society. They receive unemployment benefits and contribute very little in return.

Governments want nothing more than making sure everybody can find a job, but it's not that easy. It usually comes down to a simple business equation. If the cost of employing someone is more than the benefit they bring to the company, it doesn't make sense to hire them. Very often employers can't find enough good people for high-level jobs, while it's the low level jobs that disappear, either because of automation or the company moving to a low-wage country. Trainings to increase the skill level of unemployed people rarely help, partly because the skills that are most valued these days are exactly the kind of skills you can't be trained for, as we've already seen (creative problem solving, IQ, EQ, etc.). This involves changing people's brain and we don't know how to do that.

Until now.

What if we ask everybody who is unemployed to take a training that is proven to be effective to develop their brain potential and increase people's skill level (and market value), by letting them become Yogic Flyers. What if we ask them to come to group Yogic Flying practice as long as they receive unemployment benefits?

In the US alone there are seven million unemployed. Just imagine what turning even 1% of them (70,000) into Yogic Flyers could do for the world.

Conclusion

There are dozens of ways to create groups of Yogic Flyers without it costing anything extra for society. The personal benefits the Yogic Flyers experience more than pay for the costs.

So it's not about costs. The *only* thing that is required to create the biggest transformation the world has ever seen is awareness that these programs exist and a desire to use them.

How creating groups of Yogic Flyers can be rather profitable.

In South Africa, a good friend of mine named Taddy Blecher started a program to take poor children from the streets, teach them TM and Yogic Flying and give them a university education. His programs have been incredibly successful and have since been supported by some of the most influential people in the world, including Nelson Mandela, the Dalai Lama, Oprah Winfrey, Richard Branson, and the Bill and Melinda Gates foundation.

One interesting anecdote is that, when their university started, one of the big mining companies in South Africa decided to donate them their office building in Johannesburg (large enough to house 900 students). Johannesburg, at that time, had the *highest crime rate in the world*. It was just impossible to have an office there as it was simply too dangerous for their employees to come into the city. As a result the building was virtually worthless. (They had previously tried to sell it for $60,000 and couldn't find a buyer, so they figured it was better to give it away and get a tax benefit). But as soon as the students learned Yogic Flying and formed a group that was big enough to influence all of Johannesburg, crime rate plummeted and businesses returned. (Johannesburg is now not even in the top 50 of cities with the highest crime rate in the world anymore).

The building is now valued at $21 million.

In this case creating the group of Yogic Flyers did far more than pay for itself. Even based on the value of one single building, it was already hugely profitable.

Why We Have Good Reason to Hope: More and more governments are responding.

Other than Mozambique and Cambodia, several more governments have begun creating groups of Yogic Flyers to change the destiny of their countries, especially in Latin America:

- The government of the Mexican province of Oaxaca incorporated TM and Yogic Flying as part of the school curriculum in 450 schools, creating more than 20,000 Yogic Flyers. They now want to expand to include many more schools.

- The government of Ecuador has made TM and Yogic Flying a part of the daily routine of their military, with more than 6000 soldiers in the army, navy, and air force now practicing TM and learning Yogic Flying. They also signed a contract with the TM organisation to bring TM to 2000 schools.

- A Catholic priest in Colombia named Father Mejia started a program to provide shelter for homeless children. He has them learn TM and Yogic Flying to allow them to heal their past traumas and at the same time change the collective consciousness in the whole country. Several thousand have already become Yogic Flyers. The first result of the increased collective consciousness in Columbia? A truce between the Colombian government and the FARC rebels after more than 50 years of armed conflict.

While this is all wonderful news, the question could and should be asked again: "Why only in Latin America?"

Why don't all countries around the world follow their lead?

Well, that's really up to you now.

You know now that it's possible – even easy – to create a new destiny for your country: a destiny without war, corruption, violence, economic problems, and far less disease.

...and lower taxes.

Did I mention this already?

Hey, I'm a Belgian – we pay the highest taxes in the world, so this is a sensitive one for me. Perhaps you're happy with the taxes you're paying but I know I'm not, especially when I know they're being wasted on programs that don't work nearly as well as well as what's described in this book.

The question is: "Now that you know, what will you do with it?"

Part 4: Will You Keep This a Secret?

Insanity: doing the same thing over and over again and expecting different results.

- Albert Einstein

Now that you've discovered it's possible, and actually remarkably practical, to change the world, what will you do?

Will you allow it to remain a secret for another 40 years, or will you help to make sure everybody knows about it?

There are many things you can do to make a difference that we already mentioned in the book. Here is the full list.

1. **Stay in touch**. I'm sure there will be lots of exciting developments that we'd love to share with you, whether it is new petitions or just inspiring news about things that are happening around the world.

Sign up for our newsletter if you haven't already, by going to www.fieldparadigm/news.

Also follow us on @fieldparadigm on twitter and/or follow our Facebook page on @fieldparadigm (www.facebook.com/fieldparadigm)

2. **Share this book**. Anyone can download it for free on www.fieldparadigm.com. All you have to do is share the link and tell them to read it.

Also, if you liked the book, leave a nice Facebook comment on www.fieldparadigm.com. People are much more likely to read it if they see comments from other Facebook users.

3. **Give a copy of this book to the people you care about**. I'm sure you know somebody who could really benefit from learning to transcend, whether it is to sleep better, get over depression or an addiction, have better concentration, more self-confidence or any other reason.

You can always tell them to download the book for free, but these days people are overloaded with free e-books. If somebody really needs to know what is in this book, don't leave it up to chance. They will be five times more likely to read it if you give them an actual copy. You can get one at a minimal cost of $7.99 for the Kindle or iBook version, and $9.99 to 12.99 for a paperback copy.

By buying this book you will also directly support our cause, as it will give me some marketing budget to promote the book further. (I'll reinvest any profit from this book into marketing campaigns.) For every person that decides to buy this book, I'll have a marketing budget to reach 1000 new people on social media.

For more details on how to order your copy go to www.fieldparadigm.com

4. Contact your local politicians. Email/tweet/Facebook the link to download this book for free to your local politicians. Or send a copy of the book, if possible, as that will be 100x more effective in getting their attention. There's a much larger chance they'll read it if only a few people send the actual book than if several hundred send the link.

The closer they are to your vote, the more effective your voice will be. Find the contact details of local politicians on www.fieldparadigm.com/politics

5. **Be the light**: learn TM and Yogic Flying. This is obviously the fastest way to remove the darkness in the world. I promise you that learning to transcend and especially learning the TM-Sidhi course and Yogic Flying will be the best investment you'll ever make for yourself – and the best thing you can do for the world.

To find your local TM center go to www.fieldparadigm.com/tm

6. **Shop for peace**. Ad www.fieldparadigm.com/shop-for-peace to your bookmark and remember to use this link every time you buy something online. For each item you buy this way, participating retailers (including Amazon, Ebay and 300 others) will donate between 5 and 10% to a non-profit organization that will support professional Yogic Flyers in Fairfield, Iowa.

7. **Say "Thank you"** when you meet a TM teacher or a Yogic Flyer. A lot of them are nothing less than heroes, doing all they can do to change the destiny of the world for more than 40 years. All this while most of the outside world has been either ignoring or openly ridiculing them. They deserve our thanks. It will probably only motivate a lot of them to do even more.

8. **Go to the director of your local school, prison, business**, and give them a copy of this book, asking them to make TM and Yogic Flying part of their routine. It will be the best investment they can make to reach their own goals, whether that is the full development of the child, the best prison re-

habilitation results, or more profit for their business, while at the same time creating the effect for their city, country, or even the entire world... at no cost.

9. **Give a copy of this book to your doctor**/psychologist/psychiatrist or anyone whose job it is to help people heal. This will allow them to *really* help.

10. **If you're a student,** attend the Maharishi School boarding program (highschool) or Maharishi University of Management in Fairfield and join their group of Yogic Flyers.

We've already explained why this would be the best thing for your own development and professional career, but now you understand even better.

TM creates a profound influence on stress resistance, being yourself and brain development, all the factors that will predict success in life, but this influence will be a lot stronger still during Yogic Flying, and a lot stronger *still* when you can practice Yogic Flying as part of a big group. Currently there is no other school/university in the world where you can do this.

And on top of your own development, you'll be creating a huge influence of peace for the world as well. Did you know that every additional Yogic Flyer that joins the group of currently about 500 Yogic Flyers, creates a positive effect for a whopping additional 100,100 people. Sounds incredible? Not when you make a simple calculation of the square root of one percent formula, which predicts that additional effect of one Yogic Flyer is $((x+1)^2-x^2)*100$, so if there are 500 Yogic Flyers already it's: $(251,001-250,000)*100 = 100,100$.

So you'll be doing the best thing you could possibly do for yourself *and* for the world.

To learn more about MUM go to www.fieldparadigm.com/mum

To learn more about the Maharishi School boarding program go to www.fieldparadigm.com/maharishi-school

11. **Change the destiny of the world yourself.** This one is just in case you happen to be a millionaire or a billionaire (or happen to know a billionaire who wants to do something good for the world).

Even though governments should be supporting groups of Yogic Flyers, they are often slow to answer. Most groups so far have been created either from the little funds the TM organisation has available or through donations from private individuals.

Right now there are several projects with several thousands of Yogic Flyers in Latin America, Asia, and the United States, but they need support to be maintained and expanded.

For more information about the current groups of Yogic Flyers visit: www.fieldparadigm.com/world-peace

These are some of the ways in which you can help, but there are countless of other possibilities to make it happen. If there is a will, there is a way.

Thank you for making it happen.

All the best,

Joachim

P.S. Love your feedback on this book: Joachim@fieldparadigm.com

"The future of the world is bright, and that is my delight."

Maharishi's last words before he passed away in 2008.

Acknowledgments

Traditionally acknowledgments are written at the start of a book, but in this case, as the main person to acknowledge is Maharishi, I felt that the book itself is the best acknowledgment. Other than my purely selfish reasons for writing it - that we can elevate world consciousness to such a level that I can have magic wherever I go...and reduce my tax bill ;o) - my deepest desire was simply that more people would become aware of what Maharishi's techniques could do for the world.

In terms of Maharishi himself, I can't even begin to find the words to acknowledge him properly:

- For the role he played in my life personally, as a mentor. Without his guidance and training, this book would have never materialized.
- For the role he played in the world and for his tireless efforts to keep making it a better one.
- For his wisdom and deep insights into the truth of our existence.
- For his amazing organizing power.
- For his infectious sense of humor.
- But most of all, for his deep love and caring that affected anyone who came in touch with him, and his insatiable desire to see everyone grow and evolve.

In the end, words don't matter, and Maharishi himself was certainly never very big on words about him. He always said that the knowledge about transcending came back to the world because time required it. He was just an instrument of that omnipotent force of Nature. It was not him doing anything.

Next, the main people to acknowledge are obviously all the Maharishi Effect scientists who played a crucial role in our story. They were the ones that made it happen. Michael Dillbeck, David Orme-Johnson, Charles Alexander, Tony Nader, John Hagelin, Paul Gelderloos, Kenneth Cavanaugh, Howard Chandler, John Davies, Maxwell Rainforth, Garland S. Landrith III, Ashley Deans, Guy Hatchard, and many others.

Then, of course, there's everyone who played a crucial role in making this book happen:

- First of all my dear parents, who have basically been supporting me (both financially and emotionally) during the entire process of writing this book. There are very few people who would have had the kind of patience and trust they had.

- My dear wife, Zoya. If you talk about patience, imagine the patience a wife must have for a husband to sit behind a computer, day after day, month after month, writing a book that he then wants to give away for free, rather than providing a stable income for the family (as I hear most wives would prefer). "Heroic" is the only word that comes to mind.
- Dr. Tony Nader (aka Maharaja), for giving this project his blessing and support, and Dr. Howard Chandler (aka Raja Chancellor) for financially supporting the last phase of writing the book as well as being closely involved in the editing process himself. His guidance and advice played a huge role in making this book what it is now.
- My main editor, Lilla Nemeth. It was a real joy to spend several months together to refine and improve the manuscript. Also special thanks to Gaelen Armstrong and Dylene Cymraes who did the final editing.
- The numerous proofreaders who helped make sure everything was as perfect as it could be: Dr. Ashley Deans, Dr. Peter Swan, Lies Boonen, Jack Forem, John Bright, Mia Claes, Ian Brown and many more.
- All those who, throughout the years, just kept encouraging me to keep going: Sheila Ross, Raja Lucien, Raja Luis, Raja Konhaus, Raja Felix, Jennie Rothenburg, Stijn Vandenbosch, and many more.
- Razvan Petre, for designing an amazing book cover, and Maggie Robinson for the typesetting.
- And anybody else who played a crucial role in making this project happen. Thanks.

Appendix: How transcending works, and how it heals the damaging effect from stress

> Appendix Overview
>
> In this chapter we will:
>
> - Discuss how the technique to transcend works (and why anyone can learn), and how it got lost.
> - Discuss three ways how the damaging effects of stress get healed during TM practice

How transcending works, and how it got lost.

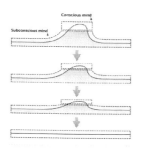

We've said earlier that people lost the ability to transcend because they lost the correct formula to teach it, which resulted in people trying to control the mind, which only keeps the mind active and only prevents the mind to transcend.

So what's the secret? It's so simple that it's surprising the technique got lost in the first place.

Using the nature of the mind, rather than trying to control it.

What is the nature of the mind?

What is every single person's deepest desire?

Happiness.

Happiness is like gravity for the mind; the mind is drawn to it. It will go to a place of more happiness by itself, completely spontaneously, without any effort from our side.

Imagine you are listening to the radio at home and the news is on, but the window is open and your neighbour's radio is playing your favorite song, where will your attention go? To your favorite song on the neighbour's radio. There is more joy for the mind there than the boring news on our radio.

Now, pay attention – you didn't have to force or control your mind; you didn't have to make any effort whatsoever. The mind went there by itself.

If you understand this, you already understand 50% of how the TM technique works. It does require a specific technique to allow the natural process to happen, which takes some training – but the rest is completely effortless.

To explain this, we'll go back to our thought bubble diagram.

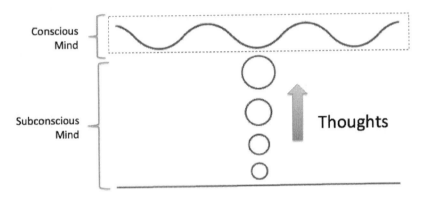

When a thought comes up, it's like a bubble of air originating from the bottom of the ocean. As the bubble rises, it grows bigger and bigger (the thought develops from abstract to more concrete) until it "pops" at the surface. This is the moment we consciously experience a thought, when it comes to surface thinking level of the mind.

What we do with TM is experience this completely natural process of thinking, but in reverse order. We learn a specific meaningless sound (called a "mantra") and then learn a specific way to think the mantra in our mind...

...and that's *all* we do.

If the technique is practiced correctly (which just depends on the right instruction), the mind will experience the mantra at deeper and deeper stages of thought by itself, until it goes into a state of complete inner silence... completely naturally and effortlessly.

Why will it go there? Because this silence, this experience of merging with the ocean and being one with everything, is the most enjoyable experience the mind can have. It's an experience of coming home and the mind wants nothing more than coming home.

By being drawn to happiness the mind is already programmed to transcend. All we have to do is activate the program.

But the moment we start to interfere, and try to control the mind, this natural process will stop, and we only prevent the mind from transcending.

> Any effort from our side will only keep the wave active, and an active wave cannot merge with the silent ocean.

Remember how I said in the prologue that TM is *not* "meditation" as it is commonly understood. All the things meditation teachers usually teach you to do are exactly the things a TM teacher will teach you *not* to do.

All this means is that, if the technique is taught correctly, there are only two requirements for *anyone* to be able to learn TM:

1. You can think a thought
2. Your mind is looking for happiness

So unless you're in a coma, or happen to be the only person in the world who wakes up with the thought: "I hope I'm going to be really *unhappy* today" you can be sure that TM will work for you.

That's why it works for everyone, usually from the very first sitting*.

A lot of attention has gone to the Mantras that are used with TM practice, but the mantra is only 5% of the technique. That's not where the secret lies (mantras have been available in books for thousands of years, and still the technique to transcend got lost). The secret lies with the technique to use them correctly. If you use mantras but start concentrating on them (which is what you'd automatically do without proper instruction) you won't be doing TM and you won't transcend

---

* Everyone is unique and will have unique experiences, and some people will experience transcending more clearly than others, and see the effect more quickly than others, but if people take the full course as designed, it rarely happens (less than 1% of the cases in my experience) that they're not satisfied with the results.

This formula to learn to transcend is a specific sequence of steps of experience and intellectual understanding that the TM teacher guides his students through, and for the technique to work it has to be *exactly* this sequence.

Intellectual understanding is actually the most crucial part. Even if we correct the big misunderstanding about meditation that we should try to control the mind and stop doing this, then still the intellect has a natural tendency to control things. Only by giving the experience of transcending, and then satisfying the intellect about the process, so it understands how it all works, will the intellect be able to let go and allow the process to happen naturally.

This is why TM cannot be learned from a book (or from the internet), because the most crucial part about learning the technique is the constant question and answer interaction between teacher and student, over a period of four evening sessions during the TM instruction, and once every few weeks for the next 6 months during the follow up sessions.

Why did the technique to transcend get lost?

When Maharishi was asked why the technique to transcend was lost, he said the main reason was because of ego.

Transcending has to be taught according to a specific formula, almost like a scientific formula. In science, $e=mc^3$ or $e=kc^2$ doesn't work. It has to be $e=mc^2$.

When a teacher passes something on to his student, however, the ego often wants to make an individual contribution. Meditation teachers had the formula to teach transcending correctly, but wanted to add something personal, something from themselves, into the equation. They wanted to *improve* the formula. The result of their contribution, however, was that the formula became something like $e=mc^2+k$, and it no longer works.

That's how gradually the idea started creeping in that meditation involved controlling the mind, and from that moment the natural technique was lost.

Maharishi's biggest contribution was not only that he was able to restore the correct formula, but also that he was able to train other teachers to properly apply this formula. This requires a lot of training, and is another big difference between a TM teacher and other meditation teachers. These days anyone can read a book on Mindfulness or read some article on the internet and start calling himself a "meditation teacher". To become a TM teacher requires an in-residence training of 5 months (and that's 5 months from early morning till late night, 7 days a week, the equivalent of almost a year of training at a normal 9-to-5 schedule).

It's easy to learn TM when it's taught correctly, but that doesn't mean it's easy to teach it. If it was, the technique would probably never have gotten lost.

All the training sessions Maharishi gave have been recorded on video, so that everyone who takes the training gets *exactly* the same training. More than 40,000 people around the world (including yours truly) have taken this training.

As Maharishi was keenly aware of the reason why the correct formula was lost, he always gave credit for everything he brought to the world to his teacher, Guru Dev. He never took *any* personal credit for anything. (When you hear people in the TM organisation say "Jai Guru Dev", it means "All glory to Guru Dev", it's basically that same reminder).

To make sure that all teachers would do the same, and resist the temptation to add something from their side, he required that every single time the TM technique is taught, the TM teacher does a short ceremony of gratitude to the tradition of teachers. This ceremony, which takes about 5 minutes, simply reminds the teacher they just are passing on the technique as they were instructed, without adding anything from themselves.

This ceremony (which Maharishi insisted should always be done in the name of his teacher, *never* in his name) is often misunderstood as something devotional, and it's not that hard to see how this could happen when you see a TM teacher waving incense and some flowers at a picture of an old man.

In reality this was just Maharishi's way to make sure that the technique would never be lost again, hopefully for thousands of years.

So if you haven't learned TM yet, I really do hope you'll give it a chance. You won't regret it.

Normally the first step is to attend a free TM infosession where the teacher will explain you how it works and what the benefits are, and will answer any questions you may have. But if you read this book, you might already be able to explain it as well as the TM teacher, and all your questions may have been already answered. In that case you can probably just contact your teacher and ask him/her to attend the preparatory lecture right away (where the practical aspects of learning TM are discussed) and sign up for a TM course.

You can find your local teacher at www.fieldparadigm.com/tm

Three ways how transcending heals the damaging effects from stress

We've said TM activates a natural inner healing power that heals the damaging effects from stress on the body and the brain, which makes us more stress resistant. There are several ways how this actually happens, which can all be objectively measured.

Healing the damaging effects of stress on the brain – increased emotional stability

If stress is damaging for our health, it's even more damaging for our brain.

Remember when we were playing God? We gave people full free will, but they *were* tied to the law of action and reaction. No escape from that one. That resulted in a problem, however. People ended up stuck in an endless loop of the same patterns of action and reaction. They didn't seem to have free will at all.

Here we'll find out why that is...and how we can get out of this mess.

Have you ever noticed that when you're stressed, you can't think as clearly and tend to act much more emotional and impulsive?

Yes? Hey, good news...it means you have a normal brain.

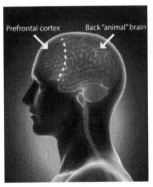

The brain has two distinctive parts; front and back. Generally speaking, the back part of the brain is what we share with other animals. It is where all the automatic processes reside, like visual processing, muscle control, maintaining the body's temperature, etc.

The front part, on the other hand, (called the prefrontal cortex) is far more highly developed in humans . It is where our self-awareness resides, and our ability to "think before we act". It allows us to first consider the long-term consequences of our actions, and control our impulses.

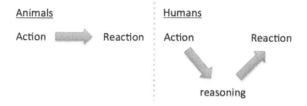

It's generally assumed that our ability to have free will is closely linked to the functioning of our pre-frontal cortex.

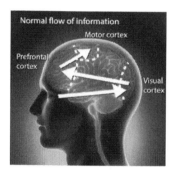

Under normal circumstances, the flow of information in the brain goes like this: we see something, the information goes from our eyes to the visual cortex, then to the prefrontal cortex, which makes a decision and then sends this decision to the motor cortex, which controls our muscles to perform an action.

In a stressful situation, however, this flow of information gets redirected.

The prefrontal cortex shuts down, and the information goes straight from the visual cortex to the motor cortex.

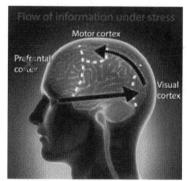

Why? For our survival.

Imagine you're in the jungle and you see a tiger running towards you. At that time you *don't* want to stop and think about it. You don't want to judge all the long-term consequences of your actions. By the time you finished thinking you're lunch.

Instead what you want to do is to act quickly, *impulsively*. So your brain will decrease the blood flow to your prefrontal cortex and essentially deactivate it, and instead will redirect the blood flow to your amygdala, your stress response center. This will raise your heart rate and release all kinds of emergency reaction hormones through your blood, and you'll have a fight-or-flight reaction. You're either going to fight the tiger or run for your life.

So during that split second, it's as if we *lose our free will* and act impulsively, almost like animals.

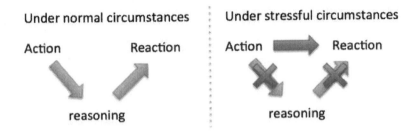

Like we said, this was designed for our survival. Sometimes a quick action is better than a well thought through action.

There is one side-effect, however.

The brain is an extremely flexible organ that constantly changes based on the experiences we have. This is how we learn habits and skills. Every time we repeat some action, like playing the violin, neural connections are made and strengthened in the part of our brain that controls our fingers, and so we get better and better at it.

Unfortunately, the same counts for stressful experiences. They will also "train your brain".

Imagine you're running late for an important meeting...and Murphy's law decides to have some fun: you get stuck in a traffic jam.

Can you feel your stress hormones pumping? You can't fight the traffic jam (you can try, but that usually only leads to more stress), nor can you run away from it, yet still the stress response is activated. The same applies to other kinds of stress: maybe you have an aggressive boss, or a lot of pressure from household duties, or from paying the bills. Soon enough, you find yourself living under *chronic stress*.

> Chronic stressful experiences will train our brain to permanently shut down the prefrontal cortex, and keep our amygdala permanently active... until it seems we can never relax anymore, not even on a holiday.

Today, this can actually be measured. When scientists look at the blood flow in the prefrontal cortex of criminals, for example, they often see that it has permanently shut down. These people have "functional holes" in their brains: areas where the brain is no longer active, as this SPECT scan shows (brain viewed from the bottom, holes are areas where there is no more blood flow).

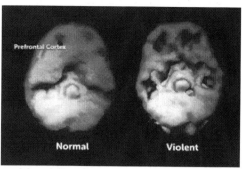

This is why people get stuck in endless cycles of action and reaction. They do something bad to someone, then one day that experience has to come back to them, but their brains get so damaged by the experience that at the moment they have to make a new choice, the part that has to make the choice is shut down.

> We put criminals behind bars *because they made the wrong choice.* It's now becoming clear that in most cases *they may not have had much of a choice.* Their ability to chose was impaired.

But what if we could give people that split second before they act? What if we give them back the ability to *think* about their action before they do it, by teaching them how to reactivate their prefrontal cortex and break the vicious circle of stress? Can you even begin to imagine how much suffering could be prevented in the world?

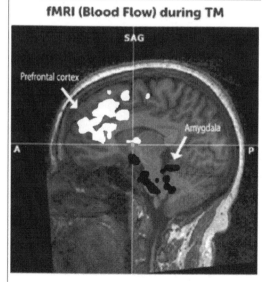

That is exactly what happens when people transcend, and this is measurable as well.

When researchers studied the blood flow in the brains of subjects while they were practicing TM, they found the *exact opposite effect of stress.* The blood flow in the part of the brain that we define as our "stress center" was decreasing, and the

291

blood flow in the prefrontal cortex was increasing*. We can now actually visually observe, in real time, how the brain is healing from the damaging effects of stress during TM.

Most people start to feel this difference after even only a few days of TM practice. They don't get upset as quickly anymore, they can more easily remain balanced. They feel more relaxed and more themselves, Etc.

Essentially we are turning around the vicious circle of stress. We are decreasing stress, and increasing stress resistance. If we can remain calm, a stressful situation won't nearly create as much stress for us.

Like with the deep rest study, these effects appear to be unique to the experience of transcending. Ordinary relaxation doesn't create nearly the same effects.

So this is one way how transcending can remove the rocks from our backpacks and heal the damaging effects from stress.

Let's look at a few more

Reduction of the cortisol stress hormone – improved stress resistance

Cortisol plays a major role in problems like obesity, high blood pressure, diabetes and the weakening of our immune system. To illustrate how this works, let's play another little game.

Imagine you are a little cortisol molecule...

There you are, packed together with all your buddies in the adrenal gland, having a party. The mood is a bit tense, you're all stress hormones after all, but you've gotten used to that.

Suddenly the alarm goes off. You get the message from central command – the amygdala – that the life of your host is in danger. *"Again?"* you think, but you know there's no time to think. You know what needs to be done, and you need to do it quickly.

So you inject yourself into the blood stream and start doing your job. And here's the fun part. Whatever other bodily processes that might get in your way get temporarily suppressed and *your work gets full priority*. Like an

---

* Newberg, Travis et al 2006

ambulance driving through a busy street, everybody else has to pull over and let you do your job. Lives are at stake here.

It kind of makes you feel important.

The first thing you do is to open the taps to flood the body with glucose – blood sugar – so that the muscles get an immediate energy source which they might need in response to whatever danger is threatening the host.

Next, you have to make sure the glucose will actually reach the muscles, rather than getting absorbed along the way. All the cells in the body love this stuff – it's sugar after all – so you actually have to make sure they don't take it away from the blood stream before it reaches the muscles which will need it. It's very easy. Cells need the help of one of your colleagues, the insulin hormone, to absorb the glucose. So you just make the cells temporarily resistant to insulin. Basically, the insulin may come knocking at the cell's doors, but the door is locked. That way it's locked for glucose as well.

Finally, as every millisecond counts, you speed up the delivery system. While another one of your colleagues (the epinephrine hormone) is already on its way to increase the heart rate, your job is to narrow the arteries (everything gets tense) so that the blood pressure increases and the flow goes a lot faster.

Okay, job done, *phew, that was close*. We saved the host's life again. Now let's turn everything back to normal and go home. After all, as soon as the ambulance is through the rest of the cars should resume driving.

But wait, you get the message from the amygdala to *keep the whole body in a state of emergency*, and eventually you have to keep it in that state for two hours.

You wonder what's going on. It's hard to imagine how a life-threatening situation can last for such a long time. It's usually only a matter of a few seconds or minutes. You either fight for your life or run away.

So you decide to check out what happened...and you're shocked. *There was never any life-threatening situation.* The host was just stuck in a traffic jam for two hours and was late for an important meeting.

You seriously start to question the wisdom of the central command in the amygdala. Don't these guys realize that keeping the body in this state of emergency is *just not healthy*?

- Long-term high blood pressure: not healthy.
- Long-term high blood sugars: not healthy (they get stored as body fats).

- Long-term insulin resistance: definitely not healthy. Not only is this essentially type 2 diabetes, but it also causes the cells to starve because they can't take up enough glucose anymore, so they'll send permanent hunger signals to the brain. So people eat, eat, eat, and still feel hungry, leading to obesity.

Plus, there are a lot of other side-effects. Processes that you're causing for a good reason for survival in the short term are now becoming long-term situations, including suppression of the immune system, memory loss, mood swings, etc.

You're seriously starting to consider quitting your job because what you're doing here is just not right. But then again, who else would give a stress hormone a job?

In the end, you just stop asking questions and do as you're told. It's their responsibility, after all.

So what did we learn from this story?

The percentage of our global population that is suffering from diabetes (8.5%), high blood pressure (22%), and being overweight (39%) is mind-blowing, and it's growing every day. More people are dying from heart disease than from any other health problem and, for the first time in history, we live in a world where more people are dying from being overweight than from being underweight.

...all largely because of one poor little stress hormone that was just doing its job.

If we could learn a completely natural way to reduce our stress, (get the amygdala to calm down and only trigger the stress response when it's really crucial) so that, and as a result, the levels of cortisol decrease, do you think this could change the world?

This is exactly what the TM researchers found.

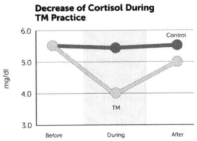

They measured cortisol concentrations in a group of TM meditators before, during and after TM practice, and did the same with a control group who didn't meditate. They found a

30% reduction in cortisol during TM, with no change in the control group*.

But even more important are the long-term effects.

Orme-Johnson exposed subjects to a series of loud sounds (a standard method to measure a stress reaction) and measured their GSR to see how quickly they habituate to the stressful situation.

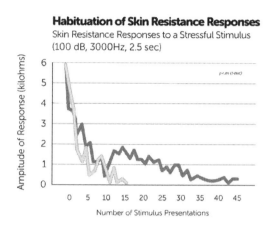

TM meditators showed a far quicker habituation to the sounds than the control group. After a mean of 11 trials the TM group showed no more response (an indication that it was no longer stressful for them), whereas it took the control group a mean of 26 trials†.

Orme-Johnson also found that the TM group showed fewer multiple galvanic skin responses to a single stressful stimulus in comparison to the control group.

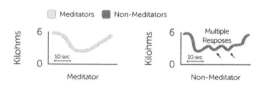

Within the TM group there is a single response, and then a recovery to normal skin resistance, while the control group showed multiple responses. This is kind of like bringing the body to a tense state where it is able to respond quickly when necessary – in case of a dangerous event – but then immediately settles down when it's no longer needed. TM meditators were able to do this, while non-meditators weren't.

This improved stress resistance appears to have a wide range of benefits. The National Institute of Health studies on the long-term of TM on reduced blood pressure, diabetes and heart disease are some of the most famous TM studies done so far. They found better results than what can usually be

---

* *Hormones and Behavior* 10(1): 54–60, 1978.
† *Psychosomatic Medicine.* 35 (4): 341–349, 1973

achieved with medicines, without negative side effects and at a far lower cost than other treatments.

Increased Serotonin hormones – spontaneous happiness

The ancient Vedic texts describe the state of transcending as a state of pure happiness for the mind, and describe that the mind's nature to always look for happiness will cause it to naturally transcend if it only gets the chance. That's why TM is enjoyable to practice, because it's ultimately just going towards your own inner happiness.

Two scientists in Vienna wanted to see if this state of inner happiness could be objectively verified, by measuring the concentrations of serotonin – our happiness hormone – in the body before and after TM practice.

To be sure that any changes were due to TM, rather than due to the natural fluctuations throughout the day, they also measured changes in a control group at exactly the same time.

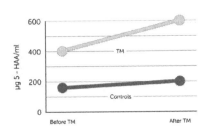

The TM group showed a 50% increase of serotonin (as measured by the serotonin metabolite 5 HIAA) after 20 minutes of TM practice. There were no significant changes in the control group*.

Even more remarkable was that prior to beginning their TM practice the levels of serotonin were already twice as high in the TM group as in the control group. This indicates a long-term general increase of serotonin.

> Happiness is the one thing money can't buy...but what if we could learn to produce it ourselves?

You probably notice that you generally don't feel very happy when you're stressed. This is largely because of the cortisol story earlier. Under stress many of the normal functions of the body are suppressed (including serotonin production) as the body prepares for a fight-or-flight response. You don't need to feel happy when a wild animal is about to attack you – you need to survive.

Under chronic stress, however, the long-term suppression of serotonin can lead to some serious mental health issues.

---

* *Journal of Neural Transmission* 39: 257–267, 1976

Other than regulating our happiness, serotonin regulates a wide range of processes in the brain, and insufficient serotonin levels have been linked to a wide range of problems, such as depression, insomnia, emotional instability, migraines, addictions, eating disorders, Alzheimer's and fibromyalgia.

> We spend *billions* every year on drugs that try to artificially regulate our serotonin levels, but these drugs have all kinds of side effects, which often are as damaging as the problem they're trying to solve.
>
> Now it turns out there's a way to increase our serotonin levels *in a completely natural way, with only positve side effects.*

So yes, TM is *very* good for stress and all its side effects, and this by itself could already change the world...but it's still only 10% of the story.

I'm glad you got to discover the full story.

Jai Guru Dev, (now you know what that means)

Joachim

References

[2] http://en.wikipedia.org/wiki/Spinoza

[3] Isaacson, Einstein His life and Universe, 2007, Simon and Schuster

[4] Anderson, Christopher (September 10, 1992). *Nature*. 359 (6391): 97.

[5] Fresling, P.: Naturligt-Övernaturligt, Forum, 1994.

[6] Conscious Universe p 97

[7] Conscious Universe p 107

[8] Supernormal, Dr. Dean Radin

[9] The Field p 156

[10] http://www.theatlantic.com/magazine/archive/2015/04/the-science-of-near-death-experiences/386231/

[11] Holographic Universe p 232

[12] Talbot, Holographic Universe, Harper Perennial, 1992,

[13] Talbot, Holographic Universe, Harper Perennial, 1992, p 224

[14] Talbot, Holographic Universe, Harper Perennial, 1992, p 215

[15] Talbot, Holographic Universe, Harper Perennial, 1992, p 217

[16] Talbot, Holographic Universe, Harper Perennial, 1992, p 219

[17] http://www.huffingtonpost.com/2013/09/25/ray-odierno-military-suicides_n_3984359.html;

[18] for all the publications go to: http://www.drfredtravis.com/CV.html

[19] *Alcoholism Treatment Quarterly* 11: 13–87, 1994

[21] http://www.cnn.com/2017/03/21/health/gop-health-care-debate-vital-directions-report/index.html

[22] http://www.cnn.com/2017/03/21/health/gop-health-care-debate-vital-directions-report/index.html

[23] http://www.statista.com/statistics/263102/pharmaceutical-market-worldwide-revenue-since-2001/

[24] http://www.bbc.com/news/business-28212223

[25] *Permanent peace*, Robert Oats

[26] *International Journal of Neuroscience* (49, 207-211).

[27] *International Journal of Neuroscience (16, 203-209).*

[28] From the book *Yogic Flying*, by Dr. Craig Pearson. *Exact details! Publisher, date*

[29] Collected Papers, vol.4, no. 335, pp 2687-2714.

[30] *Social Science Perspectives Journal 2(4), 127–146.*

[31] SAGE Open. 2016;April-June:1-16.

[32] https://ucr.fbi.gov/crime-in-the-u.s/2012/crime-in-the-u.s.-2012/tables/1tabledatadecoverviewpdf/table_1_crime_in_the_united_states_by_volume_and_rate_per_100000_inhabitants_1993-2012.xls

[33] https://en.wikipedia.org/wiki/List_of_motor_vehicle_deaths_in_U.S._by_year

[34] http://www.theglobalist.com/the-cost-of-a-human-life-statistically-speaking/

[35] G. Swanson and R.Oates, *Enlightened Management: Building high performance People.*

Made in the USA
Middletown, DE
03 January 2018